Leah Guggenheimer

About the Author

JEFF PEARLMAN is a columnist for SI.com and the *New York Times* bestselling author of four books, including *The Bad Guys Won* and *Boys Will Be Boys*. His next book, *Sweetness: The Enigmatic Life of Walter Payton,* will be released in September 2011. He blogs regularly at jeffpearlman.com.

THE BAD GUYS WON

Also by Jeff Pearlman

The Rocket That Fell to Earth
Boys Will Be Boys
Love Me, Hate Me

A SEASON OF BRAWLING, BOOZING, BIMBO CHASING,

AND CHAMPIONSHIP BASEBALL WITH

STRAW, DOC, MOOKIE, NAILS, THE KID,

AND THE REST OF THE 1986 METS,

THE ROWDIEST TEAM EVER TO PUT ON

A NEW YORK UNIFORM, AND MAYBE THE BEST

THE
BAD GUYS
WON

JEFF PEARLMAN

itbooks

AN IMPRINT OF HARPERCOLLINS PUBLISHERS

*it*books

FIRST IT BOOKS PAPERBACK EDITION PUBLISHED 2011.

The Library of Congress has catalogued the hardcover edition as follows:

Pearlman, Jeff.
    The bad guys won : a season of brawling, boozing, bimbo chasing, and championship baseball with Straw, Doc, Mookie, Nails, the Kid, and the rest of the 1986 Mets, the rowdiest team ever to put on a New York uniform, and maybe the best / Jeff Pearlman.—1st ed.
        p. cm.
    ISBN 0-06-050732-2
    1. New York Mets (Baseball team)—History. 2. World Series (Baseball) (1986).

GV875.N45P43   2004
796.357'64'097471—dc22   2003056991

ISBN 978-0-06-209763-7 (pbk.)

22 23 24 25 26 LBC 15 14 13 12 11

To Catherine and Casey Marta, mis dos Earlitas

And in memory of Walter (he got what he deserved)

Contents

	PROLOGUE	1
1	FOOD FLIGHT	7
2	THE ROAD TO 1986	18
3	"WE'RE GOING TO DOMINATE"	41
4	METSMERIZED	56
5	DRINKING DAYS	74
6	"THE KID" AND THE BLACK HATS	87
7	A LONELY TIME TO BE WHOLESOME	103
8	COOTER'S-GATE	109
9	DOC AND DARRYL	125
10	OUT OF LEFT FIELD	140
11	HOT STUFF	150
12	PLEASE STAY OFF THE FIELD	166
13	GREAT SCOTT	174
14	"IT DOESN'T GET ANY BETTER THAN THIS"	181
15	THE PASSION OF BILL BUCKNER	205
16	BOSTON AND NEW YORK	212
17	REVENGE	223
18	NEAR DEATH	232
19	WORLD CHAMPS	246
20	WHAT DYNASTY?	261
	EPILOGUE	271
	AFTERWORD	285
	ACKNOWLEDGMENTS	295

THE BAD GUYS WON

Prologue

Today's players are robots. Everybody comes to work in a black suit wearing a black tie. But fans want emotion. They want characters. They want to love you or hate you. In 1986 the Mets were loved and hated. It was the best time to be a professional baseball player.

—KEITH HERNANDEZ, Mets first baseman

IN 1986 I WAS A fourteen-year-old freshman at Mahopac High School in upstate New York, probably not the biggest nerd around but certainly pathetic enough to crack the Top 10. If that weren't bad enough, most weeks a school bully named John Degl would make sure to kick my books across the hallway floor, eliciting laughter from the general populace. It was the worst time of my life, and the one thing that kept me afloat was baseball. Because my parents considered sports to be about as important as spore collecting, I often found myself making the 200-yard walk up Emerald Lane where Dennis Gargano, one of my three friends, lived in a yellow house that smelled like sweet potatoes. What made a trip to the house special was

Dennis's dad, Vinny Gargano, the one adult I knew who considered baseball a sacred endeavor.

Mr. Gargano was born in the Flatbush section of Brooklyn in 1939, and before long he was regularly taking the trolley to Ebbets Field to sit in the bleachers and watch his beloved Dodgers. "It was the greatest place for baseball," he often told me. "You woulda loved it." Following the '57 season, the Dodgers bolted from Brooklyn for Los Angeles. Mr. Gargano was heartbroken. He refused to root for the hated Yankees and accepted that he was a fan without a team. When the Mets came along five years later, it was as if someone had been listening to his prayers. He had a reason to love baseball again.

If the Mets were on TV, there was only one place to find Mr. Gargano: in his regular position on the plaid couch, a glass of Coca-Cola on the coffee table and a pack of Viceroys by his side. From Dennis's room down the hall, I'd come running. "What do ya think of this Gooden kid?" Mr. Gargano would ask, motioning for me to sit in the nearby loveseat. "Seaver was incredible in his heyday. But this Gooden . . . he's something."

Thanks to Mr. Gargano, I had access to the greatest show on earth. The Mets were exciting and daring, and the roster represented, well, everything: superstars young and black (Dwight Gooden and Darryl Strawberry) and old and white (Gary Carter and Keith Hernandez); humble journeymen (Danny Heep and Randy Niemann) and cocky newcomers (Lenny Dykstra); contemplative sages (Mookie Wilson), bitter has-beens (George Foster), freethinking weirdos (Roger McDowell), street-hardened tough guys (Kevin Mitchell), religious zealots (Ray Knight), and Ivy League pretty boys (Ron Darling). I was in love, and even though Teresa McClure, my schoolboy crush, habitually ignored me, the Mets never let me down.

In Mahopac, a blue-collar, Irish-Italian hamlet of thirty thousand, the Mets' long-awaited success was a victory for every anti-Yankee impulse a person could muster. For years George Steinbrenner's team—with its high-priced free agent acquisitions—was the enemy of my town, which took pride in its underdog status. Mahopac was home to

Paul's Pizza and Rodak's Deli; to plumbers and electricians; to Mr. Vincent Gargano. The Yankees were McDonald's and Macy's, lawyers and doctors. No, thank you. Not here.

To many uppity New Yorkers (from the Mahopac vantage point, those who lived in the nearby towns of Scarsdale, Chappaqua, and Rye), a visit to Shea Stadium was akin to sleeping in a sewer. From the blue paint peeling off the seats and the incessant noise of LaGuardia Airport jet traffic to the charmless concrete walkways and the goofy jumbo-sized apple beyond the outfield wall that glowed with every Met home run, the place (especially compared to palatial Yankee Stadium) was a housing project surrounding a diamond. Yet it was *our* housing project, and the Mets rolled out the red carpet for the average man.

On the October night that Wilson's dribbler rolled through Bill Buckner's legs, I watched Mr. Gargano take a drag from his cigarette and smile as if the Dodgers had announced their return to Brooklyn. The Mets were about to become world champs. "Hold on to the feeling," Mr. Gargano told me. "Things like this don't happen too often. Remember what it's like. Remember how good it tastes."

I promised Mr. Vincent Gargano that I would never forget.

And then I forgot.

What can I say? When you're growing up, everything is a distraction. The girls' legs become longer. You get a job at The Great American Cookie Company. You need a date for the prom. You spend four years in college.

You become a sportswriter.

The last one—that's what really did me in. I started covering baseball for *Sports Illustrated* in 1996, and over the ensuing six years I was thrust into a new relationship with the game, one that transformed it from the magical pastime of my youth to just another professional sport. The unalloyed joy the Mets had gifted me with a decade earlier was replaced by the ugly adult traits of skepticism and distrust.

As a young teenager I would sit by the TV, glove in hand, and mimic Rafael Santana's arching throws from short to first. Now, as an adult, the last thing I wanted was to emulate the men I covered. Baseball players just seemed so *boring*. How many times could I hear some second-rate shortstop ramble on about "First I'd like to thank my Lord and Savior Jesus Christ, who made me a baseball player and brought me to the great city of Houston to be an Astro and gave me the strength to dive into the hole and catch that grounder"? Even worse, why was it that glib conversation between jock and journalist had been replaced by corporate name droppings and meaningless clichés? Yeah, Mariano, we know you just wanna win for the Yankees and play hard. We also know that Adidas is paying you $50,000 to wear that sweatshirt. What else is new?

I, like many peers in the profession, had grown up believing Jim Bouton's *Ball Four* and Sparky Lyle's *The Bronx Zoo* defined the behind-the-scenes lifestyle of ballplayers; that when they weren't at the stadium, pitchers, catchers, infielders, and outfielders gathered at the nearest pub, chasing tail and starting fights and tiptoeing the line of public decency (and often falling off). While researching a piece on the A's in 2002, I flew on the team's charter from Oakland to New York. The theme of my article was "baseball's zaniest bunch," and I anxiously anticipated loud music, fierce smack-downs, pudding-inspired food fights, and free-flowing beer. What I observed was twenty-four men quietly listening to twenty-four Walkmans. Once, three and a half hours into the flight, a pitcher named Mike Magnante went wild and crazy, asking outfielder Terrence Long if he could borrow a DVD. Long nodded. He never removed the headphones from his ears. The mood reminded me of my days studying at the Mahopac Public Library—only sometimes the librarians would at least whisper to one another.

After reading an early draft of *The Bad Guys Won*, Michael Lewis, my longtime friend and a fine sportswriter for the *Glen Falls Post-Star,* called to offer his opinion. "I enjoyed the book," he said, "but I have one complaint."

What's that?

"Except for Ed Hearn, all these guys are assholes."

I smiled. It was nearly the exact statement Bobby Ojeda had made seven months earlier when the former 18-game winner looked me in the eyes and said, "If you work on this hard, you're gonna find that we were a bunch of vile fuckers." Ojeda chuckled knowingly because it was 100 percent true and 100 percent fantastic. The Mets owned New York City because they *were* New York City. In 1986, way before the Giuliani crackdowns, the Big Apple was a cesspool of sin. In Times Square, now home to a gigantic Toys "R" Us, a person could purchase a bag of cocaine, then go around the corner and pay a hooker to snort it with him. Pornography shops were as prevalent as pizzerias. Graffiti was everywhere. At the same time the Mets were winning big in Queens, a man named Ivan Boesky was fined $100 million for trading stocks on insider information in Manhattan. He was as much hero as villain. There was a ruthlessness floating through the air, a vibe that the movie *Wall Street* summed up perfectly. Greed—arrogant, I-can't-be-stopped greed—was good in New York City. The metropolis had it, and the baseball team had it, too. Mets manager Davey Johnson guaranteed that his team would dominate, and the town didn't flinch. They expected nothing less.

That's what struck me while writing this book. Not that the Mets were unruly, but just how perfect they were for the times. Individually, away from the corrupting influence of one another, men like Ojeda, Hernandez, Dykstra, and even the troubled Gooden and Strawberry were relatively normal, run-of-the-mill human beings. Together, however, they formed an X-rated clubhouse of booze hounds, skirt chasers, and bar fighters. They played hard and partied even harder.

"What you saw was what you got," says Ojeda, "like it or hate it." So Darryl Strawberry beat on Gary Carter because he knew he could. It was one Met messing with another Met—family. New York was involved in four on-field fights that season, and they won all of them. You were allowed to dog a teammate. If anyone from the outside tried, however, he would be pummeled. "We were unique because there were no color lines, no status lines, nothing," says Knight. "We could really get on one another, but in the end, we were brothers."

There will never be another team like the '86 Mets, and it is sad. In an era of corporate synergy and political correctness, baseball today lacks the fire and panache of yesteryear. For all their greatness on the field of play, the Yankee Dynasty of the late 1990s and early 2000s will be remembered as—*yaaaaaawn!*—a skilled yet boring cast of characters, and nothing more. One day when baseball historians look back at the sport's first one hundred years, they will consider the Mets the official end of an era. It was Babe Ruth in the 1920s, Mickey Mantle in the 1950s, the Oakland A's in the 1970s, and for one wonderful season, the New York Mets of 1986.

—*Jeff Pearlman,* October 2003

Chapter 1

FOOD FLIGHT

It wasn't just guys destroying a plane. It was guys destroying a plane after an emotional roller coaster. There's a difference.

—RANDY NIEMANN, Mets pitcher

RAY KNIGHT'S ARMS were numb. Not just numb as if he'd spent a few too many minutes in the snow. Numb numb—as if he'd just swum two thousand laps in an Olympic-sized pool. As if he'd just sparred eight hundred rounds with George Foreman. As if someone had grabbed a 10-foot machete, reared back, and sliced off both limbs. "Maybe someone did," he says with a laugh. "I wouldn't have known."

It wasn't just his arms, either. Inside the head of New York's third baseman a drum was beating. His hands were shaking. His mouth was cotton-dry. His feet were on fire. His uniform must have held twenty pounds of sweat. "I couldn't walk, I couldn't talk, I couldn't move," Knight says. "I couldn't even think."

It was exhaustion, more pure and painful than any he had ever felt before. Than any he would ever feel again. "I haven't been in war," he says. "But . . ."

But this was war. Or at least the next closest thing.

Sixteen innings. In 16 beautiful, electric, heart-wrenching, gut-churning, bladder-bursting, finger-twitching, eye-bulging, throat-burning innings of baseball, the New York Mets had been pushed to the brink over and over again. On enemy turf, no less. Finally, they had pushed back.

Game 6 of the 1986 National League Championship Series:

Mets 7

Astros 6

The Mets were going to the World Series. It was everything they had dreamed of, but now—*what?* The hardest-living players in baseball entered the visiting clubhouse of the Houston Astrodome and didn't know what to do. Scream or cry? Party or pray? A couple of the men had tears streaming down their cheeks. Others slumped in front of their lockers, sandbags for shoulders and rocks for feet. "I could have slept for twenty hours," says Ed Hearn, New York's backup catcher, "and I hadn't even played in the game."

Then and there the Mets reached a collective decision. Perhaps it was inspired by the popping of a champagne cork. Or the cracking open of a beer can. Or the lighting of a cigarette. Or the primal *"Whoooo!"* bursting from Wally Backman's throat. Whatever the stimulus, the message was clear and powerful: Before they went to the World Series, the Mets would party their fuckin' brains out.

There was one problem: time.

Although the game had begun early enough, at 3:05 P.M., 16 innings was 16 innings. After four hours and forty-two minutes of baseball, it was 8:20 when the first Mets players stumbled into the clubhouse. Even as the bottles of Great Western bubbly were being distributed, Arthur Richman, the club's traveling secretary, was doing everything he could to hurry people along: *Congratulations, Ray—now get dressed! Good job, Keith—and don't forget your shaving kit!* The team had to fly back to New York immediately, and the trip was a long one. Yet in the aftermath of triumph, it didn't matter. Richman was ignored. Kevin Mitchell, the barrel-chested rookie, grabbed Bobby Ojeda around the neck and doused his head with champagne. Ojeda, in turn, doused Jesse Orosco, who doused Doug Sisk, who doused Rick Aguilera, who doused Dwight Gooden, who doused Backman. The Mets didn't just let loose, they bear-hugged and gang-tackled. They were a fraternity without classes to attend, a rock-and-roll band without instruments. Shortly after he entered the clubhouse, journeyman reliever Randy Niemann snatched a bottle of bubbly and poured it on the head of bow-tied general manager Frank Cashen, who responded with a bitter glare of death. As Phil Mushnick of the *New York Post* wrote, "Cashen's candid crankiness . . . created a national image as a party-pooper."

No matter. Some ninety minutes after the victory, a sticky, drenched Cashen, surrounded by empty bottles and crushed cans, made an announcement to his sticky, drenched players: "The World Series bus is leaving! Anyone not on it gets left behind!" This was not a joke. The Mets and their entourage piled onto a pair of buses that went to Houston's William P. Hobby Airport. En route, beers were chugged. The remaining champagne bottles were polished off and then tossed to the ground. Even manager Davey Johnson was indulging.

It was mini-mayhem.

Then they reached the plane.

Women are bad news. Very bad. They take real men—ball-playing men—and turn them to mush. They transform ruggedness and determination into sentimentality and passivity. Yes, there are good women in the world. But they are at their absolute best away from the ballpark, preparing dinner over a hot stove and tucking the children into bed. It's a simple equation, really:

$$\text{Women} + \text{Baseball} = \text{Trouble}$$

In the mind of Frank Cashen, this was established. Cashen was old school, and he wore the reputation proudly. When Rusty Staub, longtime Mets star, commonly referred to the players' wives as "cunts" and the players' extramarital girlfriends as "special cunts," he was speaking Cashen's language. In his eighteenth year as a baseball executive, Cashen was a throwback to the good old days when a ballplayer would never use the opposite sex as an excuse. Baby due any day? Tough luck—you're staying with the team. Wife sick? Send her a note. Honeymoon? Not during the season, kid. Cashen's philosophy could be summed up in one sentence: Frank Robinson never missed a day for no friggin' broad, and neither should you. Now, in the midst of the playoffs, this news: The Mets players wanted their wives to fly with the team.

Cashen knew there had been rumblings concerning this issue, but he tuned them out until two of the more respected Mets—Knight and pitcher Ron Darling—requested a meeting. In Cashen's office they made an impassioned case for women in flight. "The wives cook, they raise the kids, and they've stood behind us through a long season," said Darling, New York's assistant player representative. "They've contributed to this as much as anyone."

While Cashen still felt—no, *knew*—that it was a terrible idea, he and the players reached a compromise: The wives could fly with the team, but only on the two return trips from Houston.

This news was great for several of the Mets, insignificant for many of them, and terrible for a few. Gary Carter, the straight-out-of-Mayberry catcher, considered each new day with his wife, Sandy, as blessed as a budding rose. Keith Hernandez was in the midst of divorce proceedings with his wife, Susan, and was unaffected by Cashen's decision. And then there was Darryl Strawberry, the combustible twenty-four-year-old right fielder. Strawberry's relationship with his wife, Lisa, was troubled and, at worst, bloody. Two years earlier, when Strawberry told his teammates that he was about to propose, the reaction was bad. Lisa Andrews rubbed many of the Mets the wrong way. Unlike the typical ballplayer wife—a petite, large-breasted, dumb-as-a-shoe platinum-blond trophy with an extensive Hooters background—Lisa was big, hard, and loud. In the ocean of beautiful, submissive young women who hungered for ballplayers, *this* was Strawberry's grand find? "She was a tough girl," says Vinny Greco, an assistant equipment manager. "His wife could probably knock out half the guys on the team." And the way she spoke to Strawberry in public! Bossy, even downright demeaning. "There may have been affectionate feelings, but they were just a match and a bomb," says John Rufino, also an assistant equipment manager. "They brought the worst out in each other, and guys told him and told him and told him not to do it. But he didn't listen."

During the National League Championship Series, the marriage of Darryl and Lisa reached new lows. When Lisa accompanied her husband to Houston (on a separate plane) to try to work things out, the yelling and pushing were fit for *Jerry Springer*. In their hotel room at the Westin Galleria, the bickering was nonstop and—to neighboring rooms—audible. In his 1992 autobiography, *Darryl*, Strawberry said that, combined with the intensity of the playoffs, it was all too much. "There was no backing off and no backing down as Lisa and I kept fighting. I could feel the violence rising inside of me like the howling of so many demons. I was out of control. I was being paid to be out of control and physical. I'm sorry for what I did, but I did it at a time when everybody around me wanted violence and a display of raw power. I tried to tell her to stop. I almost begged her to just wait another week or so. Go back to California. Go to New York. Go stay with your mother, for heaven's sake. Just don't mess me up while I'm trying to play this game."

But Lisa didn't listen. She stuck around and, from Darryl's vantage point, nagged and nagged and nagged. Before the games she would nag. After the games she would nag. During games—during at-bats—Darryl could hear his wife, in his head, nagging. The night before the now-famous Game 6, Strawberry lost control. He took a swing and nailed his wife square in the face, sending her backward and breaking her nose. It was an ugly, bloody moment, and that image—Strawberry out of control—would define him for the next decade.

And now, to Cashen's chagrin, Lisa and Darryl and all their troubles would be on the plane, surrounded by beer, bubbly, whiskey, and God knows what else.

For much of the 1970s and 1980s, Ozark Airlines was the charter company for major league baseball. They handled the air transportation for some fifteen to eighteen teams a year, and did so with the class and dignity of a five-star hotel.

Along with safety and promptness, the good folk at Ozark prided themselves on cleanliness. They might not have had the fleet size of Delta or American, but Ozark's planes—primarily DC-9s—were the most sparkling in the business. Carpets were vacuumed after every flight, magazines were neatly stacked, the tray tables were wiped down, and the armrests shined like a new nickel. "We went above and beyond," says Bill Mihsk, the airline's vice president of marketing. "Our mission was to provide great service in a wonderful atmosphere. First class."

Like any other corporation that relies on image, Ozark routinely put a happy public face on the world of jock transportation: *Ozark is proud to be the airline of choice of the* [FILL IN THE TEAM)! *Ozark wishes* [FILL IN THE TEAM] *luck in their fight for the World Series!*

But truth be told, many members of the Ozark family—primarily flight attendants—detested the sporting life. Ozark's athletic clients were primarily hockey, football, and baseball teams, and there were enough horror stories to fill Vincent Price's memoir. More than one flight attendant found herself the target of sexual barbs ranging from the forgettable to the stupid to the mean to the detestable. (Usually, the detestable ones were accompanied by a pinch on the rear.) Several male staffers were stuffed in overhead compartments. Oftentimes athletes turned the plane's minuscule bathroom into an Olympic-style venue. *(Do you believe in miracles? Yes! The Cowboys have stuffed a football down the toilet!)* On one memorable voyage Mihsk watched as members of the California Angels, angry over a less-than-delectable meal, picked the steaks off their trays and taped them to the bottom of their shoes. Even this was better than the Raiders, who enjoyed dumping their entire meal—salad, soup, dessert, and all—into the seat pocket. "It seems that some teams were always finding things to do with food," says Mihsk. "Most other people just ate it."

But as Mihsk well knew, athletes aren't like most other people. Far from it. And the '86 Mets weren't even like most other athletes. They were, hands down, the most unruly team Ozark had ever transported. On June 29 of that 1986 season, Ozark was flying the Mets from Chicago to St. Louis when a half-dozen dinner rolls were fired through the air, lifting off near the airplane's rear and landing twenty rows up. The flight attendants ducked for cover, then stood up and continued service. In the back, the culprits—pitchers Jesse Orosco and Doug Sisk—snickered with delight. But there was a problem. Cliff Day, Ozark's supervisor of charter sales and operations, had accompanied his crew on the flight, and he wasn't happy. He stood at the head of the plane and made an announcement. "Here's what we're gonna do," he said. "You're gonna straighten up immediately, or we're gonna land and you can take a bus to St. Louis!"

The response was loud, angry, and unanimous: Fuck you! Fuck you! Fuck you!

On another trip from New York to Los Angeles, according to an ex–Ozark official, Darryl Strawberry and Dwight Gooden, the team's two marquee stars, exposed their penises and were "inviting the women to lick this and lick that." The Ozark official says the Mets front office was immediately made aware of the incident (Cashen denies any knowledge of the event), but the flight attendants declined to pursue any legal action. "Strawberry and Gooden were just horrible guys on that flight—absolutely terrible human beings when they drank," says the Ozark employee. "There could have been sexual harassment suits all over the place. How those guys got away with what they did is a shame."

"The Mets were animals," adds Day. "They were worse than Philly, and that's when the Phillies had Greg Luzinski and Larry Bowa. But the Mets were the worst. They had some real dickheads."

Women and dickheads. They filed off the bus together—a few composed, most in advanced states of inebriation—and onto the airplane. Welcome to hell.

Because the Mets' playoff traveling party was too large for Ozark's DC-9s, the team hired a United DC-10 for the trip. It was New York's first dealings with the airline, and United's executive staff hoped it would be the beginning of a long relationship.

As everyone boarded, flight attendants distributed glasses of champagne to the already buzzed clientele. Some players—Hearn, Knight—politely took one. Others—Sisk, Orosco, Heep—grabbed two or three or four. Or ten.

Sisk, Orosco, and Heep. They were the Three Musketeers of the Mets, only this trio was as dashing as a scrum of street rats. Their collective nickname was the "Scum Bunch," and it fit perfectly. The "Scummers" took pride in antics that made *Porky's* look like a documentary on convent life. By day they were mild-mannered baseball players. But by night, watch out. The Scum Bunch ran the back of the plane on team flights, holding drink-a-thons and sometimes, as a result, puke-a-thons. And now the wives were here, equally indulgent but unfamiliar with the effects of getting wasted thirty-five thousand feet above ground.

After takeoff the boozing reached epic levels. The champagne was followed by beer, beer, and more beer. Almost everybody—even Carter—partook. (He had only one.) On this night the Scum Bunch were magnets, drawing people to the rear of the aircraft. "It was the loudest flight I've ever been on," says Michael Rufino, one of the team's batboys. "It was sheer craziness."

"It was the one time when everybody—and I mean everybody—was drinking," says Wally Backman, the team's second baseman. "It was all-out partying."

For the first hour the all-out partying was little more than drinking and yelling. But then, the United crew committed the ultimate mid-celebration error: They served cake. It was the kind you see at childhood birthday parties—spongy yellow with chocolate icing on top. The flight attendants distributed a piece to every person on the flight. Rufino remembers sitting in his seat and biting into his piece when—*Whoooosh! Splat!*

What the?

Whoooosh! Splat!

What the hell?

Whoooosh! Splat!

What the hell is that?

Whoooosh! Splat!

It was cake. Lots of cake. It started with Jane Heep, who chucked a piece at her husband. Suddenly—*Whoooosh! Splat!*—pieces of cake were—*Whoooosh! Splat!*—everywhere. On the backs of seats. On the fronts of suits. In hair. Covering eyes. Brown icing was all over the carpet. Brown icing on the ceiling. Soon it was a free-for-all. Bottles of champagne rolled down the aisle. Peas were smooshed up and used as shampoo. "Tore up that plane like *Bebe's Kids*," says Kevin Mitchell. "I couldn't believe the things I saw going on."

More and more alcohol made its way from United's refrigerators to passengers' throats. When the beer ran out, the airline distributed small bottles of hard liquor. To a man the players insist that this was where the real trouble began. The wives were able to handle champagne and beer, but not the strong stuff, especially combined with the altitude and the food. Who was the first to throw up? Eighteen years later it's hard to say. One thing is certain: At least three wives did so, and none seemed to feel that the toilet or a barf bag would serve them any better than the seat pocket.

Meanwhile, a couple of players—demonstrating the '86 Mets trademark intellectual curiosity—decided to see if with some jiggling the seats could unfold into a couch. Strawberry, for one, pushed and pushed until—crack!—the seat folded down.

"It was like watching *Animal House,* with John Belushi having the food fight in the cafeteria," says Vinny Greco. "You were just ducking from stuff the whole time. It got to a point where even I was like, 'Whoa, what the hell is going on here? What are we doing to this plane?'"

In his autobiography, *Heat,* Gooden recalls his most vivid image of the flight. "At one point the partying was so out of control, the lavatory door accidentally flew open and there was one of my teammates, his face in front of lines of cocaine," he writes. "I wasn't shocked that he was using. I was shocked that he was so high, he didn't even realize the door was open."

Meanwhile, the airplane was a disaster area. Upon landing, two or three wives had to be carried off the jet. Others weren't quite sure of their whereabouts. Half the team exited wearing T-shirts and ties. Sisk wore one shoe. Fans who had waited for hours at Kennedy Airport to greet the team were shocked at what they saw. "To have the wives in their snazzy North Beach Leather outfits, covered in vomit, it didn't make for a pretty picture," says Mets pitcher Ron Darling. "And the guys were coming off in various forms of disarray of dress. We were gross."

The plane was even grosser. A few days after the flight, Cashen received a bill from United for $7,500, along with a note saying that the Mets' business was no longer welcome. Besides the innards of the craft being layered in food, three rows of broken seats had to be completely removed. Cashen was furious—at his players for turning a DC-10 into a toilet; at his manager, Davey Johnson, for displaying the disciplinary skills of a fig; and at himself for allowing the wives to fly.

He called Johnson into his office and, after a good bout of back-and-forth screaming, insisted the manager tell his players that they would be financially responsible for the damages.

That afternoon Richman, the travel secretary, held a closed-door meeting with the team. In front of the disbelieving players, Richman let them know that Cashen was livid, that the New York Mets were a first-class operation and would not stand for this and blah, blah, blah.

Once he left the room, Johnson spoke. This was one of his shining moments as Mets manager.

"Guys," he began, "do you realize how much damage we did on the plane? I mean, does anybody in here have anything to say? Does anybody in here feel guilty?" Johnson was pacing back and forth, a copy of the United bill rolled up in his hand. The players were awkwardly staring at the ground, quiet and motionless. "Men, what are we going to do about this? What should we do?"

There was silence.

"Well," said Johnson, "do you know what I think? I think in the next four games you'll probably put enough money in these guys' pockets to cover this. So fuck this bullshit!"

With that, Johnson ripped the bill in half, crumpled it up, and threw it into a nearby garbage can. The room exploded with comments.

YEAH! FUCK THEM!

FUCKIN' A—!

MOTHERFUCKERS!

The Mets were heading to the World Series.

Chapter 2

THE ROAD TO 1986

What was the impact of Frank Cashen? When I came, the Mets were a laughingstock. When I left, the Mets were a powerhouse.

—ED LYNCH, Mets pitcher

THE FACE OF THE NEW YORK METS is standing here, inches away, snickering like a hyena as tears stream from your eyes. You want a two-by-four plank of wood to slug the back of his oversized head. You want to spit on his shoes and piss in his cap and rip his hair out. And then, when he's crouched over in agony, you'll slip on a pair of Gene Simmons's steel-toed boots and kick him in the g'nads.

But (sigh) you can't.

He's Dave Kingman.

You're just a kid.

Look, you knew the guy was an ass. Hadn't your father told you so? *David Friggin' Kingman is the biggest no-good, #$%^^$@.!$%#! since Adolf Hitler.* Think about all the things he's done throughout his career. Pouring a glass of ice water over the head of a sportswriter who dared—the nerve!—ask about his low batting average. Cursing out a female reporter in the clubhouse because she was, well, a female reporter in the clubhouse. And what about last year when Kingman was playing for the Cubs? Hadn't he all but begged for a Dave Kingman T-shirt day at Wrigley? And when those morons in the front office finally gave in, what happened? Kingman, on the DL with an injured shoulder, goes AWOL. He blows off his own day—which he requested—to pitch water bikes for Kawasaki at some Windy City summer festival. Thirty thousand Dave Kingman T-shirts, zero Dave Kingmans. An ass.

But you didn't listen, did you? It's February 1981, and you and your family drove all the way down from New York for spring training. You thought, *Man, it'd be great to have Dave Kingman—the mighty Kong—autograph my baseball!* You even sat here at Huggins-Stengel Field through a nasty St. Petersburg rainstorm, begging your dad to stay just a little longer. And when the clouds cleared, the magic began. Mookie Wilson signed your ball. Joe Torre and Mike Cubbage, too. They looked you right in the eye and called you son and sport and pal! And magically the crisp white baseball you had bought for $1.50 at Toys "R" Us became the most beloved possession you'd ever owned. This was the best day of your week. Your year. Your life! And it's about to get better. Oh, my God—here comes Dave Kingman!

He's jogging along the first base line from right field, staring down at the rain-drenched grass at his feet.

Daaaave! you scream.

Again: *Daaaave! Mister Kingman!*

Miraculously, he slows down, looks up, and grins. He's motioning for you to toss him your baseball. Me? Yeah, kid, you. And in a flash you think to yourself: *See? This guy's okay. The media makes him out to be a jerk, but really he's a great guy! Who knows? Maybe we'll be friends. I'll go out to Shea, he'll wave. Wow!*

So you toss him your baseball, the most magical possession you've ever owned. And as he takes two steps back, this becomes the moment that you first realize Santa Claus is a fat guy on parole, the tooth fairy is your mother, your favorite third grade teacher is an alcoholic, Max isn't in doggy heaven, and the noise late at night from your parents' bedroom isn't furniture being moved.

Kingman makes no effort to catch the ball. He just watches it drop into a globe-sized puddle of mud, spit, and rainwater. And he snickers. Your baseball is ruined.

This is the face of the New York Mets.

Frank Cashen is a funny-looking man. Not ugly, just funny. One imagines that he always has been, what with those chubby cheeks and that Mr. Potato Head nose and the way he waddles back and forth, arms chugging at his side. Cashen is short—five feet seven inches in loafers—and with his ever-present bow tie, he somehow seems even shorter. In his second year as general manager the Mets are the laughingstock of baseball.

Sometimes when the New York press is calling for his head (or, at the least, questioning his judgment), Cashen wonders what he is doing here, standing on a marshy field in St. Petersburg, watching boorish slugger Dave Kingman abuse the approximately twenty-six paying customers—*Cashen's* paying customers—as if they were cockroaches beneath his Nikes. This was not baseball the way Cashen understood it, the way things were in Baltimore where honor and respect were words that weren't just uttered but were branded into your conscience.

Ah, Baltimore. Now that was a place for a baseball man: the home of Jim Palmer and Brooks Robinson, of Earl Weaver and Mark Belanger. Cashen was born there in 1922, and his heart never left. He grew up a feisty yet undersized sandlot second baseman and spent much of his youth in the stands at old Clifton Park. Young Frank was a ballplayer's ballplayer—not the best but the most enamored of the game. Cashen went on to play four mediocre seasons at Loyola College, where he turned a smooth double play but hit almost everything on the ground. He was "bad even in wartime baseball," Cashen once said to *The Washington Post*. Then he labeled his game in scout-speak: "I was CP and NC—'can't play' and 'no chance.'"

Once he was done not playing well for Loyola, Cashen—thinking the game was a thing of his past—joined the staff of the *Baltimore News-American*. He started on the prep school beat, but spent fifteen of his seventeen years as an award-winning sportswriter and columnist. During his first few years at the paper, Cashen attended the University of Maryland law school at night. He was young and ambitious, and he assumed his career would amount to either fifty years in journalism or fifty years in law. "Truthfully, all I ever wanted to do was work in newspapers," says Cashen. "But I had all my kids [he and Jean, his wife, have seven children], and I couldn't afford just doing something for the love of it."

In 1959 a life-changing twist of fate occurred. A local businessman named Jerry Hoffberger offered Cashen a substantial salary increase to become the director of publicity and promotion for the Baltimore Raceway and the Bel Air Race Track. Impressed by his work, Hoffberger soon asked Cashen to take over as the advertising head for his National Brewing Company. Again, Cashen dazzled Hoffberger, who admired his keen business sense. "He knew how to do a lot," Hoffberger told *Newsday* in 1989, ten years before his death. "Frank's organized, methodical, puts little slips of paper on his desk with his jobs on them, and moves them around according to priority. He had a well-organized and fertile mind."

In 1965 the National Brewing Company purchased the Orioles, and Hoffberger, who knew little of sports' inner workings, approached Cashen about the job of executive vice president. He didn't have to ask twice. Although he was hardly one to exude emotion, Cashen's heart fluttered with each Oriole success, and sank ritually with defeats. He was as much a baseball diehard as the fans in the bleachers. Over the next ten years Cashen's Orioles won two World Series and four pennants. He oversaw the drafting of such Baltimore future stars as Eddie Murray, Mike Flanagan, Bobby Grich, and Doug DeCinces, and he dealt for fixtures like Ken Singleton and Mike Cuellar. Perhaps his greatest achievement came after that debut season when, in his first trade, Cashen acquired outfielder Frank Robinson from the Reds for a popular right-handed pitcher named Milt Pappas. At the time, Robinson's temperament and his dark brown skin cloaked him with the dreaded "malcontent" label. The Reds couldn't wait to ship him out. Cashen—

blind to color and 20/20 toward talent—couldn't wait to bring him in. He was dedicated to building the best club possible, and if the Reds were dumb enough to peddle their star player, it was their loss. In two and a half years with Cincinnati, Pappas won thirty games. Robinson, meanwhile, became a Baltimore legend, winning the 1966 American League MVP and leading the Orioles to a shocking World Series upset over the pitching-rich Los Angeles Dodgers. In six seasons with Baltimore, Robinson would be selected to play in five All-Star Games. Pappas for Robinson stands as one of the more lopsided deals in baseball history.

Cashen's reputation as a shrewd but fair operator spread throughout the game. He served not just as a sound judge of talent but as the manager of all aspects of Baltimore's operations, from stadium maintenance to broadcasting to ticket sales to concessions. In 1975 when a group of major league owners attempted unsuccessfully to unseat commissioner Bowie Kuhn, Cashen was their leading choice for the gig. Several years earlier he was mentioned as a strong candidate for the American League presidency. But in November 1975, Cashen—worn out from the fifteen-hour-a-day grind of baseball—resigned from the Orioles to return to Hoffberger's brewery as senior vice president of marketing and sales. He stayed there until 1979 when Kuhn named him to the supervisory post of administrator of baseball.

In 1980 the Mets came calling.

The Mets? Was there a more pathetic operation in baseball? In 1979, New York had landed in last place in the NL East for the third straight season, finishing 35 games behind the champion Pittsburgh Pirates and a comical 17 games behind the Cubs, the next-to-last-place finishers. They played in the largest city in the United States, where baseball remained the most beloved sport in town. Yet home attendance, 788,905 fans (9,739 per game), ranked rock bottom in team history. To be a Met fan in the mid-to-late 1970s was to watch center fielder Lee Mazzilli throw baseballs every which way but straight or second baseman Doug Flynn struggling to hit the ball past the mound or starter

John Pacella's hat falling off pitch after pitch. It was peek-through-your-fingers baseball—bad pitching combined with bad fielding combined with bad hitting combined with bad attitudes combined with bad management combined with an ugly stadium and no minor league system to speak of. These were the Mets: During a spring training B-game against the Cardinals at Payson Field in 1979, New York mistakenly failed to enlist enough players. With no right fielder available, a coach turned to Brian Cazeneuve, the club's fifteen-year-old batboy, and ordered him to, "Go out there and watch your head!"

Shortly after they purchased the club from Charles Payson for $21.3 million in January 1980, Nelson Doubleday and Fred Wilpon, a pair of wealthy businessmen with minimal baseball know-how, received unsolicited telephone calls from Hoffberger, whom neither had ever met. Said Hoffberger: "I understand you just bought the Mets. Well, the best general manager around is Frank Cashen. Get him while you can." Skeptical, Doubleday and Wilpon contacted other team owners to ask for permission to interview their general managers. As Doubleday told *The Sporting News* in 1980, "Three or four times the answer was 'Sure, but I don't know why you're looking here when the best guy for the job is in New York.' Then they named him: Frank Cashen. I figured, after all those totally unsolicited recommendations, that we'd better talk to him."

During the interview process, Cashen peppered the new owners with questions and got the answers he wanted:

Are you willing to spend money on players?

Yes.

Are you willing to develop a farm system?

Yes.

Will you be patient?

Yes.

Will you leave me alone?

Yes.

Are you sure you'll leave me alone?

Yes.

Will you definitely leave me alone?

Yes.

Seriously—never, ever bug me.

Okay.

"I said, 'Are you looking for a quick fix, where we just go out and sign some veteran ballplayers, or are you looking to build a team?'" says Cashen. "They said they wanted to build. I said, 'Okay, but it's gonna take four or five years.'" The Mets never interviewed another candidate. Cashen agreed to a five-year, $500,000 contract, and the uphill climb began. "I took over a huge mess," says Cashen. "Talent-wise, we had nothing. Fan support, there was nothing. In my estimation it was as ugly as you could get. Just terrible. We needed a complete overhaul of everything." Cashen knew where to begin. As a former journalist he recognized that showbiz sold the sport, not vice versa. Yes, customers wanted to see great baseball, but they would tolerate something less if it was presented in a funky, bright-colored package. Cashen was aware that while the Yankee Stadium press box was brimming with buzz, Shea Stadium was a media ghost town—a couple of print guys and a TV camera or two.

So, no, the Mets wouldn't compete for a few years. They didn't have any true stars, their base-to-base brand of baseball wasn't exactly thrill-a-minute pizzazz, they weren't an especially nice group of fellas, and their stadium was hardly the Magic Kingdom. But did that mean they couldn't generate some buzz of their own?

Cashen took a big step to erase the Mets' hangdog image. In a groundbreaking move New York established a $300,000 marketing budget and hired Della Femina, Travisano & Partners, a well-known Madison Avenue advertising agency, to develop a strategy. Nowadays teams in all four major sports employ an army of PR experts and marketers to generate excitement. In 1980 such devices were rare.

With little to market in terms of actual success, Della Femina, Travisano & Partners came up with a new slogan—The Magic Is Back!—and a series of television advertisements featuring not Mazzilli or Flynn but old Brooklyn Dodgers stars like Jackie Robinson and Ralph Branca. Truth be told, there was no magic now, and there was little reason to believe magic was on the way. "We sold the past and promised the future," Jerry Della Femina, the firm's president, told *The New York Times Magazine* in 1985. "And prayed no one would remember the present."

Cashen was no idiot. Spin control might spice up the atmosphere and serve as a temporary distraction, but nobody wanted to watch a dead horse. In 1980, Cashen completed only one trade, obtaining a journeyman outfielder named Claudell Washington from the Chicago White Sox for minor league pitcher Jesse Anderson. This was the way the GM thought it should be. Slow paced. Step by step. There was no pressure on Cashen to deal for the sake of dealing, to appease the dwindling loyalists with cosmetic makeovers. No, the Mets needed to make some real progress; to show that, while not much magic yet existed at Shea, a couple of spells were brewing. To Cashen the only way to accomplish this was by seeking out young talent.

Ever since their debut season in 1962, the Mets had done wonders with the amateur draft—wondrously transforming their high picks into hapless scrubs. Indeed, it took years for fans to forget the debacle of 1966 when GM George Weiss bypassed Arizona State slugger Reggie Jackson for a high school catcher named Steve Chilcott. Jackson, selected second by the Kansas City A's, is in the Hall of Fame. Chilcott is a nice guy.

In the ensuing years the Mets' first-round selections included such noteworthies as Randy Sterling, Richard Puig, Butch Benton, and Tom Thurberg. It was one train wreck after another. Then in 1980, New York faced its latest make-or-break decision. Because of their dismal record in 1979, the Mets were awarded the Number 1 pick in the amateur draft. This was Cashen's first huge personnel moment as New York's GM. The Mets' scouting department was split between Billy Beane, a speedy, hard-nosed outfielder out of San Diego's Mt. Carmel High School, and Darryl Strawberry, an immature yet gifted kid from Crenshaw High in Los Angeles. Strawberry didn't have Beane's overt passion for the game (as a junior, he had twice quit the baseball team when coach Brooks Hurst disciplined him for not hustling), but he was six feet four inches with the grace of a swan and the power of a tornado. Oklahoma State had offered him a scholarship to play baseball and basketball. Long before his first professional game, Strawberry was branded "the black Ted Williams." Hugh Alexander, a scout for the Philadelphia Phillies, called him "the best prospect I've seen in the last thirty years."

Roger Jongewaard, the Mets' amateur scout for Southern California, watched both prospects play on multiple occasions, and he begged the club to select Strawberry. "Darryl had greatness written all over him," says Jongewaard, who recalls the prodigy's 400-foot homers and 93-mph fastballs. "He was a beautiful athlete who would become a beautiful baseball player. Beane was talented, but Darryl was special." Besides immaturity, the primary concern about Strawberry was background. The third of five kids, Strawberry spent most of his youth surrounded by the drugs and guns of low-income southwest Los Angeles. He was hardened in that way; not an especially bad kid, but unafraid to see a bullet-punctured body or line of cocaine. Was he an incredible athlete? No doubt. How would he adapt to new environments, surrounded by mostly white teammates in a mostly white game? Nobody knew. Still, the Mets were intrigued. Cashen trusted Jongewaard and picked Strawberry first overall, then watched with glee as Beane stuck around for selection number 23. With the twenty-fourth pick (New York received the two extra first-round selections as compensation for free agent losses), the Mets landed catcher John Gibbons of San Antonio's McArthur High. All of a sudden New York's barren farm system boasted the nation's two top-rated high school outfielders and the draft's third-ranked backstop. All three would reach the majors.

By virtue of his surname alone, Strawberry brought the Mets a huge dose of media cachet. (Looking for an amateur star to profile before the draft, *Sports Illustrated* heard the name "Strawberry" and, sight unseen, decided he was their subject.) Cashen asked Jongewaard to accompany the green Strawberry to his professional debut with New York's Rookie League club in Kingsport, Tennessee, where fifteen out-of-town reporters attended his makeshift press conference. Jongewaard still remembers a quiet, somewhat overwhelmed eighteen-year-old soaking in the surroundings, his head spinning like a Tilt-a-Whirl. Following that evening's game (during which Strawberry singled in his first at-bat),

Jongewaard wanted to take Strawberry out for a celebratory dinner. But nothing was open in tiny Kingsport. "So I said, 'Darryl, do you like McDonald's?'" says Jongewaard. Strawberry's eyes widened. "You bet I do!"

"And this part," says Jongewaard, "I'll never forget. The cashier asked for his order, and Darryl said, 'I'll take a hamburger and a milkshake.' Then the cashier wanted to know what flavor he'd like. Darryl smiled like the big kid he was and said, 'Strawberry, of course!'"

A star was on his way.

The Mets finished 67–95 in 1980, and the only on-field bright spot was that by winning three more games than the Cubs, they avoided the cellar for the first time since 1976. On August 14, New York trailed first-place Philadelphia by 7½ games, and the Phillies were in town for a 5-game series. "I remember thinking, 'This is our chance to do some damage and prove we're for real,'" recalls Flynn. "And then they swept us like we were a bunch of dogs. They beat the tar out of us."

Away from the diamond, things were slowly starting to turn in the right direction. Because the reigning position players were so weak, Cashen felt it was time to give some of his prospects a major league look-see. When the team reported to spring training in 1981, its new third baseman was twenty-four-year-old Hubie Brooks, and their center fielder was a twenty-five-year-old speedster from Bamberg, South Carolina, with the memorable name of William Hayward (Mookie) Wilson. Both were rookies.

Though it wasn't obvious at the time, the emergence of *Moooookie!* (as the fans joyfully called him) was the beginning of the end for Lee Mazzilli, the Brooklyn-born local favorite who for the past four seasons had stolen the hearts of New York's female fans. Born and raised in the Sheepshead Bay section of Brooklyn, Mazzilli was a local phenomenon from the age of ten when he won the first of eight national speed-skating championships. The ambidextrous Mazzilli was the Mets' first-round pick in the June 1973 amateur draft, and within three years he reached Shea Stadium. It was a lovefest from the very beginning. Mazzilli was Tom Cruise cute and more than happy to hit the nightlife, and if anyone in baseball had tried to wear tighter uniform pants, his circulation would have been cut off below the waist. "Maz was a matinee idol," said Jay Horwitz, the team's media relations director. "He was our movie star."

The hype didn't match the reality. Mazzilli had some skills, but he grew up witness to New York's love affair with Willie Mays, Mickey Mantle, and Duke Snider, and he, too, longed to roam the legend-making pastures of center field. One problem: Defensively, Mazzilli was bad. "Lee could aim to left and throw the ball right," says former Met pitcher Pat Zachry. "He could never get the throws down."

As Mazzilli's Q-rating increased, his attitude went polar. He pouted when, to make room for Wilson, manager Joe Torre made him play first base or a corner outfield position, and he irked older teammates by strutting around the stadium like a ten-year veteran. Cazeneuve, the bat-boy-turned-right fielder, remembers sitting at a table in the clubhouse before a spring training game, quietly eating an egg and imitation bacon sandwich, when out of nowhere Mazzilli picked it up and took a big bite. "What's this shit?" he mumbled. Cazeneuve, a vegetarian, explained to Mazzilli that it was homemade and healthy. "Okay," said Mazzilli. "If that's the case." He then shoved the entire sandwich in his mouth, leaving Cazeneuve stunned. Cashen loathed egos, especially piggish ones that accompanied so-so skills.

Wilson, on the other hand, was perfect: Quiet. Respectful. Beautifully innocent and beautifully skilled, and fast enough to cover the deepest reaches of Shea's outfield. Torre loved the pup's hustle, and Horwitz loved his Magic Johnson–esque 10,000-watt smile. As Terry Leach, a longtime Mets reliever, says, "If you didn't immediately take to Mookie Wilson, you didn't take to anybody."

Progress was slow for the Mets. In an effort to add more pop to the lineup, Cashen acquired Kingman from the Cubs for outfielder Steve Henderson in 1981. That season Kingman did as well as expected—22 homers, 105 whiffs, and innumerable crude moments. "Look, we needed some faces around to show the fans we were interested in winning," says Cashen, whose team finished 41–62 in a strike-shortened run that year. "We knew Kingman wasn't the star to get us over the hump, but he represented something."

In the off-season, Cashen pulled off the blockbuster that Mets fans had been anticipating. On February 10, 1982, New York sent catcher Alex Trevino and two pitchers to Cincinnati for outfielder George Foster, the menacing, black-bat-twirling former National League MVP. Foster immediately signed a five-year, $10 million deal, the second largest contract in major league history. This was Cashen's statement not just to Mets fans but to the team across the city as well. One year earlier the Yankees had outbid the Mets for Dave Winfield who became the game's first $2 million man. Now the Mets had their own, and they were anxious to crow about it. At his introductory press conference, Foster—normally soft-spoken and aloof—fired the first shot. "I'd like to warn the airplanes and the airport," he said, "not to fly too low." Those gathered roared in delight. This was Cashen's moment. His team's moment. Finally, a real star for the Mets.

Two months later any goodwill toward the club evaporated when Cashen shipped Mazzilli to Texas for a pair of minor league pitchers. Although his production had slipped from his all-star season of 1979, Mazzilli remained the city's biggest heartthrob. When the deal was announced, Shea's switchboard lit up for hours with angry phone calls. Rangers GM Eddie Robinson, a desperate star seeker with a questionable baseball IQ, had called the Mets a few weeks earlier, eager to find a marquee center fielder. Coincidentally, so did Cubs GM Dallas Green, who thought Mazzilli would be a nice fit for Wrigley's cozy confines. When Chicago offered closer Lee Smith and outfielder Mel Hall for Mazzilli, Cashen believed he had a deal. But minutes before completion, Green tried substituting Doug Bird, a nobody middleman, for the dominant Smith. Cashen exploded, screaming at Green over the phone for ruining what would have been, in the New York GM's mind, the deal to rule all deals. The Mets went back to Robinson, who ignored his scouts and presented New York with Ron Darling and Walt Terrell, the Rangers' top two mound prospects. On the day the swap was announced, Joe McIlvaine, New York's assistant GM, was at Tampa's Hillsborough High to check out a young pitcher named Dwight Gooden. Suddenly a man charged toward him, screaming, "How could you do this to me? How could you rob me like that?" It was Joe Klein, the Rangers' scouting director. "I knew from the moment we made the deal," says McIlvaine, "that this was one of the best trades I'd ever be a part of."

He was right. Darling became an all-star, and in 1984, Terrell was sent to Detroit for Howard Johnson, the top third baseman in Met history. Mazzilli, on the other hand, played a total of 58 games with Texas. Robinson never lived the transaction down.

Shortly afterward, Cashen and his staff made a move that would eventually exorcise the ghost of Tom Seaver, the most popular player in franchise history. Seaver had been the Mets' first superstar, leading them to their miracle World Championship in 1969 and to a National League pennant in 1973. But in a salary dispute in 1977, the Mets' troglodyte chairman, M. Donald Grant, traded Seaver to Cincinnati for a batch of forgettable spare parts.

Now with the fifth pick in the June 1982 amateur draft, New York selected a kid they hoped would become their new Seaver: a lightning-armed right hander named Dwight Eugene Gooden. Widely considered the field's fifth or sixth best prospect, Gooden had been monitored extensively by New York. The organization sent eight scouts to watch him pitch, and McIlvaine visited several times on his own. He was easily sold. "Gooden blew me away with his package—he could throw hard, he had good command, he was confident," said McIlvaine. "It was easy."

Most important, Gooden graded off the charts for makeup and personality. Raised in the mostly black working-class neighborhood of Belmont Heights, Florida, this was a seventeen-year-old kid whose aw-shucks demeanor was 100 percent legitimate. His worst youthful transgression was throwing stones at passing cars. "I knocked out a lot of windows," he told *Time* magazine, "and got a lot of whippings." Big deal. Most of his time was spent on the local Little League fields, showing up hours early to play catch and take batting practice, then staying late for extra work. Baseball was a magnet, and Gooden couldn't stay away. On weekends he and Floyd Youmans, his pal and a future major-leaguer as well, would while away their days playing home run derby and pepper, stepping outside at eight A.M. and usually not returning until the dinner bell. It was a classic American boyhood, and Gooden was a classic American boy. As opposed to the draft's top pick, Brooklyn shortstop Shawon Dunston, who went to the Cubs, there were no worries with Gooden about rough surroundings or a street-tough attitude.

The Mets *thought* he would become a top-shelf pitcher. But they *knew* he would always make them proud.

From a developmental standpoint, nearly everything was going right for the Mets. This did not translate into immediate on-field success. Foster's debut season resulted in 13 homers and 70 RBIs, pathetic for a man who once led the league with 52 dingers. Unlike Cincinnati fans, who clapped whether a player hit 4 homers or bungled 4 grounders, New York crowds booed Foster mercilessly, and it ate him up. "I thought George might blossom when he came to New York," says Zachry, who played with Foster in Cincinnati. "But you have to be thick-skinned to thrive in that town. And George wasn't." Wilson and Brooks, though, both lived up to the hype, and Kingman was Kingman. But all through 1982 and early 1983, the Mets lacked the killer instinct that defined baseball's best teams. Manager George Bamberger had replaced Torre in 1982, and he and Cashen often lamented the Mets' minimal snarl. When the Phillies came to town, Pete Rose would charge from base to base, clouds of dust following his steps. The Dodgers' Davey Lopes played as if every inch of Shea Stadium belonged to him. And worst of all were the Cardinals, who had that damned Keith Hernandez. Not in years had Cashen seen a more intense, more obnoxious competitor than the St. Louis first baseman, a man who would stand on the dugout's edge and scream threats at the opposing pitchers: "We're gonna kick your ass! You suck! Is that all you've got, punk?"

Oh, Cashen had loved and hated Hernandez for years. Loved the way he played the game, hated the way he slaughtered the Mets. Every time the two teams met, Hernandez seemed to come through. When it wasn't a clutch hit, it was a great defensive play. He was a modern-day

Frank Robinson: equal parts ass and god. "Man, I couldn't stand playing against Hernandez," says Ed Lynch, a Met pitcher from 1980 to 1986. "He was just so fierce. It drove you crazy. You wanted to kill him."

But it wasn't opponents who had the most vivid murder fantasies. The man who *really* wanted to kill Hernandez was his manager. Whitey Herzog came to St. Louis from Kansas City, where his star was a down-in-the-dirt third baseman named George Brett. When he joined the Cards in 1980, Herzog had a Brett blueprint in his mind, a way the best players should walk, talk, and act. It was a "when men were men" sort of philosophy, and Hernandez didn't conform. Whereas Brett was instinctive, Hernandez was analytical. Whereas Brett would eat and sleep baseball, Hernandez was engrossed by Civil War novels and *The New York Times* crossword puzzle. Brett was a Skoal man; Hernandez was a thinking man's man. During his first season with St. Louis, Herzog invited Hernandez to go on a fishing trip. "It'll be great," he told his first baseman. "A chance for the two of us to talk things over and catch some fish and . . ." Hernandez declined. He just didn't think managers and players should do that sort of thing. It pissed Herzog off.

By 1983, Herzog had had enough of the anti-Brett. He was tired of Hernandez's attitude; tired of watching him jog down the first base line on routine grounders to the infield. He also began hearing rumors of Hernandez's involvement with cocaine, and, proof or no proof, it didn't sit well. Laziness was one thing; drugs were another. On June 15, 1983, the day of the trading deadline, Herzog called the Mets to see if they would consider parting with Neil Allen, New York's young closer (whose well-known drinking problem didn't seem to bother Herzog). "I said, 'No, I really hadn't thought about it,'" recalls Cashen. "And Whitey said, 'If you think about Neil Allen and another pitcher, we'll give you Keith Hernandez.'" That was all Cashen needed to hear. Three hours later Hernandez was a Met, swapped for Allen and Rick Ownbey, the erratic right-hander best known for throwing a Frisbee with his feet. It was one of the biggest trades in Mets history. It was the worst day of Hernandez's life.

Hernandez didn't just hate New York, he feared it, too. When he came to town with the Cardinals, it was, he says, "time to catch up on my sleep." During Hernandez's rookie season, a Cardinals coach pointed to Manhattan's Central Park from the safe distance of a hotel window and warned, "Never, ever go there."

Worst of all, the Cardinals had just won the 1982 World Series, and the Mets were the league joke. At the Mets' spring training facility, management hung a sign that read THROUGH THESE PORTALS PASS THE BEST PLAYERS IN BASEBALL. At Shea, one of the Mets took his own brush and painted a different message outside the clubhouse: THROUGH THESE PORTALS PASS THE BIGGEST LAUGHERS IN BASEBALL. When he learned of the deal, Hernandez immediately called Jack Childers, his agent, to ask if he could afford to retire and live off deferred income. The answer was a big no. He was trapped in hardball hell, in a city where muggers beat up old ladies and on a team where ballplayers cared more about post-game hoochies than compiling winning streaks. That night Hernandez bawled himself to sleep.

The Mets were in Montreal at the time of the trade, and Arthur Richman arranged Hernandez's flight. This was a very important moment for the franchise. Hernandez was a star in his prime who would be eligible for free agency after the season. In the name of respectability, New York needed to impress (and re-sign) him. With this in mind, Jay Horwitz took a limousine to Dorval Airport to meet Hernandez. "Our plan," says Horwitz, "was to show Keith that the Mets were a first-class organization." The limo parked outside the wrong gate. After waiting for twenty-five minutes, Hernandez caught a cab. Says Horwitz, "I felt like a real idiot."

Luckily, Rusty Staub, New York's longtime pinch hitter and goodwill ambassador, convinced Hernandez to give the city a chance. Staub took Hernandez to plays, museums, restaurants, and bars; he pointed out the beautiful women on every street corner. It was a tour Staub had offered before, but few players were more impressed than Hernandez. New York was his kind of town after all. And even though the Mets finished last again in 1983, Hernandez signed a five-year, $8.4 million deal to stick around. The next year he reported to spring training and noticed something shocking: pitching. Oodles of pitching. Young left-handers throwing 95 mph. Young right-handers throwing 95 mph. Sinkers sinking, sliders sliding. Electric movement. There was Gooden, the kid drafted two years earlier. There were Darling and Terrell, the two studs once condemned by a Mazzilli-worshiping public. There was Allen's replacement as closer, a quirky left-hander named Jesse Orosco. There was Dougie Sisk, whose pitches danced with the unpredictability of drunken sailors. There was Rick Aguilera and Calvin Schiraldi and Floyd Youmans. "Pitching," says Hernandez, "out the ass."

Plus, in 1983, Hernandez had been downright astounded by the talents of Strawberry, who hit 26 home runs to be named NL Rookie of the Year. Strawberry was the graceful type of player who made everything look simple. The ball jumped off his bat like a firecracker. He ran like a deer. Hernandez immediately compared the youngster to Willie McCovey, the Giants' future Hall of Famer. "You could see what was coming for the Mets," says Hernandez. "The team was about to explode. I decided I wanted to be a part of it."

Cashen's makeover had taken effect. Egotistical veterans like Kingman and Ellis Valentine were let go in favor of vigor and promise. Strawberry was a fixture in right. Wilson patrolled center with grace. Hernandez was at first, Brooks was at third, and the new second baseman was a feisty kid named Wally Backman. Finally, there was actually enough life to support Della Femina's latest slogan: Catch the rising stars!

To cap it all off, Cashen hired a new field general.

Davey Johnson's first interview for the job of manager of the New York Mets was in a lounge in Atlanta's Fulton County Airport in the winter of 1983. It was a strange place to hold such a meeting, but Cashen had grown suspicious of the snooping metropolitan media, which to his mind existed for the sole purpose of mocking him and his franchise. Just a few years earlier Phil Pepe of the *Daily News* had all but called Cashen a flop and publicly dared him to resign if the Mets failed to improve. It stung.

Not one to waste words, Cashen began by handing Johnson a list of the ten qualities he was looking for in a manager: Fearless. Intelligent. Good communicator. Energetic. Tough. Dedicated to player development. Patient. Hard working. Cooperative. Positive.

Johnson didn't flinch. "I've got those," he said. "What else do you need?"

Cashen laughed. This was the Davey Johnson he knew, the man who, as Baltimore's second baseman from 1965 to 1972, never met a task too challenging. As a player, Johnson was baseball's Renaissance man, dedicated to becoming more than just a stereotypical jock. In no particular order Johnson earned a degree in mathematics from Trinity University in San Antonio; spent off-seasons working as an associate with Major Realty, one of the Southeast's largest brokerages; owned a motel (David Johnson's Second Sack in New Smyrna Beach, Florida), a fifty-acre horse ranch, three shopping centers, and six apartment complexes; earned licenses as a pilot and a scuba diver; and edited an investment newsletter for five hundred major-leaguers.

He was nicknamed "Dum-Dum" by a couple of Oriole teammates in backhanded honor to his erudition. In a game against the Yankees in 1970, Johnson called time-out and approached the mound where Baltimore ace Jim Palmer was struggling. "Jim," he said, "have you ever heard of the unfavorable chance deviation?"

Palmer just stared.

"Well, Jim, you're in an unfavorable chance deviation, and what I recommend is that you aim this ball right down the heart of the plate instead of trying to hit the corner, because then you will hit the corner, and it's as simple as that."

"Davey," said Palmer, "shut the fuck up."

Johnson's great passion was technology. Following the 1968 season he took a course on computers at Johns Hopkins University, and it was love at first sight. Hours would be spent reading books on programming and hardware and typing away on a clunky, old-school system the size of a desk. The next year he developed a program, The Optimization of the Oriole Lineup, that analyzed pitcher versus hitter matchups. He eagerly handed the data to manager Earl Weaver, who snarled, "What's this shit?"

"Ah, he didn't understand it," says Johnson. "I'd say, 'Weaver, the standard deviation chart says you need at least a thousand chances to predict within 5 percent.' He'd just bark at me."

Three years after his retirement as a player in 1978, Johnson was hired by the Mets to manage their Double A minor league club in Jackson, Mississippi, which he immediately guided to the Texas League championship. Two years later Johnson led another Met affiliate—Tidewater, Virginia—to the Triple A World Series crown. It was perfectly clear that here was a man who knew how to run a ball club. "Look," he told Cashen at the airport, "to me you don't have a choice. I know your system, I've been successful, I'm a former major leaguer, and I'm a winner. Why would you hire anyone else?"

A convinced Cashen offered his soon-to-be new manager a $50,000 salary, which was met with a chuckle of disbelief. "Frank, I don't think so," Johnson said. "This is New York. I won't be able to pay my rent." At $100,000, they had a deal.

New York was once again picked to finish last in 1984, but Johnson was not discouraged. Darling and Terrell, both of whom were penciled into the rotation from the start, had performed well in stints with the Mets the previous season, and the new skipper was hoping to reel in one more wunderkind.

Two years earlier, in 1982, the Mets had asked Johnson to fill in at Class A Kingsport for two weeks while Manager Ed Olsen was away on personal business. It was on Johnson's first day that he stood behind a catcher in the bullpen and watched seventeen-year-old Dwight Gooden throw a baseball. The kid was built like a pretzel stick, with tiny shoulders, a scrunched-down posture, and a long neck. He was quiet, too; not a peep. Then he let loose: *bam!* "His fastball was like a shotgun blast coming at you," Johnson says. "I still remember the sound." When the session ended, Johnson pulled Gooden aside and asked him to explain the mechanics of his pitching. "Well, I grip the ball across the seams if I wanna get a little giddyup on it," Gooden said, "and I grip it with the seams if I want some lateral movement." Johnson was incredulous. The kid wasn't old enough to vote or drink a beer, and he sounded like Jim Bunning.

One season later Gooden dominated at Class A Lynchburg (19–4, 2.50 ERA, 300 strikeouts in an incredible 191 innings pitched), then advanced to Tidewater that September to pitch for Johnson in the Triple A World Series. There was no doubt in Johnson's mind: If he was hired to guide the Mets, Gooden was coming along.

Through much of spring training, manager and GM bickered over the teenage phenom. Just three seasons earlier Cashen had allowed Joe Torre to keep twenty-two-year-old super-prospect Tim Leary, and the right-hander injured his elbow 2 innings into his first major league start. This spooked Cashen, and he saw it as yet another reason that a club was better off waiting than rushing. Leary should have been dominating the league by now, and instead he was slumming in Milwaukee, just trying to stick it out as a major leaguer. Gooden was clearly physically ready, but what about his emotional state? McIlvaine had reason to worry. As president of the Florida Diamond Club (an organization of active and retired baseball scouts), he phoned Gooden the previous off-season to inform him that he had been named the group's Best Young Player from Florida. Gooden agreed to speak at the award banquet, then never showed. "I was furious. I couldn't imagine why he did that to me," McIlvaine says. "When I finally tracked him down, it was very sad. He said he didn't come because he was afraid of standing up and talking."

In the end, Johnson won with this point: Gooden didn't have to talk, just pitch. "He's ready, I know it," Johnson said in his final sales pitch to Cashen. "And don't worry because I'll protect him. That's what I do with young arms."

New York wound up finishing second, 6½ games behind the Cubs, and the revival of the 90-win Mets was—along with Chicago's resurgence—the National League story of 1984. Gooden's 17–9 record, 2.60 ERA, and 276 strikeouts (an NL rookie record) earned him Rookie of the Year, and Strawberry was selected to start in his first All-Star Game. "We were too young to be great at that point," says Johnson, "but you could see it on the horizon. We just needed to mature, and we needed another big piece."

Gary Carter speaks French.

In the history of major league baseball, there have been thousands of catchers—mostly dirty, angry creatures just waiting for the next home plate collision to dislocate some base runner's gums. How many of these men do you think spoke French? Three? Four, max?

Gary Carter speaks French because in 1983 that's what the Montreal Expos wanted him to do. Charles Bronfman, the team's owner, was paying Carter $14.1 million over seven years, and he demanded more for his money. That's the kind of guy Bronfman was—one of those wealthy aristocrats who, with the signing of a contract, think they own a player's life. So Carter roped off a section in the Olympic Stadium outfield and paid for underprivileged kids to watch games. And he took a Berlitz French course.

Carter was sure this would win Bronfman over, or at least stop his yapping. The owner had been ripping Carter's "lack of commitment," and when the Expos' highest-paid player compiled a measly 17 home runs and 79 RBIs in 1983, it hardly helped things. Although it was tendonitis in Carter's left arm, not lack of commitment, that had led to the disappointing year, it made no difference to Bronfman. He whined and whined about Carter not earning his pay, even when in '84 he led the NL with 106 RBIs and ranked third with 27 homers. The Expos weren't making money, and the owner found a scapegoat. That off-season Expos GM John McHale called Cashen. "We're thinking about trading Gary," he said. "How interested are you?"

He didn't have to ask twice. The two teams spent the next month crafting a deal that would shift the balance of power in the NL East. At first the Expos nearly sent Carter to Atlanta. But when the Braves backed out, New York was in. On December 10, 1984, the Mets acquired Carter in exchange for Brooks, Mike Fitzgerald, Youmans, and outfielder Herm Winningham. The trade was such a blockbuster that in the second quarter of a *Monday Night Football* game between the Los Angeles Raiders and the Detroit Lions, Howard Cosell stopped everything to make an announcement. *"Lay-dees and gent-el-men, this just in . . ."*

When he first learned of the deal, Carter was shocked. He had done all he could to remain in Montreal, even if it meant being bullied by an owner he didn't especially like. "I wanted to be one of those guys whose whole career is with one team," he says. "I had a real sense of loyalty to the Expos organization."

If anyone knew loyalty—real dyed-in-the-wool loyalty—it was Carter, who had spent most of his adult life desperately trying to honor the memory of his mother. Growing up in Fullerton, California, Carter had enjoyed a relatively normal boyhood of baseball, basketball, and football until his mother, Inge, died in 1966 of leukemia. He was twelve. It was, Carter once told *Sports Illustrated* in a rare introspective moment, "a bad time. I've spent a good portion of my life without her, and I'd give up my contract now to have her back. It's still hard for me to believe." On the morning Inge was taken to the hospital, Carter said, "Mom, I love you, and I'll see you soon." She died six months later at age thirty-seven. It scarred her son for life.

An extremely religious man, Carter has always had complete faith that his mom is somewhere on a cloud, smiling and looking down on her family with tremendous pride. In many ways that is what kept him going through knee injury after knee injury. That is why he played hard, why he never took for granted a day in the majors, and why he regularly donated large bags of money to Leukemia Canada. He was loyal to the memory of his mother and, in a way that's not entirely separate, loyal to the Expos, too. Montreal was the franchise that nurtured him.

Now, it was over. Carter was a Met, and the Mets were stacked. "To a team that won ninety games, we added a dominant force behind the dish," says Johnson. "There would no longer be any moral victories. We were made to win."

For the first time in more than a decade New York entered the year as a serious playoff contender. Gooden, a phenom as a rookie, was deified as a sophomore, going 24–4 with a 1.53 ERA. At age twenty he became the youngest pitcher ever to win the Cy Young

Award. Darling emerged as one of the best number 2 starters in the game, with a 16–6 record. Carter's 32 homers and 100 RBIs led the club, and Hernandez won his eighth straight Gold Glove. When the season ended, the Mets finished 98–64. They were eliminated by St. Louis on the next to last day.

To Cashen it wasn't the wins and losses that mattered so much as the buzz. Even in spring training he had expected his team to need another year of growth. He was right. The excitement, the energy—the team's home attendance (2,751,437 fans over 81 games, a 33,968 average) established a record for New York baseball—were a sign that for the first time in his tenure a phony marketing slogan was no longer needed. The rising stars were here. The magic truly was back.

And the 1986 season was only five months away.

Chapter 3

"WE'RE GOING TO DOMINATE"

People ask how many of the guys knew that our team
could be good. A better question is: Did any of us think we
wouldn't be great?

—TERRY LEACH, Mets pitcher

DAVEY JOHNSON WAS NEVER a big fan of meetings. To him 99 percent
of them were a waste of time and the other 1 percent were an excuse to
relax in an air-conditioned room. The morning of February 26, 1986,
however, was a special moment: the first mandatory spring training
workout for all position players. It had been a wonderful, surprisingly
smooth first two years for Johnson in New York. With Cashen's impressive talent collecting and the manager's ability to get the most from his
players, the Mets were on the threshold of something big. Second place
would no longer cut it. The skill level was high. The expectations were
higher. New York was a real title contender, and Johnson wanted to set
the tone for the forthcoming season.

The Mets gathered in the tiny home clubhouse of ancient Huggins-
Stengel Field where the ventilation was poor and the benches were made

of old wood. Most of the players were still nursing the numb sensation of a winter without bats, balls, and screaming fans. Just one month earlier the space shuttle Challenger had exploded over Cape Canaveral, killing a seven-member crew that included Christa McAuliffe, the teacher-turned-astronaut. It had been front-page news ever since, and the world remained in a state of mourning—except at spring training. Here there were sleepy eyes and empty minds and dreams of six-packs and fishing poles. The conversations ran from the mundane ("Did you watch *Miami Vice* last week?") to the inane ("Who's cooler—Crockett or Tubbs?"). When Johnson walked in, many were set for yet another rendition of the boring old "It's my way or the highway" managerial blather. Departed manager George Bamberger had once even kicked off the season by enthusiastically telling his troops, "Fellas, if we can finish .500, that'll be a real achievement!"

Now, just when they prepared to tune their skipper out, Johnson delivered the unexpected. "Men," he began, "I'd like to welcome you to spring training and the New York Mets. I'm gonna keep this short. There are two rules I have on this club:

"Number 1. Be on time.

"Number 2. Don't embarrass the team.

"Otherwise, you'll be treated as a professional, which all of you are."

With that, several Mets—assuming the speech was *really* short—began looking for the exit. Johnson continued: "This is our year. I know the Cardinals won last year, but that's done with. We're not just going to win, we're going to win big. We're going to dominate. We're going to blow the rest of the division away. I have no doubt about that. And neither should you. Now let's get to work."

There have never been—and never will be—comparisons drawn between Johnson's address and the speeches of Abraham Lincoln and Martin Luther King. Yet few words have had a greater impact on the entire roster of a major league baseball team. At St. Louis's camp, manager Whitey Herzog was telling his troops to play hard and keep up last year's good work. *Yawn.* At the Cubs' camp, manager Jim Frey was insisting that this could be a new year for the perennially sorry franchise. *Yawn.*

At the Mets' camp, Johnson was making a guarantee. Not just success. Domination.

"For a manager to come out and say, 'You will not just win but win decisively,' was unheard of," says Hernandez. "It can only work with the right group of guys. But Davey was cut from the same cloth as us, and he knew it. We would win—no questions asked."

Johnson relayed those same thoughts to the media, explaining that his club should wipe out the NL East. When Cashen heard this, he fumed. He quickly wrote a note and placed it on the manager's desk: *Davey, how in the world can you say that? You're making it harder on yourself and the team.* Johnson crumpled up the letter and deposited it in the nearest trash can.

This was the Mets' manager in a nutshell. *Screw the press. Screw the opposition. Hell, screw my general manager. We're the best team. I know it, my guys know it. So why the hell shouldn't the world know it?* In a city where image was everything, Johnson couldn't care less about what the public thought. *Love me, hate me—we're gonna romp.*

The Mets were coming off a 98-win season, and they were—in nearly all areas—more skilled, more intense, and more arrogant than the Cardinals, Cubs, and the rest of the NL East. All you had to do was look around. New York featured the league's best catcher (Carter), first baseman (Hernandez), and right fielder (Strawberry); a speedy top of the order (Wilson, Dykstra, and Backman); three power threats (Carter, Strawberry, and Foster); and enough young hard throwers to form a Bob Gibson tribute band. By the end of '85 the Mets knew for a fact they were superior to St. Louis, that only a lucky break here or there had allowed the Cardinals to win the division by a game. *One game.* "It should have been us," says pitcher Rick Aguilera. "We knew that in our hearts."

Johnson's confidence had grown exponentially three months earlier, when Cashen completed a trade that in the manager's mind vaulted the Mets from World Series contender to World Series favorite. New York sent four young prospects—pitchers Calvin Schiraldi and Wes Gardner and outfielders John Christensen and LaSchelle Tarver—to Boston for left-hander Bobby Ojeda and three minor leaguers. Many rival GMs laughed off the deal as a huge gaffe by the Mets. Once the Number 1 pitcher on a University of Texas staff that included Roger Clemens, Schiraldi threw his fastball in the mid-90s and could start or relieve, and Gardner was projected to be a solid Number 3 big league starter.

And they traded them for . . . *Ojeda?* If the world was in need of a spokesman for its mediocre major league pitchers, here was the ideal candidate. In six seasons with the Red Sox, he went 44–39 with a 4.21 ERA. Not only was his best pitch a change-up, but Ojeda was brash and opinionated. The Sox front office bemoaned what they considered a spotty attitude, and in the stuffy Fenway Park clubhouse, where strait-laced veterans ruled in silence, such was not tolerated. "Let's just say I wasn't their type," says Ojeda. "I didn't fit the mold."

At Shea Stadium, being brash and opinionated was all but a require-ment. Cashen was well aware of Ojeda's reputation, but he also knew the Cardinals struggled against left-handers (a .257 average versus left-ies, as opposed to .268 versus righties). That's why, as soon as the '85 season closed, Cashen went snooping around for a left-handed starter. He nearly pulled a deal off that winter until the Padres, shopping Craig Lefferts, demanded Dykstra—too steep a price. Now the Mets had their lefty, and Johnson was thrilled. Assuming Ojeda pitched well that spring, he would join New York's first three starters—Dwight Gooden, Ron Darling, and Sid Fernandez—in a young, deep, and rubber-armed rota-tion. "It was the best group I'd ever caught," says Carter. "I had some great individuals in Montreal, but never this type of quality, back to back to back to back. That's probably where the confidence of our club came from. With good pitching you can do everything. We had pitching. Nobody could touch us."

The we-shall-rule-the-earth attitude of the Mets was obvious from the start, and Johnson loved it. The Mets weren't just loose. They were zany and goofy and a little warped, and it took, oh, twenty minutes into the first day of workouts for behavioral patterns to emerge. Doug Sisk, a hard-drinking, hard-laughing right-handed reliever, did the honors, taking a dump in the clubhouse bathroom, emerging with a piece of soiled toilet paper, and dangling it over a hanger in Gooden's locker. This was hardly new material for Sisk, who excelled in torturing the team's young pitching phenom. But it was certifiably disgusting, and it never failed to repulse its target. Upon approaching his locker, Gooden turned to Darling. *Sniff, sniff, sniff.* "Do you smell something?" he asked.

With Sisk guffawing from across the room, Gooden reached for his shorts and grabbed the stained tissue. "Dougie!" he screamed. "Dammit, Dougie!"

Equally vile was another spring gag. Every day after workouts Ojeda and Aguilera would bolt from camp and head for the nearest lake to go fishing. Invariably they'd catch nothing and return to be mocked by Vinny Greco, the Bronx-born assistant equipment manager. "Do youse guys have skills at all? Youse s'posed ta put da fish in da net." Ojeda and Aguilera would laugh along, but inside they boiled. "We'll get this punk," Ojeda promised. "No question about it."

At the time the Mets had their equipment staff sleep in a small side room of the Huggins-Stengel complex. The chamber was the size of a coffin, with ventilation to match. Greco's bed was a perfect target.

One night Greco and a couple of coworkers went out to party at the heart of St. Petersburg's white-hot social scene: Bennigan's. They stayed until one A.M. drinking beer and downing steak fries. When Greco returned home, he washed his face, brushed his teeth, and pulled back the covers to slide into bed. There on his sheets was revenge in the form of the chopped-up remains of a large sea bass, bloody and gooey and, *peeeeeeeeeeeeeeew!* "It was probably there from two o'clock that afternoon," says Greco, recalling the impact that 95-degree temperatures have on a fish. "It stunk like all hell."

The next morning, Greco was greeted in the clubhouse by Ojeda and Aguilera. They were laughing and pointing with delight. "Now," Greco snarled, "you've opened up a war."

One week after the fishy incident, Aguilera and Ojeda were scheduled to play in a charity golf tournament with several Mets corporate sponsors. On the morning of the event, the pitchers brought their bags to the stadium. At the same time the players hit the field, Greco was in the clubhouse peeling the shells off four-dozen hard-boiled eggs. One by one he replaced every golf ball with an egg. That afternoon, as they repeatedly reached into their bags for balls, the pitchers' fingertips found the slimy surface of a peeled egg. As unbearable as the stench of bed-bound bass is, it does not compare to the rankness of rotting, sun-exposed egg.

When they came back to the stadium, Greco was smiling from ear to ear. "Do you want to end this now?" the equipment man asked. "Or do you want to see some of my other tricks?"

Ojeda and Aguilera called a truce. Score one for the little guy.

Unfortunately for the Mets, the early springtime hype was temporarily quashed by a series of spirit-sucking turns. Five months earlier, seven current and former major leaguers testified under immunity before a U.S. District Court in Pittsburgh in the case of Curtis Strong, a Philadelphia-based caterer on trial for sixteen counts of cocaine distribution to baseball players. Among those called was Hernandez, who, in a public hearing, admitted to using the drug from 1980 to 1983 as a member of the St. Louis Cardinals. Under oath Hernandez called cocaine "a demon in me" and "the devil on this earth." It was torturous humiliation, and by virtue of being the best-known of a group of players that included Dave Parker, Joaquin Andujar, Enos Cabell, and Lonnie Smith, Hernandez became the image for drugs in baseball. Indeed, the first time he returned to St. Louis after testifying, fans cruelly serenaded him with a chorus of "Coke is it!"

By cooperating at the trial, Hernandez was granted immunity from prosecution. But he still had to deal with major league commissioner Peter Ueberroth, who desperately wanted to establish himself as the antidrug czar. In his sixteen years on the job, Bowie Kuhn, Ueberroth's predecessor, had done a credible job of marketing the game to the modern fan—expanding the playoff format, incorporating the designated hitter, and presiding over the addition of six franchises. Yet when it came to substance abuse, Kuhn was mostly clueless. His was a Don't Ask, Don't Tell operation, and even though cocaine abuse had infiltrated many a clubhouse, Kuhn seemed either ignorant or unconcerned. On his watch the game was poisoned. Ueberroth made decontamination his top priority.

After several months of delaying disciplinary action, Ueberroth issued a heavy-handed decision. Hernandez had a choice: He could either face a one-year suspension or donate 10 percent of his 1986 base salary to a drug-prevention program, undergo mandatory testing for the rest of his career, and provide two hundred hours of drug-related community service.

The ruling stung the prideful Hernandez. Sure, he could understand *some* penalty. But two hundred hours of community service? Was *Ueberroth* on drugs? Even Hernandez's closest friends considered him guarded, almost a bit shy. Talking to kids about drug abuse—his drug abuse—would be torture. "Knowing Keith, he'll mostly resent the service," Darling told *The New York Times*. "I volunteered to do drug appearances and probably spent twenty-five hours all winter. It's a lot of time."

Worse than the service was the immediate impact on the Mets. Although no one believed that the fiercely competitive Hernandez would accept the suspension, the episode put a damper on what was supposed to be a prelude to dominance. On the day of the ruling, Hernandez made only a brief statement, and most of his teammates publicly avoided the issue. Hernandez was the team's undisputed leader, and there was a loyalty there. "Nobody wanted to hurt Keith," says Knight. "We had to handle it delicately."

When it came to doing so, few set a better example than Mookie Wilson, who treated every day as if it were 75 degrees and sunny. Wilson had the ideal response to Hernandez's troubles, which was an unambiguous "We will stand by Keith and help him make the best of this." Behind the scenes he pulled Hernandez aside and quietly pledged his support. It was typical big-hearted Mookie.

Yet beneath the warmth, Wilson, too, was having trouble. His was caused not by drugs but—quite possibly—by damp baseballs.

———

It traces back to a mid-February day in 1983 when Frank Howard was an off-his-rocker bench coach with the Mets. The team's morning workout was washed out by a tremendous thunderstorm, so most of the players retreated to either the clubhouse or the batting cages. The last man to come in from the field was Howard, who was carrying a basket filled to the brim with baseballs. "The balls are soaking wet, just drenched," recalls John Rufino, an equipment manager. "And Howard sees me and says, 'Excuse me, son. Do you mind if I use this dryer here?'"

Rufino assumed Howard wanted to throw in a shirt, maybe a pair of socks. Moments later he heard the sound: Batabump! Batabump! Batabump! Batabump! Rufino rushed back to the room where twenty-four baseballs were banging around in the dryer. "Son," said Howard, "these balls have to be dry. As soon as this here storm passes by, we've gotta be ready."

Rufino was stunned. "Frank, what are you talking about? We have tons of new balls you can use."

Howard refused, insisting that there was no need to waste fresh rawhide when a simple dryer could do the trick. A few minutes later the rain stopped. Howard emptied the machine, returning now half-damp baseballs to his basket. For the next forty-five minutes he hit deep fly balls to Wilson, who with each throw back to the infield felt more and more discomfort in his right shoulder. "Sure enough, after the workout there's Mookie on the trainer's table," says Rufino. "His arm is dangling off, and the trainer is trying to get these knots out." Despite the pain, Mookie had apparently just kept on throwing "seventy-five shot puts from left field."

In spring training 1986, Mookie Wilson was still trying to fully recover from a chronically bad shoulder. He missed much of the previous spring with a shoulder problem, and twice in 1985 had corrective surgery. Much of his arm strength was gone, making one of the league's fastest center fielders also one of its weakest throwers.

At least he was on the field; having been a Met during the darkness, he was now part of the rebirth. Wilson was coming along slowly, mildly working the shoulder while taking regular batting practice. "I was excited because we had so much talent out there," he said. "Nothing could hold us back."

And then—*bam!*—horror. On the morning of March 5, Wilson and some teammates were participating in a routine rundown drill between first and second. Wilson was the base runner, Carter played first, and Rafael Santana was at short. As Wilson ran from first to second, Carter threw Santana the ball. Before Wilson could turn his head, Santana whipped the ball toward first, accidentally striking Mookie just above his right eye, shattering his sunglasses and sending him crumpled to the ground. Carter was the first to reach Wilson. His voice—high, quivering—and words told the story: "Watch it! Goddarnit, Mook! Are you all right? Just stay where you are! Did it break the glass? Did it break the—? Oh, God! It did! Stay where you are!"

As teammates gathered around, they took in a gruesome sight: Broken glass on the ground. Small shards in Wilson's eye. Blood trickling down his cheek. "I was very scared," says Wilson. "Anytime you get hit in the eye like that, there's the fear whether you'll regain your sight 100 percent or not."

Wilson did. But he was out for two months.

Luckily for Johnson, depth wasn't his primary concern. By not trading Dykstra for Lefferts, the Mets held on to a fast, fearless center fielder who could easily step in for Wilson. Dykstra was cocky, too. "All I need to do is play every day," he told the *Daily News*, "and I'm gonna hit .300 and I'm gonna steal over fifty bases." At second base New York added right-handed–hitting Tim Teufel in an off-season trade with the Twins to platoon with Wally Backman. At third, incumbent Ray Knight was scheduled to split time with Howard Johnson.

Of all the positions this one caused the most concern. It was difficult for Knight to get excited about the upcoming season because throughout the winter and spring he was unsure whether he'd be around. During the off-season Cashen had gone from team to team, desperate to shed Knight's $600,000 contract. It wasn't just that the Mets thought Hojo had the abilities to be a front-line major league player. No, Cashen had been around, and he knew when a horse was ready for the glue factory. Knight looked an awful lot like Elmer's. Two seasons earlier he batted .237 for the Astros and Mets. In 1985 his numbers dropped to .218, with 6 home runs and 36 RBIs. "He was thirty-three years old, an age when guys start to really decline," says Cashen. "His end was near."

There were only two pro-Knight voices among the team's decision makers, and they belonged to the manager and hitting coach Bill Robinson. Johnson believed that his third baseman's drop-off was more a result of injuries (over two years Knight had battled a bad elbow, a torn shoulder, a battered Achilles heel, and kidney stones) than of aging, and near the beginning of spring he and Cashen had engaged in a heated closed-door debate. "Ray's my third baseman, Frank, so stop trying to screw with the situation!" Johnson screamed. "He has more than enough left!" In the back of his mind the manager was unsure, though. Knight's bat had looked awfully slow in '85, especially during a horrific mid-summer stretch. Maybe his time had passed.

Knight knew Cashen had little confidence in his abilities, so he did something about it. During the off-season he worked six days a week digging fence holes around his new home in Albany, Georgia. By winter's end his callused hands were regular-season tough, his biceps were bulging, and his weight was down to 190 pounds, the lowest since his rookie season twelve years earlier. But he had more to overcome than just physical issues. When Knight slogged through the first few exhibition games, doubt crept in. *Maybe I am finished*, he thought to himself, a painful concession for a proud man. *Have I lost it?*

One day, after Knight had gone 0 for 4 with four strikeouts, Strawberry walked by and cracked, "Hey, Ray, is your wife making more money than you again?" Strawberry and Knight were pals, but now was not the time for a zinger, especially about his wife, pro golfer Nancy Lopez. Robinson spotted the dejected player sitting by his locker, head in hands. It was the opening that the hitting coach had been waiting for. "Are you ready to work?" Robinson asked. "Because I know we can turn this thing around."

The two men strolled to the batting cage, where Robinson broke down—and rebuilt—Knight's swing. In hindsight, a simple adjustment was all it took. Robinson believed that with a slight raising of the hands, Knight would significantly increase his bat speed. The normally stubborn third baseman had reached the depths of baseball's Death Valley. He listened. The next day Knight went 2 for 4. Then 3 for 3. Then 1 for 3. Then 2 for 3. He ended the exhibition run with a .292 average.

Nine months later Knight told Robinson that he was going to buy him a gift for saving his career. He purchased a Remington 20-gauge pump shotgun and gave it to the coach. Robinson, an avid shooter, continues to fire away with the gun in the backyard of his house. "Ray was always one of my favorites," says Robinson. "He just needed a little help."

Dwight Gooden needed help, too, only no one saw it. Not yet. How could they? He was the golden god of baseball: the *Time* and *Sports Illustrated* coverboy, the reigning Cy Young Award winner, the owner of a sizzling fastball and a drooping curve. After watching Gooden pitch, even the legendary Sandy Koufax said, "I'd trade my past for his future." On the heels of his historic '85 season, New York signed him to a one-year, $1.32 million deal, making him the youngest millionaire in major league history. Additionally, a memorabilia company paid Gooden $10,000 cash in exchange for sixteen dozen autographed baseballs. He was the hottest name on the hottest team in the hottest town. But as Carlene Pearson, Gooden's fiancée, later told the *Post*, "Publicity and money changed him."

As soon as Gooden's contract was announced, it seemed that every old-school pal from Tampa was back in his life, deeply concerned for his well-being. In his first two seasons Gooden was hailed as the rare youngster capable of handling the New York spotlight. But as he surrounded himself with an increasing number of undesirables, Gooden's ability to make wise decisions waned. It wasn't that he looked for trouble. But, as Davey Johnson says, "Doc never wanted to disappoint anyone or let people down. His worst trait was kind of a quality—he didn't know how to say no to others. He wanted to please."

The first sign came in January, nearly a month before pitchers and catchers were scheduled to report. While shagging some fly balls with some friends near his home in Tampa, Gooden tripped and sprained his left ankle. Instead of contacting the Mets, he kept quiet. Ten days later an anonymous caller informed Cashen that Gooden was hurt. When the GM asked the pitcher what happened, Gooden admitted that he had a minor ankle sprain but claimed it was the result of jogging in the outfield of Hillsborough High's baseball diamond.

Several team executives suspected Gooden of telling a fib, but none confronted him. He was just a kid, and kids—especially those with million-dollar contracts—make mistakes. "We expected so much out of Dwight," says Al Harazin, an assistant GM, "that it was easy to forget he was barely old enough to drink." Gooden told the Mets that he would immediately fly to New York and have the ankle examined. Instead he went to Manhattan to sign some Dwight Gooden collector lithographs and hours later flew back to Tampa. No exam.

Again, the Mets passed the situation off as a minor youthful indiscretion. Then, on April 5, Gooden called Johnson from Tampa to inform his skipper that he had been in a car accident and was too emotionally upset to play in that afternoon's spring training game against the Pirates in Bradenton. Johnson couldn't help but envision the worst—a twisted piece of metal, Gooden in a hospital, blood and guts—and told his pitcher just to take care of himself. "Dwight was like a son to me," Johnson says. "I loved him." The next day there were stirrings that— surprise!—the accident was a hoax. Gooden insisted otherwise, awkwardly explaining to the media: "We were coming out of downtown Tampa and were joining the interstate there, and a car just ran us off the road. There was no crash or contact, really. My friend hurt his arm a little. I'm okay." Oddly, there was no police report and no sign of car damage. Johnson, livid, fined him $500.

Still, the Mets ignored the warning signs. They saw what they wanted to see. At the ball park Gooden seemed to be as carefree and happy as ever. When reporters asked, "What's wrong with Dwight?" Johnson offered the simplest of answers: "Absolutely nothing." It was not a lie but the product of his look-the-other-way managerial approach. As long as Dwight Gooden was smiling and in good physical shape, Johnson requested no knowledge about the pitcher's private time. Johnson was a manager, not a baby-sitter. When he claimed ignorance, Johnson wasn't fibbing. He just didn't know.

Dick Young, the *Post*'s veteran columnist, seemed to have some idea. On April 8 he wrote a piece titled "Success May Turn Dr. K into Mr. Hide."

> [Gooden] is such a good kid, I didn't think he would lie, or scheme, and it makes me worry about the future. Now that he is 21, a man, does he think he can get away with things?
>
> The line between greatness and mediocrity is not wide. A slim loss of desire can make a fatal difference. The kid who would have made the trip to Bradenton becomes the man who ducks it. It makes you wonder, and worry just a bit.

It was overall a miserable spring for Gooden; when he wasn't recovering from a faux fender bender, he was getting hammered by opponents to the tune of 10 earned runs in his first 21 innings. Certainly, part of the problem had to do with his increasingly disturbing off-the-field behavior. Yet Gooden would never again come close to the Cy Young showing of '85, and some of that blame must fall on pitching coach Mel Stottlemyre.

Throughout the previous season Stottlemyre would watch Gooden perform and think, *Boy, this kid is amazing, and all he throws is fastball-curveball! Imagine if he had another pitch.* That's what he set out to do—teach the best pitcher in baseball how to be even better. Stottlemyre had a reputation that was beyond reproach. He had been a five-time all-star with the Yankees in the late 1960s and early '70s, and New York's hurlers loved that he was the rare coach who crouched down and worked as a catcher during bullpen sessions. Many on the staff had, in the course of their careers, been forced to deal with at least one pitching coach who considered it his role to yell and scream and make life miserable. Not Stottlemyre. He was a gentle man with an easygoing demeanor and a soft touch. He spoke, they listened—no questions asked.

All through that spring Stottlemyre had Gooden toy with a change-up and a two-seam fastball, two pitches he did not throw. It was hard to watch. Gooden was a trouper, but the confidence he exuded on his fast-ball and curveball never attached itself to the other pitches. He felt awkward and unsure. There were four catchers with the team—Carter, Ed Hearn, Barry Lyons, and John Gibbons—who had handled Gooden at one point or another. All four agreed that Stottlemyre's plan was poorly thought out. "I remember catching him one day in the bullpen, and they were working with him on the two-seam," says Hearn. "I'm thinking, *What the hell is this?* He was a power pitcher with tons of movement, and they're trying to teach him *movement?* What the hell for?"

"I always thought they should have left Doc alone," says Carter. "Mel thought teaching him a third pitch would be to his advantage. But he didn't need it. He needed someone to say, 'Hey, you've been success-ful. Just keep going at it.' But they didn't."

Stottlemyre's plan had an immediate impact. Gooden's release point—once as stable as Ayers Rock—changed from pitch to pitch. So did his confidence. "I also think it hurt his shoulder," says Carter. "The pitches didn't feel natural to Doc, and pitching was so natural to him. It just wasn't smart."

Had New York's decision makers been present in 1506 when Leonardo da Vinci was painting the Mona Lisa, they would have insisted on a mustache and larger ears. Here they had Gooden, called "the most dominant young pitcher since Walter Johnson" by *Sports Illustrated*, and it wasn't good enough. Stottlemyre wanted the third pitch. Cashen urged Gooden to shorten his leg kick in order to make it harder for opposing teams to steal freely. McIlvaine, a former minor league pitcher, advised Gooden against trying to strike out so many guys. "If we can reduce Doc's pitches, we can save his arm," he told Davey Johnson more than once. "He doesn't need 200 strikeouts to succeed."

In the pursuit of excellence, Gooden made a tremendous mistake. He listened to everyone.

On the final day of spring training, Davey Johnson took a moment to evaluate his club one last time. It had been a terrible two months. His first baseman was humiliated. His meal ticket ace was struggling on and off the field. His center fielder wore a patch over one eye. New York's 13–13–1 record wasn't quite what Johnson had in mind.

But this was a team of badasses, and the manager smiled just thinking about it. In a meaningless exhibition game against the Phillies, Roger McDowell shattered Philadelphia shortstop Tom Foley's wrist with a tight pitch to the midsection. As soon as it happened, several Phillies players began shouting at the pitcher from the dugout, calling him every vulgar name in the book and accusing New York's pitchers of intentional beanings. Johnson's boys barked right back. "Screw those dicks," Doug Sisk told McDowell afterward. "They're just jealous 'cause we're gonna kick their asses."

The Mets were about to take on the world.

The world didn't stand a chance.

Chapter 4

METSMERIZED

The Mets had this arrogance thing all year. You can be a winning team and still be likable. You can still have class.

—OZZIE SMITH, Cardinals shortstop

ON THE FIRST DAY of the 1986 season, the Mets beat the woeful Pittsburgh Pirates, 4–2.

On the second day of the 1986 season, the Mets recorded a rap album.

But not any ol' rap album. *Get Metsmerized.* Picture Vanilla Ice on crack, MC Hammer with half a tongue, and Kurtis Blow without one iota of rhythm. Now put them all together and subtract any remaining shreds of harmony, flow, cadence, and talent. Oh yeah—make sure the lyrics don't exceed a second-grade reading level. That's *Get Metsmerized.*

Here, take a listen:

> *My name is Hojo, I'm here to say*
> *Our team is going all the way*

> *With pitching, power, speed and style*
> *Results guaranteed to make you smile.*

Or . . .

> *When they want a batter filled with terror*
> *They call on me, Rick Aguilera*
> *Slider's hot, I'm on the mound*
> *With cool control I mow 'em down.*

The song was inspired by the Chicago Bears, whose *Superbowl Shuffle* rap of 1985 earned multi-platinum status as the team went on to the NFL title. There was, however, one gigantic difference. At the time Walter Payton, Jim McMahon, Willie Gault, and company recorded the *Shuffle*, Chicago was 10–0 and the class of an overmatched league. The Mets were, ahem, 1–0 and making ludicrous boasts:

> *I'm George Foster, I love this team*
> *The Mets are better than the Red Machine.*

The idea smelled like money to George Foster, who had a weakness for get-rich-quick schemes. A year earlier Foster managed to enrage half the league by selling knockoff Polo golf shirts for $25 in the Shea Stadium visiting clubhouse. Whenever a new team came to town, Foster would send one of the equipment guys over with a bundle of merchandise. "If you looked closely, the horse on the shirt had three back legs," says Vinny Greco, an assistant equipment manager. "The next time the team came to town, the shirts would be the size of a wallet. They'd yell at me, 'I want my money back!' I'd say, 'Hey, go talk to George.'"

This time Foster smelled gold. Two New York–based "record producers" with thin credentials, Jeff Gordon and Aaron Stoner, told Foster that if he gathered up some teammates, the three of them could make oodles of money. The Mets' left fielder didn't have to be asked twice. On April 9, Foster, Gooden, Strawberry, Dykstra, Santana,

Aguilera, Teufel, Kevin Mitchell, and Howard Johnson congregated in a Pittsburgh recording studio to lay down a tune that sixteen years later Teufel accurately describes as "unlistenable."

With the exception of Aguilera, none of the Mets seems to understand the concept of rapping along with the beat. The Dominican-born Santana, who spoke English as well as he hit (he batted .218 in '86), is 97 percent unintelligible. Dykstra sounds as if he's chewing on rocks. Strawberry is illiterate. Foster squeals like a teenage prom queen. "They were terrific!" Gordon told the *Post*, obviously unaware that "terrific" and "torturous" are not synonyms. "Darryl was so good, he did his bit just over drums!" *Ooooooh.*

Even worse than the catastrophic rapping was the arrogance: from the players, who felt comfortable making their *Superbowl Shuffle* with 161 games left to play; from Foster, who believed in such an asinine plan and never thought to give a portion of the proceeds to charity; from Gordon and Stoner, who assumed the public would buy a nugget of manure as long as *Mets* was inscribed along the side; from Gooden and Strawberry, who, inspired by the masterpiece, went on to record solo rap singles. (For a brain cell–sucking treat, dig up a copy of Strawberry's *Chocolate Strawberry,* featuring Richie Rich.) "There were people who should have retired off this record," says Stoner, still upset eighteen years later. "It was a brilliant idea."

"We were," adds Foster, "ahead of our time."

Just how bad was *Get Metsmerized?* Instead of hiring backup singers to do the chorus, Stoner recruited free agents from around his block. One day, for example, Stav Birnbaum, a fourteen-year-old girl whose family lived next to Stoner on Manhattan's Upper West Side, was walking her dog, Cyrus. "Hey, kid," said Stoner. "Do you wanna see the inside of a studio?" Did she! Not only did Stav attend, but so did her older brother, Elam, both of whom carried tunes like choking ostriches. Another participant, Kirsten Van Brunt, was Foster's twenty-year-old live-in nanny. "I'm not a good singer," she says. "But I don't think that mattered."

Get Metsmerized flopped. Initially, Passport Records printed one thousand copies on a twelve-inch "collector's edition" record. Approximately 120 were sold. The first obstacle was the music: It was awful. The second was the Mets: In spite of repeated requests from Foster, Gordon, Stoner, and the record company, the franchise refused to peddle *Get Metsmerized* at Shea Stadium or promote it with signs, ads, or announcements. In fact, thanks to the organization's stalling, the record wasn't released until August, by which time Foster was with the Chicago White Sox. "When the team name is behind a product, the product had better be good," says Drew Sheinman, the Mets' former director of marketing. "And that song was a joke."

For a juggernaut that was supposed to mop up the world, so were the Mets. After one week New York was 2–3 and in fourth place, 2½ games behind the Cardinals. Did reports of *Get Metsmerized* irk the opposition? You be the judge. "I figured we might as well go out there and play them, even though they say they have the division and the playoffs won," St. Louis manager Whitey Herzog said after his team's 6–2 opening-week victory. "The Mets have an outstanding team. I like them, but I like us, too. I don't think they have the lock that they think they do."

Performing as if they were still lollygagging under the spring training sun, the Mets of '86 looked like the Mets of the late '70s and early '80s. In the third game of the season, a humiliating 9–8 loss against Philadelphia, New York blew a 3-run lead in the bottom of the ninth, then a 1-run lead in the bottom of the fourteenth. Hernandez went 0 for 7 and committed a huge ninth-inning error to open the floodgates. (Six years later the gaffe became lore when it turned into the theme of an hour-long *Seinfeld* episode, "The Boyfriend.") "This," said Backman, "is the kind of game you might look back on in the last week of the season when you're fighting for something."

Things got worse in the 6–2 loss to the Cardinals, the Mets' home opener. It was a gala day at Shea Stadium, which—after massive off-season renovations—featured everything from thirty new luxury suites to a revamped press dining room to state-of-the-art bathrooms. The sun was shining and Shea was nearly packed, but the good vibrations didn't last. Gooden allowed only 2 runs in 8 innings; then, with the bases loaded and the game tied at 2 in the thirteenth, a roller found its way through Howard Johnson's legs at third. The Cards crowed with glee. "I don't think we're gonna see a two-team race," said Ozzie Smith, the boastful St. Louis shortstop. "If we play good ball, we'll win."

The Cardinals were licking their chops while watching the Mets falter. Other clubs struggled, and the league noticed with casual indifference. But these were the high-and-mighty Metropolitans, self-proclaimed dominators of the baseball landscape. The Mets told everyone they would kick ass and take no prisoners, and they couldn't back up their boasts. The result was humiliation. It wasn't merely poor play. It was Hernandez, woozy from the cocaine ordeal and also in the midst of a messy divorce. It was Knight attempting to adjust to a new stance. It was Dykstra stepping in as a full-time replacement for the injured Wilson. Most strikingly it was their ace. Two days after the loss to the Cardinals, Gooden found himself in a new mess, one that led to the ugly *Daily News* headline: I'M NOT A VIOLENT PERSON.

While returning a rental car to LaGuardia Airport, Gooden and two women—Betty Jones, his sister, and Carlene Pearson, his fiancée—got into a shouting match with Dorothy Taylor, a thirty-four-year-old Hertz employee who was working the desk that night. According to Taylor, Jones verbally abused her, then threw a drink. Another witness told the *Daily News* that Gooden and his companions all carried drinks into the service area and that they got "bent out of shape" when Taylor asked them to go out in the rain and double-check the vehicle's mileage. Gooden, the witness said, became "abusive and nasty" and called Taylor "a stupid bitch." Jones was charged with Class C harassment.

Abusing rental car agents isn't often cause for alarm. In some sectors it's hailed as public service. But this was yet another glimpse at a new, different side of Dr. K. There would be no free passes. The next day the writers and TV cameras camped out in front of Gooden's locker, still expecting the same happy-go-lucky kid to answer their questions, no matter the negativity of the subject matter. They were greeted by bitterness. "I can't do anything right anymore," he said. "Everyone seems like they're waiting for the first big thing you do. Anything, and then *boom!*

It's a big issue. I'm not looking for trouble, it just happens, and there's no way to avoid that." (In a funny epilogue, four months later Gooden was hired to endorse National Car Rental. Greg Hahn, the company's account supervisor, told *Newsday*: "Gooden has had experience with other car-rental companies, but he prefers the treatment he gets from National.") To Gooden it felt like the world was caving in on him.

There was a black cloud hovering above the team; everything was going wrong at the wrong time. The Mets were losing, their brightest star was cursing out Hertz employees, a slumping Foster was being booed every time he approached the plate, the tabloids were smelling blood, and NBC's Len Berman was wondering aloud, "Are the Mets doomed for disappointment?"

And Flash-quick, things changed. The '86 Mets became the '86 Mets. It began, appropriately, on April 18 when Rodney Dangerfield threw out the first pitch at Shea. New York had spent the opening week of the season getting absolutely no respect from opponents, many of whom wondered why a team that hadn't won a World Series in seventeen years was cocky enough to declare themselves the favorites. They quickly found out. After allowing solo home runs to Milt Thompson and Mike Schmidt in the first, Darling shut down the Phillies, holding them to 2 hits and no runs over the next 6 innings. The big blow came in the seventh when Foster's bases-loaded single down the first-base line drove in 2 runs. Foster received his first standing ovation of the season, and the Mets won, 5–2. The moment was a landmark for the slugger, until that point a target of intense fan hostility. Foster was the quietest member of the team, and most fans interpreted this as indifference. Why wouldn't Foster smile? Why wouldn't he crack more jokes? If he was simply a declining player, perhaps the Mets faithful would have cut him some slack, but Foster was overpaid and, personality-wise, undynamic. Hence he was despised. "We're here to bring a flag to Shea, and we need George," Hernandez said after the game. "George is under a hell of a lot of pressure because the boos are affecting him. Anybody would be tense under those conditions."

The following day the Mets beat Philadelphia again, this time 3–2 behind a 6-hit, 10-strikeout complete game gem by Gooden. The day was a strange one for the Doctor, who pitched beautifully but found himself in yet another puddle of controversy. The Government Employees Insurance Company had filed suit against Gooden for a traffic accident that occurred three years earlier. On December 14, 1983, Gooden allegedly struck the back of a van driven by Dorothy Guess of Odessa, Texas. According to the insurance company, the car he was driving belonged to his brother-in-law and was uninsured. The accident, GEICO claimed, caused "bodily injury, pain and suffering, mental anguish, medical expenses, loss of wages and earning ability and the capacity to enjoy life."

What could Gooden do besides shrug his shoulders, laugh, and pitch his butt off? *This*, he wondered, *is the price of fame?* Fortunately, his teammates had better senses of humor than Dorothy Guess, sufferer of mental anguish. Throughout the year the New York clubhouse would be a place of heavy-duty mocking, and it bloomed here. Gooden, according to Strawberry, was about to open a new business: a driving school with Leon Spinks, the equally accident-prone boxer. Gooden, according to McDowell, was kindly employing Helen Keller as his chauffeur. Gooden, according to Sisk, had been hired as a new spokesman for Rent-A-Wreck.

No, the Mets were not going to let distractions squash destiny. Or dampen their fun. New York rolled with a 3-game sweep of the Phillies and a 2-game stomping of Pittsburgh. On April 21 the Mets trailed the Pirates 4–2 in the eighth inning when, with two outs and Foster on first, Ray Knight was scheduled to hit. Cecilio Guante, the Bucs' top right-handed reliever, was pitching, and Knight was certain Davey Johnson would send up Howard Johnson as a left-handed pinch hitter. "I looked in the dugout," recalls Knight, "and Davey said, 'Go ahead. Go get him. It meant everything to me. So many people doubted me. My manager didn't.'" Knight cracked a fastball beyond the left field wall and into the rear of the Pittsburgh bullpen, some 460 feet away. The Mets went on to win, 6–5. "That was the hardest ball I've ever hit in my life and the most important," Knight says. "It proved I was still a player." With Ojeda's 7-inning 7–1 triumph over the Pirates the next afternoon, New York (7–3) took hold of first place. It was a spot they would never relinquish.

Later in the season as New York compiled win after win, some would argue that the division had been wrapped up since the start of spring training; that their talent and arrogance made the Mets too powerful a beast for even the strongest division rival. But throughout baseball history plenty of teams that were "destined" to win had sunk like old boots. Like all other clubs in all other years, New York possessed soft spots. Gooden may have possessed one of the greatest arms of his generation, but he was just as emotionally vulnerable as any other pitcher made of flesh, bone, and blood. The bullpen could be spotty. The defense was below average. Davey Johnson, a great manager in many ways, was only a so-so game strategist. No, the Mets had to dig in and decide that talent and dedication would equal success. That happened on April 24 when they traveled to St. Louis for a four-game series against the evil Cardinal empire.

Up until the early to mid-'80s, Cardinals versus the Mets was no more of a rivalry than Hulk Hogan versus Molly Ringwald. "The Mets were another team to beat, and that's about it," says Ken Oberkfell, a Cardinals infielder from 1977 to 1984. "People ask what our rivalry was like. When I was there, it didn't exist."

That began to change in 1983 when Cardinals manager Whitey Herzog made the worst personnel decision of his otherwise magnificent ten-year St. Louis reign. Convinced that his team would be better off without the quirky Hernandez, he pawned the all-star first baseman off on the Mets.

Hernandez taught the Mets how to win. He took pitchers under his wing, and with rookie catcher Mike Fitzgerald behind the dish in '84 and the brand-new Carter around in '85, he controlled the on-field operations. If the first baseman spoke, people listened. When Aguilera jogged in from the bullpen to make his major league debut at Philadelphia on June 12, 1985, his palms were covered with sweat, and the opposing hitters all looked like King Kong. "I was terrified," he says. "Keith saw that." Hernandez casually strolled to the mound. "Aguilera—you're a Spaniard, right?" the first baseman asked. Aguilera nodded sheepishly. "Us Spaniards got sack," Hernandez said. "Let's do it!" Aguilera held the Phillies hitless for 2 innings.

Following an unsuccesful start against San Diego, Darling deject- edly returned to his hotel room. When he opened the door, a bottle of iced Dom Perignon was resting on the night table. It was from Hernandez. Attached was a note: "Enjoy this. I hope it will help you forget."

Hernandez knew that St. Louis would likely be the club standing be- tween the Mets and the playoffs, so he made it abundantly clear that New York should do anything—absolutely anything—to turn the Cardinals into bacon bits. This meant that whenever Backman slid into Ozzie Smith, he would do so with a little extra elbow-to-chest action at the end; that Gooden's fastball, 94 mph versus the Padres and Expos, would be just a little faster (and closer to the chin) with St. Louis around; that Carter's tags—usually strong yet peaceful—would carry a bit more oomph when Tommy Herr charged the plate. "It was heated," says Knight. "I've been in some good rivalries. But we didn't like the Cardinals and it showed."

Until he was traded, Hernandez had what he calls a "respectable ad- miration" for Herzog. They weren't friends, but he could admit that Her- zog possessed a brilliant baseball mind. "The best manager I ever played for," says Hernandez. When he switched uniforms, whatever goodwill there had been died. Hernandez believed he was sent to New York as a punishment. Heck, why else would the 1979 NL MVP be dealt for Neil Allen and a mid-level prospect? He was not wanted.

So when the Mets traveled to St. Louis for the first big series of '86, Davey Johnson didn't have to say much to rally his troops. They were all professionals who had been in similar situations before. Pressure was nothing new to the major league baseball player. But somehow this was different. The usual clubhouse banter was kept to a minimum. Hernan- dez sat intently by his locker in the small visitors' clubhouse, and many followed suit. The World Series was months away, yet somehow this felt like a World Series. Ever the psychologist, Johnson sensed the buzz. He stood before the team and asked for silence.

"Men," he said, "let's send a message right here, right now. We have a chance to take command of this thing early and put ourselves in these guys' heads. If we dominate this series, they'll curl up and die. Let's kill 'em." The Mets stormed the dugout like pit bulls after a cat. They were ready.

In the first game, a Thursday night affair in front of 33,597 rabid spectators, New York ripped the Cardinals' hearts out. With Herzog's club winning 4–2 in the top of the ninth, the fans stood on their feet in anticipation, expecting Todd Worrell, the league's nastiest closer, to finish things. But with Foster on second, Howard Johnson took a Worrell fastball and—*thwack!*—launched it deep into the right field stands, tying the score at 4 and knocking the wind out of a city. The next inning Foster poked an RBI single to left, scoring Backman from second for the 5–4 win. The moment was a huge one for Davey Johnson, who wanted Herzog's skull on a platter nearly as badly as Hernandez. "Oh, they were the enemy," says Johnson. "Believe it or not, Whitey was my mentor. From day one he thrived at matchups. I learned that from him. So when he brought in Worrell, it was 'check.' Well, now I had Hojo against Worrell, and he could always hit that guy. It was 'checkmate' for us." It was the first time in 90 games that the Cards had blown a ninth-inning lead, and the setback was gut-wrenching. New York's players poured out of the dugout to mob Backman, coating him in head pats and high-fives. Hernandez smiled as his nemesis looked on with disgust. "The Mets are the team to beat," Herzog said, smoke rising from under his cap. "Hell, they think they won the last two years anyway."

The following morning the *St. Louis Post-Dispatch* featured a full-page advertisement that read: THE BAD GUYS ARE BACK IN TOWN. The picture was of Gooden, and the ad was right—Gooden was bad. *Nasty* bad. For a guy confronting countless off-the-field distractions, Gooden pitched masterfully. On the second night of the series he held the Cardinals to 5 hits in a 9–0 Met rout, backed by Knight's team-leading fifth and sixth homers. "All series are big," Knight told the *Daily*

News afterward, "but this is bigger because the Cardinals are the best team in the division—next to us."

After the game several Mets were shocked to find Hernandez alone in the shower, crying under the streaming warm water. Hernandez was the team's Mr. Stoic, but the drugs and the divorce and the abusive St. Louis hooligans had finally cracked him. Everywhere Hernandez turned, Busch Stadium's obnoxious fans pounced, screaming "Traitor!" and "Druggie!" When he was kneeling on deck, someone threw a bottle that whizzed past his head. "He was hurting," says Carter. "Keith was a very proud baseball player. He didn't want the distractions, and they really beat on him." That the Cardinals fans—*his* old fans—would act this way was devastating. Despite his toughness Hernandez was desperate for approval and affection. In many ways it stemmed from his childhood in Pacifica, California. Hernandez's father, John, worked as a member of the San Francisco Fire Department, but his background was in baseball. In 1940, a few months after signing a $1,000 bonus to join the Brooklyn Dodgers organization, John was playing in a minor league game in Georgia when a wayward pitch nailed him in the face. His eyesight was permanently damaged, his career over before it started.

Unable to play himself, John made Keith his project. "Baseball was like Dad's vocation," Gary Hernandez, Keith's older brother, once told *Sports Illustrated*. "The fire department was something that put food on the table and paid the bills. His passion was baseball and teaching us to play it." Keith and Gary were subjected to written baseball exams and hours upon hours of grounders on the nearby field. If John detected even the slightest lack of effort in a game, he would rip into his kids at length. Even when Hernandez finally reached the majors in 1974, John remained unsatisfied. Encouraging words were rare. Reprimands were common: "Your hands are too low," "Your back foot is sticking out," or "You're not going the other way enough." Their relationship became strained and remained that way for years. Hernandez wanted a hug, a pat on the butt, something. Instead, it was either a complaint or a suggestion.

In a 1989 Q&A with *Playboy*, Hernandez summed it up: "My big problem with Dad came . . . when I was in the major leagues and told him, 'Hey, I am a man, and I want to go it on my own. If I get into a slump and it becomes critical enough, I'll ask for your advice. But I want to play ball by myself and not have you to lean on.' That was in 1978, after I'd hit .340 the first half of the season and slumped in the second half. I wanted to pull away from him, which caused a big stir. He just couldn't let go. Some people have said we have a love-hate relationship, but I don't think of it that way; I know I've never hated him."

Sitting under a shower, tears running, Hernandez needed a father. Not a hitting coach.

The third and fourth games of the Cards series were both relatively close. Sid Fernandez struck out ten in Saturday's 4–3 win, then Ojeda went the distance in the sweep-clinching 5–3 finale. When the dust cleared, the Mets had an 11–3 record and a 4½-game lead over the sinking Cardinals. It was the best start in franchise history and a clear signal to St. Louis: You guys are toast.

The Cardinals were never a factor again. They suffered multiple injuries throughout the season, at one point fielding a starting lineup with a combined 9 career homers. Thanks to a strong run during the final month, Herzog maintained respectability, finishing 79–82 and *just* 28½ games out of first. But they were never able to recover from the Met-delivered ass-whuppin'. No one was happier than Hernandez.

During the sweep a truth emerged that, come series end, Herzog humbly called "the difference between the Mets and most everyone else": New York was deep enough to have two first-rate third basemen (Knight and Johnson), two first-rate second basemen (Backman and Teufel), a fourth outfielder with pop (Danny Heep), and, in Dykstra, one of the organization's four highly rated center fielders (Wilson was on the DL, and Stanley Jefferson and Terry Blocker were in the minors). "Davey just had a matchup for everybody," says Knight. "That made us very dangerous." At the end of '85, Cashen and Johnson thought it necessary to address a glaring vulnerability against left-handed pitching, with St. Louis ace John Tudor specifically in mind. So the right-handed-hitting Teufel arrived, and contrary to the wishes of several front-office executives, the team promoted a twenty-four-year-old rookie with an ungodly right-handed pop, the skills to play six positions, and the reputation of a thug. His name was Kevin Mitchell.

In the 5–3 series-closing win, Mitchell hit leadoff for the first time in his life and played shortstop for the first time in his life, too. He did both with aplomb: a fourth-inning homer off Tudor and an errorless game in the field. Carter immediately anointed Mitchell "World B. Free" (after an NBA player with the strange appellation) because, he says, "Mitch could play any position on the globe."

Soon every Met was calling Mitchell "World." He loved it.

When Kevin Mitchell was fourteen years old, he was shot in the back. The bullet, fired by a random hoodlum somewhere in the rough streets of gang-infested San Diego, left a scar that to this day protrudes like a Hershey's Kiss. Physically, Mitchell can look in the mirror and see the scar. Emotionally, it remains as raw and odious as month-old milk.

To borrow a line from *Pulp Fiction*, Mitchell is "a bad-ass mother-fucker." When he was twenty-three years old and playing for Triple A Tidewater, Mitchell's stepbrother, Donald, was killed in a gang-related shoot-out. Ed Hearn, a teammate that season, remembers Mitchell in the Tides' clubhouse, tears welling in his eyes, openly plotting a way to leave the team, go home, and seek revenge. "He was a bull in a china closet," says Hearn. "I said, 'Mitch, think about this. Think about what you're about to do to your life.'"

Wisely, Mitchell never departed. But his notorious image—angry, violent, ferocious—grew exponentially. Throughout the Mets minor league system Mitchell had already become something of a legend from an incident that took place in 1981, when he and Darryl Strawberry were both with the organization's Instructional League club in St. Petersburg, Florida. It was a scorcher of an afternoon, and six members of the team were playing pickup basketball on a blacktop court near Al Lang Stadium. At one point during the action, Strawberry—a better hoops player than Mitchell—became enraged by a unnecessarily rough foul. "What's with the pussy shit!" he yelled Mitchell's way. At the time he knew Mitchell only as another outfielder trying to move up the ranks—a face, a name, and nothing more. "You're playing like a fucking pussy!"

Mitchell walked up to Strawberry, a devilish smile tattooed on his mug. Pop! He punched him in the face. Pop! Pop! Two more times. Strawberry tugged Mitchell by the hair and then bit his right arm. With this Mitchell *really* got mad. He grabbed Strawberry around the waist, lifted him up, and—wham!—slammed him headfirst onto the pavement. He dove on top of Strawberry before the two were separated. "Who the fuck do you think you are?" Mitchell yelled at his battered, bloodied opponent. "Do you know who you're fucking with?"

Dazed but not confused, Strawberry shot back: "You're the one who's gonna get released, not me! I'm a first-round pick! I'm Darryl-fuckin'-Strawberry! Who the fuck are you?"

Mitchell was shocked. Darryl Strawberry? *The* Darryl Strawberry? "I thought Darryl Strawberry was white," Mitchell says now. "I had no idea." Instead of being intimidated, Mitchell flipped. He went to his hotel room, grabbed a baseball bat, and returned to the court, anxious to bash in Strawberry's skull, as well as those of the players—Met prospects Lloyd McClendon, Randy Milligan, and Mike Davis—who broke up the brawl. While Mitchell was gone, Miligan picked Strawberry off the ground, dusted him off, and offered a word of advice. "This Mitchell guy is crazy," he said. "He comes from the ghetto, and he will kill you." The players, Strawberry included, dashed off before Mitchell could come back to finish the job.

If Mitchell had been another soft-hitting middle infielder with moderate skills, it is unquestionable that he would have been released and shipped back to the rough streets of San Diego, never to be heard from again. Yet even though he wasn't a Strawberry-esque prospect, Mets coaches loved Mitchell's quick bat and kill-or-be-killed instincts. While playing for Double A Jackson in 1983, he engaged in yet another scrap, only this one endeared him to the organization. In a game against the Midland Cubs, the opposing pitcher beaned a Met player in the head. Mitchell, who was on third base, began cursing at Tommy Harmon, the Midland manager. Harmon charged from the dugout, reached Mitchell, and—

splat! Mitchell grabbed Harmon's right arm, twisted him into a head-lock, and flipped him on his back. "Mitch beat the living shit out of him," recalls Calvin Schiraldi, a former teammate. "It was all-time ugly."

By 1984, Mitchell was a top prospect at Tidewater, and in 1986 he reported to spring training with a real shot at sticking with the big club. During the exhibition season he batted .353 with a team-high 4 homers. Davey Johnson tried Mitchell everywhere: third base, shortstop, left field, center field, right field. Wherever he was asked to play, the kid excelled. But there were still questions about his attitude.

The day before Johnson was to tell the youngster that he had made the team, Bill Robinson, the first-base coach, pulled Mitchell aside. Robinson was a skinny, bookish man with the intimidation rating of a snail. Mitchell was barrel-chested and muscle-packed and the owner of an SOB scowl. "You know, Kevin, the world doesn't owe you a damn thing—certainly not baseball," Robinson said, jabbing a finger into the player's chest. "If you don't wise up and do the things you're capable of doing, you're gonna be out of this game. You have a chance to do some great things. You also have a chance to fuck up your life. It's your choice."

Mitchell was stunned. Nobody had ever spoken to him that way, at least not without winding up in the emergency room. Why, he could kill this old coach with one hand, one finger.

Instead, he listened.

"I had a chip on my shoulder," says Mitchell. "And Bill made me realize that I wasn't in San Diego. I was a baseball player making a nice salary in a great city, and I had to make the most of it."

As the Mets went on their greatest roll in franchise history, it seemed as if the club would never lose. Following the flogging of the Cardinals, New York traveled to Atlanta and took the first 2 games of the series. The second victory, an 8–1 smacking in which Strawberry had 5 hits and Gooden held the lowly Braves to 1 run over 8 innings, tied the organizational mark of 11 straight wins.

Although they finally fell to Atlanta the next night, Hernandez was unshaken. "No big deal," he said. "We'll start a new streak tomorrow."

Miraculously, they did. The Mets ran off another 7 in a row, including sweeps of the Reds and Astros. By mid-May, New York was 21–7 and 3½ games up on game-yet-overmatched Montreal. When the team flew to San Diego for a 3-game series against the Padres, Mitchell rented a white stretch limousine and took three Mets to his grandma Josie's house for a soulful spread of chicken, ribs, chitlins, biscuits, and collard greens. As they pulled up to Granny's driveway, dozens of fans were standing in the yard, anxious for a picture or autograph. It was one of the first signs that the Mets were becoming more than a New York phenomenon. "Mitch got out of the car, and people went crazy," says Hearn. "Then Straw, and they screamed even louder. Then Ed Hearn. It was dead quiet, like, 'Who's the white guy?' Mitch's grandma pulled me aside and said, 'Now, Ed, you might not like chitlins, so I got you a chicken breast.'"

The Mets were eating up baseball. Strawberry, Hernandez, and Carter powered an order that at that point ranked sixth in the NL with 31 homers, and the starting foursome of Gooden, Darling, Fernandez, and Ojeda had combined for a 20–4 mark. The closer tandem of McDowell and Orosco was one of the league's best. There was also one serendipitous breakout, and it was huge. With Wilson still on the DL for the early part of the season, Davey Johnson figured that for a while at least the top of his lineup would struggle to spark the offense. Instead, New York fell deeply in love with Dykstra and Backman, a pair of peanut-sized, dirt-covered, cigarette-smoking scrappers who shared the bonds of rejection and stole the spotlight from their superstar teammates. To many fans they were—together—*Dykman*. Or *Backstra*. As the Mets' leadoff (Dykstra) and Number 2 (Backman) hitters, the duo thrived on wreaking havoc on a league that had mocked their talents. Wasn't it just five years earlier that the five-foot-ten, 160-pound Dykstra, an obscure, unwanted rug rat out of Garden Grove High in Santa Ana, California, attended a Mets' tryout camp and was asked by one of the coaches, "Kid, are you the batboy?"

Dykstra's livid response: "My name is Lenny Dykstra, and I'm the best fuckin' player in California." Chosen in the twelfth round of the

1981 draft, Dykstra did not regard himself as a mid-level prospect. He told Roger Jongewaard, New York's veteran West Coast scout, that he deserved a higher salary than the top overall selection and demanded that he skip Rookie Ball and begin at Class A. The first wish was ignored, the second granted. "He was crazy," says Jongewaard. "We loved that about him."

Backman, meanwhile, was the Mets' Number 1 draft pick out of Aloha High in Hillsboro, Oregon, in 1977. But because he was five-nine and 160 pounds, the team's brass always seemed to find a Brian Giles or Jose Oquendo to hand the position to. "Those other guys had greater talent," says Davey Johnson, "but they didn't focus 100 percent." It became a predictable routine: Backman would hit .300 with 20-plus stolen bases in the minors, attend spring training, and *almost* make the club. *If you were just a little more . . .*

"I always thought I would get an opportunity to play at some point," Backman says, "but there were a lot of people who just didn't want my type of ballplayer."

Davey Johnson *loved* his type, affectionately referring to Backman and Dykstra as "my down-and-dirty guys." In 1983, Johnson was Backman's manager at Triple A Tidewater, and he made a promise: If I'm ever the Mets' skipper, you're my second baseman. The next season Johnson was in New York, and so was Backman.

For years Mets fans had been forced to watch a lethargic group of so-called professionals go through the motions. Now they had two electric water bugs, and the results were mesmerizing. Dykstra hit safely in 12 of the first 15 games of '86, and in the 8-1 win over Atlanta, his 3 hits, 2 runs, and 2 stolen bases had Braves pitchers' heads spinning. Defensively, Dykstra routinely slammed into the center field wall like a wrecking ball. After Cincinnati's Dave Parker was robbed of a homer, he gave Dykstra the ultimate backhanded compliment. "He's a gritty little player," Parker said. "What tees me off is he's only four-eleven." Dykstra's nickname—"Nails"—was perfect. Nobody was tougher.

Except maybe Backman. The guy with the dirtiest uniform in baseball hit .407 in his first 17 games, and like Dykstra, he would have happily traded his spleen for a couple of victories. At the start of every game Backman and Robinson had their own dugout ritual. "I'd get in his face and say, 'You little motherfucker! You little son of a bitch!'" says Robinson. "He'd say, 'Bill, I love when you talk to me like that.'" In the ninth inning of New York's 4–3 win at St. Louis, Backman saved the day with an out-of-nowhere, stretched-to-the-limit snag of a Terry Pendleton line drive. As soon as the ball was caught, Pendleton slammed his bat to the ground.

The Dynamic (Runt) Duo had done it again.

Chapter 5

DRINKING DAYS

You don't win a World Series drinking milk.

—DOUG SISK, Mets pitcher

AS THE METS CONTINUED to win, they continued to drink. *And drink. And drink. And drink. And drink. And drink. And drink.*

On May 10, Wilson returned to center field for his first start of the year, and the Mets beat the Reds, 5–1, at Shea. It was the club's twentieth win in 24 games, the third-best start in baseball history. "The Mets don't have a weakness right now," Cincinnati manager Pete Rose said. "When you're on a roll like that, everything works."

And drink. And drink. On May 15, Danny Heep clubbed a Nolan Ryan curveball over the Astrodome's right field fence in New York's 6–2 win over streaking Houston. "It's got to be discouraging to the other teams," said Carter. "They must be thinking, 'Gee, when are the Mets going to take a dive?' Well, we don't plan on it."

And drink. And drink. On May 21, Darling held the Giants to 3 hits over 7 innings in the Mets' 7–4 triumph at Candlestick Park. It was the club's third straight victory. "I think other teams are picking up the paper and saying, 'God, the Mets won again,'" said Darling. "We're saying, 'Guys, you're gonna have to catch us.'"

And drink. And drink. Following every New York victory the team would enter its clubhouse and be greeted by a bountiful chest of icy Budweisers (as opposed to every New York loss when the team would enter the clubhouse and be greeted by a bountiful chest of icy Budweisers). There was a ritual on the days the Mets were leaving a city: a few beers immediately after the game, shower, a few more beers, board the bus for the airport with three or four beers in pocket, chug-chug-chug, board airplane, more beers, arrive in new town, board bus to hotel, one or two more beers, arrive at Hilton/Marriott/Hyatt, pass out on hotel bed (with beer in hand, groupie optional).

Ed Hearn, one of the team's few abstainers, loves telling the warm, fuzzy stories of his championship season. Once, for example, the Mets were on the bus from Greater Pittsburgh International Airport to the downtown Hilton. It was a late night, and Hearn was dozing off in his seat, eyes slowly shutting . . . slowly shutting . . . slowly shutting . . . slowly . . .

Pssssssssssssssssssssssssssssssssssssssss.

Hearn popped from his slumber. Moisture was seeping into the back of his seat. Warm moisture. At first he thought the air-conditioning was leaking from above. Then he turned around. There, passed out, was shortstop Rafael Santana, penis in hand ("Cock the size of a bat," Hearn says with a laugh), spraying urine like a fire hydrant. "He's drunk, pissing all over himself," says Hearn. "Eight out of ten guys would have drilled him. I was nice enough to straighten him up in his seat."

Hearn didn't blame Santana, the team's resident wine connoisseur. How could he? The shortstop was another victim of the Scum Bunch, kings of the Mets' nighttime world.

There was no escape.

The rules to the card game were simple. If a player drew a red card, he drank. And if he drew a black card, he picked again. It wasn't complicated because, well, who needed complications? Up toward the front of the Mets plane, Carter and Wilson could sleep and read their Bibles all they wanted, but here in the back, the issues of the world were as noteworthy as a fat stewardess. Why? Because this was the land of the Scum Bunch. Only Scum allowed.

Nobody seems quite sure how the moniker came to be, just that it fit perfectly. According to team historians the Scum Bunch debuted three seasons earlier when five Mets pitchers—Orosco, Sisk, Carlos Diaz, Scott Holman, and Walt Terrell—turned grape tossing into an unsanctioned Olympic event. On days when the hours felt long and there was little to do, the five would sit at a table in the New York clubhouse, find the softest grapes, and chuck them at the overhead TV. *Splat! Splat! Splat!* Invariably Charlie Samuels, the gruff Shea Stadium clubhouse manager, would notice the damage, mutter "Sons of bitches" under his breath, wipe off the screen, and ban grapes from the room. The next day there would be a bowl of peaches. *Splat! Splat! Splat!* Then a bowl of plums. *Splat! Splat! Splat!* Then a bowl of mangoes. *Splat! Splat! Splat!* Finally, the fruit was taken away altogether. "Sons of bitches."

Samuels was embraced by the Scum Bunch because, as targets go, he was as easy as they come. Whenever a chair was out of place or a helmet scuffed, the short, chunky Samuels was first on the scene to fix things up. As a result, Sisk and the gang found every opportunity to ruffle Samuels's feathers. A drop of fruit punch on the carpet here. A couple of spilled sunflower seeds there. Sisk even gave Samuels his own nickname, "The Big Fig Newton," after the cookie company's mascot. Like the original Big Fig Newton, Samuels was wide, wobbly, and sort of crusty on the outside. Over time "The Big Fig Newton" was shortened to just "Fig." It stuck for years.

The Scum Bunch were not bonded merely by a love of torturing the clubhouse manager. Their primary shared passion was alcohol consumption. When a game at Shea Stadium ended, Samuels and Vinny Greco, his assistant, would comb the clubhouse, sweep the carpet, and polish the helmets. Gradually the players would drift off. "And there'd be Sisk, Heep, and Orosco, three hours after everyone else went home," says

Greco. "They'd be there completely wasted in their underwear and a T-shirt with a six-pack of beer, picking their noses and comparing booger sizes or rubbing hot balm in each other's jocks or crushing beer cans and throwing them on the floor." Sometimes Greco found the trio in the batting cage, laughing hysterically over nothing, tossing beer cans up in the air and whacking them with bats. Greco would make an announcement: "Time to go home!" And another announcement: "Really, time to go home!" Finally, he'd start flicking the light switch: "Guys, get the hell out!"

"Meanwhile," says Greco, "their wives were waiting outside the clubhouse the entire time, desperate to leave."

Over the years the official Scum Bunch lineup changed slightly (Heep, who joined the team in an '83 trade from Houston, replaced Diaz, Holman, and Terrell), but the heart and soul remained. While Orosco represented your typical goofy left-hander and Heep was the quietly mischievous sidekick, the Scum Bunch was all about the tortured Sisk, who needed a drink—lots and lots of drinks—more than anyone.

From the end of the 1982 season through all of 1984 there was no better National League reliever than Sisk, owner of the game's most wickedly unpredictable sinker. At his peak in '84 the right-hander was unhittable, with a 2.09 ERA and 15 saves in fifty appearances. But then *poof!* His touch was gone. A few bad outings led to a bunch of bad outings, and Sisk's confidence eroded to the point where one good pitch felt like an accomplishment. This was a fragile psyche. Sisk's ERA jumped to 5.30 in '85, and as he blew game after game, the crowds at Shea heckled him like a rejected stand-up comic. Once when Sisk was leaving the stadium after a blown save, a fan jumped in front of his car, pulled a gun out of his jacket pocket, and pointed it at the reliever's head. On second glance it was only a finger. But it scared Sisk to death.

Things got no better the following year. Before a home contest against Philadelphia, New York entertained the fans by holding a computer-generated game between the '69 Mets and the '86 Mets. The back-and-forth action was described on the Diamond Vision scoreboard, and when the '86 Mets won, 5–2, there was a huge cheer. Two seconds later WINNING PITCHER: SISK appeared. The boos were deafening. "Do people think that because I was wearing a uniform, I couldn't be hurt?" says Sisk. "I'm human. The negativity ate me up." Repeated visits with pitching coach Mel Stottlemyre offered temporary relief, but only until Sisk took the mound, and allowed, oh, 6 hits, 4 walks and 3 earned runs in one-third of an inning. Sisk lost sleep. He paced back and forth. His appetite was gone. After yet another poor outing, Carter approached Sisk in the back of the airplane, trying to console the battered pitcher. "Look, Dougie, I know what you're going through," Carter said. "Just try and be tough and—"

Orosco, sitting nearby, angrily interrupted: "Gary, you have no fuckin' idea what he's going through. You've never been booed in your life. So shut up!"

The Scum Bunch was Sisk's cocoon, the one place he knew nobody was waiting with a jeer or a curse or a gun (real or imaginary). As a result he devoted himself to the group's unambiguous mission: to corrupt as many Mets as possible. At this Sisk excelled.

While the thirty-two-year-old Carter fancied himself the leader of the Mets, he was not reflective of the team's overall off-the-field persona. Most of the players were twenty-something, naïve, and determined to live the New York City baseball player lifestyle to the fullest. They were men like Sid Fernandez, immensely talented but, well, not exactly the next Albert Einstein.

Early on in spring training, Fernandez sat down on the couch in his manager's office and confessed to having a serious problem. There was this house, and it was right on a beach along the Pacific Ocean in the pitcher's hometown of Honolulu. "It's my dream home," Fernandez said. "It's perfect for me, and it's for sale." The place was selling for $160,000.

Johnson, owner of a real estate license, didn't understand the problem. "Sid, you're a pitcher in the major leagues," he said. "You're making $200,000 this year. Why don't you just buy the thing? It'll be a good investment."

Fernandez nodded, left the room, and over the course of the next two weeks thought long and hard about the house. Before an intrasquad game, Johnson pulled him aside. "Well, Sid, did you make the big purchase?"

The question was met with a frown. "Nah, Skip. I couldn't do it," he said. "I'm just not so sure that I can live on $40,000 for the entire year."

Huh?

Fernandez failed to grasp the concept of a mortgage. This was the same pitcher who was convinced the WWF was 100 percent real. Who once visited a teammate's house, spent three hours speaking to his Honolulu-based parents on the telephone, and was shocked when he was angrily handed a bill for $600. "Imagine someone who doesn't know what anything outside of the clubhouse is about, and that was Sid," says Paul Greco, a team batboy. "Guys were like, 'Sid, *never* leave the stadium.'"

For the Scum Bunch it was almost too easy. They would invite Fernandez to partake in a couple of beers. Soon crushed cans would litter the airplane's aisle, and the normally mild-mannered Hawaiian would be buzzed and in the middle of Insult Fest '86. "Hey, Sid," Sisk would say to the hefty left-hander, "you really pitched your asses off today."

FERNANDEZ: "Fuck you, Doggie! Nice pink shirt!"

SISK: "Whatever, Fat Boy. At least I only need one to cover my body."

FERNANDEZ: "Yeah, but at least . . . umm . . . whatever."

To be a Met was to have all your vulnerabilities and weaknesses exposed like a root canal. Nearly every man was referred to by his nickname, and it wasn't pretty. The media-obsessed Carter was, of course, "Camera" and "The Kodak Kid." Hearn, the nerdy backup catcher, was "Ward," after the straight-and-narrow father in *Leave It to Beaver*. Barry Lyons, a balding reserve catcher, was "Barry Hairline" and "Mattress Head." The grimy-looking Backman was "Finster" for the dirty Looney Tunes character. Knight was "Mr. Nancy Lopez." Strawberry was so laughably lean and muscular that he was granted a sobriquet that stuck for years: "Pulled Muscle Face."

Indeed, no Met was more heavily influenced by the Scum Bunch than "Pulled Muscle Face." When Strawberry first arrived in New York in May 1983, he was twenty-one years old and wise enough to know that rookies—no matter how highly touted—were meant to be seen and not heard. Veteran teammates would walk by, and Strawberry's eyes stayed focused on the ground. He was cautious and polite.

Straw, how's it going?

"Umm, fine."

Straw, you're hitting the stuffing out of the baseball.

"Well, thanks."

Straw, your cat is on fire.

"Okay."

"Straw had a warm heart," says Dave Magadan, a rookie first baseman. "One on one he was as good a person as I'd ever played with. But when he'd get around the guys on the back of the plane and have a few beers, it'd get ugly. When people egged him on, Straw became a different person."

Like sharks scenting blood, the Scum Bunch smelled it. Strawberry had spent most of his life in an odd sort of baseball isolation, separated from the rest of the world by the blessed skill of hitting a round object very far. Everywhere he went, he aspired more to fit in than to be special. But when you are tall, strong, good-looking, and gifted, it is a near impossibility. Here, however, was his chance—not to rule the world but to be just another stumbling drunk. Nobody cared that Darryl Strawberry was a superdooperstar with millions of fans and gobs of talent. Nope, just sit down and crack open another beer. By '86, Strawberry was a rear-of-the-aircraft regular, downing brews at a Carl Lewis–like pace. Some of the Mets—Fernandez, Leach, Ojeda—were friendly guzzlers. Put a few beers in their system, and it was all smiles and laughter. "I might have drunk like Dean Martin," says Ojeda, "but I wasn't a bad guy." This was definitely *not* true of Strawberry. Give the star right fielder one or two Budweisers, and he was as mellow as a hippie at Woodstock. But by his fifth beer, things changed. Strawberry would become agitated and mean and, most of all, vicious. For a large man it took Strawberry a remarkably short amount of time to go from blissful to blasted. "You never knew when Darryl would lash out or embarrass you," says Hearn. "It was absolutely brutal. A lot of the guys made you feel good. Darryl made you feel like a ball of crud."

The targets were numerous. Backman, the scrappy second baseman, had acne marks covering his back. To some it was an opportunity for light zingers. But Strawberry took it too far, too often, calling Backman "an ugly motherfucker" and "zit boy." "Darryl," says Darling, "needed a good ass kicking when he was a kid." Equally subjected was Carter, wholesome, decent, and the spark to Strawberry's match. During a spring training interview two seasons earlier, Strawberry had said that he considered himself the leader of the Mets. The comment was met with amused disbelief. "Darryl will find out," said pinch hitter Rusty Staub, "that you don't lead with your mouth, you lead with your actions." On a team picture hanging in the clubhouse, Strawberry's face was circled with a black marker and the sarcastic comment, "Yeah, Straw! Our Captain!" was written on the side. It was all a big joke, with Strawberry the punch line. But because of his terrible sense of self-vision, Strawberry didn't see it. Even after showing up late time and time again, he still sought to lead. *This is my team*, he often thought. *I'm the star. I lead. They follow.*

Then along came Carter, calling the shots from behind the plate, filming commercials, signing countless autographs, and making a substantially higher salary. To Strawberry this was the ultimate threat to his authority. Hernandez was a great leader, but he was quiet in the clubhouse and hit with only so-so power (in Strawberry's odd mind, power equaled status). Plus, he intimidated Strawberry. Hernandez was cerebral and read thick books. How could Strawberry compete with that?

Carter, on the other hand, was loud, accessible, and a bountiful home-run source. It was good old-fashioned jealousy, and it could get nasty.

In the midst of a July trip to Houston, Carter stopped to sign autographs before boarding the team bus. It was practically a daily routine, and while the Mets always made fun of him ("Gary's in the trainer's room," Terry Leach once cracked good-naturedly, "icing his cheeks"), there was an overall sense of respect for his dedication to the paying customer—except from Strawberry. "Hey, Camera, get on the fuckin' bus!" Strawberry yelled. "I don't see any cameras out there." Carter did not find this funny—especially in front of fans. "Doberman," he yelled, "why don't you shut up!" It was Carter's typical style of retort (lame), but the pointy-eared Strawberry did sort of look like a dog.

"Why don't you make me?"

Carter, certainly strong enough to hold his own in a brawl, backed off. Instead he invited Strawberry to chapel service. Strawberry declined.

When he drank, Strawberry did not aim just for Carter. According to *Heat*, Gooden's autobiography, even the two close friends—mockingly tagged "The Knuckle Brothers" by teammates—got into it. On a post-season flight to Boston, Gooden ordered a drink from the flight attendant, and when it was not promptly delivered, he ordered again.

"Doc, you think she's your servant or something?" said Strawberry.

"Hey," countered Gooden, "all I want is a beer."

"Then wait your turn, man. She's busy. Can't you see that?"

"Why don't you mind your own business, cuz? I ain't talking to you."

"It is my business."

Several teammates rushed in to separate the two.

On one of the team's visits to St. Louis that season, Hernandez purchased a dozen Grade-A steaks, sealed and frozen in an airtight package. After a few drinks on the bus to the airport, Strawberry started to rag on New York's first baseman about his reception from the Cardinals fans. This was not a laughing matter. Hernandez yanked a steak from the box and whipped it at Strawberry. *Thud!* The meat hit his stomach and slid to the floor. Strawberry charged Hernandez but was held back. "There was this meat fight," says Hearn, "just because Darryl was acting like Darryl." Soon steaks were flying like Frisbees. It was the epic carnivore free-for-all. "By the time we reached the airport, guys were eating the steaks raw," says Ojeda. "Taking bites out and breathing hard and hitting each other. It was that psycho mentality."

Fully loaded, Strawberry feared no man. There were days when Davey Johnson, as all managers do, would mosey down to the back of the jet, either to make small talk or check on an injury. Sometimes Strawberry would be as warm as a teddy bear; other times he'd loudly rip his manager to shreds. "Why the hell are you playing Lenny more than Mookie?" he'd ask. "What are you fucking thinking?" When the mood struck him, Strawberry screamed from the rear of the aircraft: *"Davey, you ain't worth shit! Davey, you're nothing!"* Did Johnson, sitting twenty rows up, hear his star? Of course. "But what was he going to do?" says Hearn. "Darryl was strong, and when he was tanked, he couldn't be stopped."

Of all his teammates Strawberry reserved the most boisterous abuse for Tim Teufel, the club's new second baseman. Nobody had a gentler soul than Teufel, a warmhearted Christian from Greenwich, Connecticut. His wife, Valerie, was expecting the couple's first child, and Teufel was as giddy as could be. In three seasons with Minnesota, Teufel had grown accustomed to the buddy-buddy stylings of the team's superstars, Kirby Puckett, Kent Hrbek, and Tom Brunansky. "If you had a problem or a question, the guys in Minnesota were great," he says. "Very supportive." New York was different.

For some reason, it struck Strawberry as funny that Teufel's random nickname was "Richard." It struck Strawberry as especially funny when he was three or four sheets to the wind. Strawberry thought up his own riff on Richard as a new moniker for Teufel: "Richard Head." During the day Strawberry was kind. "Hey, Timmy, go get 'em!" or "What's up, Teuf?" But on the charter, things changed:

"Yo, Richard Head!"

"Hey, Mr. Dick Head."

"How's your dick, Head?"

"Darryl would get on the plane or the bus, and he always had to have the one-upmanship," says Carter. "That's what used to irritate me the most about him. He'd make stupid comments, and we'd just shake our heads and go, 'That's Darryl.'"

Teufel didn't shake his head. He didn't wag his finger. He didn't spit or cry or laugh. He took the high road and ignored Strawberry. What else could he do? Teufel was a part-time player. Strawberry was a star. So "Richard Head" it was. Richard Head this. Richard Head that. Richard Head on the bus to the plane. Richard Head on the plane to the bus. Finally, during a flight to Los Angeles in August, Teufel heard one "Richard Head" too many. Sitting a couple of rows in front of Strawberry, he stood up, walked toward his teammate, and pointed. "Listen, this is the last time I'm taking your bullshit!" he said. "I'm tired of hearing that crap! Stop screwing with me!"

For a moment Strawberry was stunned. Then he put down his beer, stood up, and pointed a finger at Teufel. "Are you seriously talking to me?" he growled.

Teufel was. And if a half-dozen teammates hadn't stepped in between the two men, who knows what would have happened? (Las Vegas odds favored Strawberry, 900 to 1.) "There's a breaking point to every person in their pride and character and who they are," says Teufel. "No man is just going to sit there and be a marshmallow."

Strawberry was so impressed by Teufel's bravado that the two actually developed a friendship. And as if the confrontation snapped him out of a malaise, Teufel came alive. In the first half of the season he batted a putrid .228. With a new dose of machismo, that rose to .268. Not great but respectable. "From that day forward Teuf became a better ballplayer," says Ojeda. "He was just pushed and pushed and pushed, and he was tired of it. It woke something up inside him. He wasn't gonna take shit from nobody anymore. And that included Darryl Strawberry."

Even though the Mets' terrible behavior can be traced directly to the Scum Bunch, the rear of airplanes is where the blame begins, not ends. For while Heep, Orosco, and Sisk were in many ways the straws that stirred the (alcoholic) drink, they were not the bartenders. That job fell to Johnson, the manager.

A hard-drinking wild child as a player, Johnson never felt comfortable in the role of disciplinarian. Johnson was a great game-time manager, but he genuinely hated dealing with away-from-the-field discipline.

His mantra—"As long as you play hard, I'm gonna treat you guys as men"—was repeated over and over, and soon it took on an unintended meaning for many of the Mets. There was a feeling that Johnson got anytime he had to badger one of his troops after hours, and it was akin to nausea. He absolutely *hated* to lecture baseball players on proper decorum. He found it annoying to receive as a player, and nightmarish as a skipper. Johnson didn't take this job to play principal. He simply loved baseball. "Davey had been a veteran player, so he knew how veterans wanted to be treated," says Harazin. "Keep the reins loose and don't make too many rules."

When the noise coming from the back of the aircraft got too loud, Johnson, who referred to the area as "The Ghetto," would occasionally check in—to drop off a garbage bag. "They'd throw their crumpled beer cans all over the place," he says. "I just didn't think it was right." Part of Johnson's problem was that at the same time his men were getting sauced on beer, he was gulping his third or fourth vodka. Under the manager's rule, players were not allowed hard alcohol on flights, but the coaching staff was. Every so often one of the assistant GMs, Harazin or McIlvaine, would accompany the team on a road trip, and the reports back to Cashen were rarely good. Cashen was alarmed by the partying, but as a crusty baseball man he knew that beer was no less a part of the game's culture than sunflower seeds and chewing tobacco. Baseball players drank, smoked, and chased pussy. That was understood. What really got him was the gambling.

The airplane was divided into sections of cliques, and although the Scum Bunch had the strongest gravitational pull, there was also a gang of men who spent an inordinate amount of time playing poker and casino. Of course, if Aguilera, Backman, Dykstra, Ojeda, Teufel, and Howard Johnson—the primary culprits—were betting Goldfish crackers, there would not have been an issue. But as the pots grew, from $400 to $500 to $600 to $1,000 and more, Hernandez, like Cashen, became concerned. Johnson was generally mute. "Guys were losing serious money, and that can cause some big problems," Hernandez says. "What if someone's a sore loser? Or what if someone can't afford to lose that much? All of a sudden you have an issue in the clubhouse. If I were the manager, I wouldn't have allowed it."

Davey Johnson once halfheartedly requested that his men not play for insane amounts. But instead of backing down, they just changed tactics. Toothpicks replaced bills, with the debts to be settled later that night. It reached a point where poker games began on the plane, continued on the bus, and finished in a hotel room at 5 A.M. To stroll into one of the players' suites late at night was to see boxes upon boxes of cold pizza, ashtrays filled with dozens of cigarette butts, and empty beer cans lining the dressers. The most intense practitioner was Dykstra, whose reckless, balls-to-the-wall card philosophy resembled his style of baseball (or vice versa). "Man, Lenny was a gambler," says one teammate. "He always had to put a wager on everything, no matter how stacked the odds were against him. He didn't know how to let up."

Did it hurt the Mets? Maybe, maybe not. Did it hurt Dykstra? Four years later he was put on probation by commissioner Fay Vincent for losing $78,000 in poker and golf to a Mississippi gambler.

Chapter 6

"THE KID" AND THE BLACK HATS

We were throwbacks, man. We were like, "Gimme a steak, gimme a fuckin' beer, gimme a smoke, and get the fuck out of our way."

—BOBBY OJEDA, Mets pitcher

GARY CARTER IS A GEEK.

This sounds strange, doesn't it? How many major league Hall of Famers with bulging muscles and boyish good looks have been grouped with Screech, Steve Urkel, and Potsie Webber on the all-time uncool list?

The facts, however, are indisputable. Carter is the anti-Fonzie, as koolamundo as a pair of neon pink leg warmers and the L.A. Gears to match. He doesn't:

Drink.

Smoke.

Do drugs.

Curse.

Cheat on his wife.

Wear the latest fashions.

Embrace an entourage.

Speak of himself in the third person.

Carter *does* drive a Lexus, a black LS330 with all the trimmings. But even in that attempt to be hip, Carter falls flat on his face. Not only does he have a vanity license plate reading KID 8, but surrounding it is a border that says BASEBALL'S BEEN VERY, VERY GOOD TO ME.

All together now: G-E-E-K.

The thing is, there's a certain authenticity to Carter's geekdom that in limited doses makes him endearing. When Carter speaks glowingly of his wife, Sandy, he radiates love and compassion. When he tells you that his daughter, Kimmy, was a catcher for the Florida State softball team, there's a beaming pride in his smile. Once when *Good Morning America* asked Carter to compete in an on-air bubble gum–blowing contest, he agreed on the condition that his gum be sugar-free. "Gary is a great man," says Knight. "And if a lot of people emulated his lifestyle, they'd be a lot better off."

By all accounts Carter was born a geek, raised a geek, and sent off into the world as a geek. By 1986, at age thirty-two, he was *the* geek—baseball's cleanest, most wholesome, most photogenic, most accessible, *most despised* player.

Yes, despised. In high school the geeks are either ignored or smacked around. But in major league baseball—where nerds are few and far between—there was little tolerance for the gosh-darn-it, gee-whiz, holy-cow world of Gary Carter. Especially in Montreal, land of his baseball roots.

While there are those in New York who would argue (with some merit) that Carter's greatest days came as a Met, he spent eleven of his eighteen seasons starring for the Expos, the franchise that drafted him out of Sunnyhills High in Fullerton, California, in 1972 and molded him into baseball's best catcher. In 1974, when Carter was with Triple A Memphis and word of his inevitable rise reached the Montreal clubhouse, players with the big club began teasing Barry Foote, the gruff starting catcher, that his job was in jeopardy. Many of the Expos had met Carter in spring training, and sparking a trend that would last for two decades, they didn't much care for him. "He rubbed a lot of people the wrong way," says Warren Cromartie, a former Montreal outfielder. "Gary was just . . . different."

It is humorous to see KID printed on Carter's license plate because the nickname was spawned from anything but affection. Expos pitcher Don Carrithers was the first to call Carter "the Kid," and he did so mockingly behind his teammate's back. It was a way to get Foote's goat: "Hey, Barry, the Kid sure had a ton of heart!" or "Gosh, that Kid owns a nice smile!" The truth was, most of the Expos resented Carter from the beginning because with talent radiating from his body, it became clear that the popular-yet-ordinary Foote's future was grim. Like a gaggle of Girl Scouts, the Expos' older players would routinely talk trash behind Carter's back, giggling and mocking the youngster's enthusiasm and naïveté. Whenever he entered the clubhouse, Carter would be met with silence. "It hurt," he says, "but I tried to succeed that much harder." In June 1975, just nine months after Carter's first big league game, Foote was traded to Philadelphia. The Kid was The Man.

Over the next decade nobody could argue with the Expos' decision. Carter was a horse—big, strong, fast, reliable; a potent home run hitter and the perfect guy to build a lineup around. "There were only two catchers of that caliber in baseball—Johnny Bench and Gary," says former Expos outfielder Jerry White. "Every year you knew Gary could be the MVP. He was that good."

And *that* abhorred. For much of the late 1970s and early 1980s, there was no stranger fit in baseball than Gary Carter playing for the Montreal Expos. To better know the community, Carter moved his family from their home in West Palm Beach to a full-time residence in Montreal. He made countless public appearances and never turned down an autograph request. Simultaneously, according to one person close to the Expos, "ten, maybe twelve players on the team had some type of drug issue." Right fielder Ellis Valentine snorted lines in the back of the team bus. Left fielder Tim Raines learned to dive headfirst so as not to puncture the bag of coke in his back uniform pocket.

What kind of environment was this for Mr. Wholesome? Carter

watched his addict teammates run lazily around the base paths, and he
also became the defenseless victim of their attacks. Tired of calling him
"the Kid," several Expos thought up two new ones—"Lights" and
"Camera Carter"—to express their disgust over his love affair with the
media. In the team's Olympic Stadium clubhouse, Carter's locker was
directly to the left of the main entrance—the perfect place to greet the
press. "At the time there were a lot of black guys on that team who
weren't getting any publicity," says Raines. "We had Andre Dawson and
Ellis Valentine being ignored, and Gary would be late to the field
because he had to do his commercials. I don't think people were mad
that he was getting attention, but we felt that he was taking away from
the team. Sometimes he seemed more concerned about Gary Carter
than the Montreal Expos." The ridicule did not stay behind clubhouse
walls. Cromartie talked to a Cub, who talked to a Red, who talked to a
Dodger and Padre and Cardinal and Phillie and Giant. Before long,
Carter's reputation as a do-gooder fraud was everywhere. You could see
it in the sneers of rival players, who avoided Carter in the stadium hall-
ways and treated him like dirt. Did it hurt? Of course. "I carried a lot of
baggage with me," Carter says. "I'd go to a new team, and guys were saying they wondered how I was in the clubhouse, whether I had a big head
or was a team player."

Carter arrived in New York in 1985, and the Mets players saw what
they wanted to see. Those who considered Carter a media hog watched
with disgust as he accepted any and all interview requests, be they from
NBC's Sal Marchiano or *The* (Nashville) *Tennessean*'s Larry Woody. Those
who embraced Carter as an answer to the franchise's backstop prayers
found him gregarious and helpful. The rest just shook their heads,
laughed, and realized their offense was a hundred times more potent
with Carter in the middle. "Look, we all disliked Gary when we played
against him," says Hernandez. "He was just a little rah-rah varsity collegiate type even though he didn't go to college. He just had a way about
him that pissed you off. But I respected him as a player. And when he
came to New York, I appreciated him, too."

To Carter's delight there was something entirely different about the way his Mets teammates treated him. In Montreal the behind-the-back trash talk had eaten Carter up. When Cromartie called him "Teeths," it stung all the more because he did so out of earshot. Where was the camaraderie? In New York the ragging was equally voracious, but the Mets weren't afraid to laugh three inches from Carter's face. Did Carter enjoy the exchanges? No. "But at least it was *to* me, and there was some respect," he says. "I've got big shoulders, and I can accept all that stuff. Just not when it's sniping."

The Mets had their most fun with Carter's Cousteau-like search for endorsements. Whether it was 7UP, Ivory Soap, Sassoon, or Gillette, Carter seemed to be on every billboard and commercial in the tristate area, hawking some god-awful product. Perhaps no player has ever looked sillier than Carter did in a magazine advertisement for Northville Gasoline. There, above the quote "When it comes to high performance gasoline, Northville's got a lot on the ball" is The Kid, wearing pinstriped uniform pants and a Northville pump attendant windbreaker and hat.

Strangely, at the same time Carter was becoming a Met, the Mets were becoming Carter. With the successes of '84 and '85, more TV cameras and out-of-town scribes were heading to Shea. There was ample attention to go around. If Carter was "Camera Carter," then Strawberry was "Camera Strawberry," Gooden "Camera Gooden," and Hernandez "Camera Hernandez." Before The Kid's arrival, the Mets were a relatively mild-mannered collection of players. Strawberry had his swagger and so did Hernandez. But otherwise it was mostly "Put your head down and play the game right." Carter changed that. In his first game as a Met on April 9, 1985, the catcher hit a game-winning tenth-inning homer against the Cardinals for a 6–5 opening day win. As he rounded the bases, Shea Stadium's rafters literally wobbled. Carter pumped his arm in the air, then did so again. When he reached home, he was swarmed by teammates. Carter jumped out of the dugout for a rousing curtain call. It summed up everything the Expos disliked about their ex-teammate, and everything the Mets were about to adopt.

By '86, curtain calls were more common at Shea than they were at *Les Misérables*. Howard Johnson started another obnoxious trend by introducing rally caps to the dugout. On the rare instances when New York trailed late in a game, Hojo would think up inventive ways to wear his hat. There was "desert style" (a towel dangling from the back), "cummerbund" (hat tucked into belt), "baseball hat" (ball balanced on the brim), and "the Amish" (hat folded and twisted to look like an Amish farmer's lid). When Hojo selected a look, his teammates followed. "All the colleges have 'em," Johnson told *The New York Times*. "Why not us?" From across the diamond, the fashion statements were accurately interpreted as brazen. How could a team mess with their hats when *they're losing*? "They had so much over-the-top swagger," says Keith Moreland, a former Cubs outfielder. "Yeah, they were good, but not good enough to do stuff like that."

By season's end the Mets would have a music video, two songs ("Get Metsmerized" and "Let's Go Mets!"), two *GQ* covers (Darling and Hernandez), countless *Sports Illustrated* features, and enough enemies to fill Madison Square Garden. The cockiness spread through the clubhouse like a case of chicken pox, jumping from player to player with uncontrollable ferocity. It was impossible to be a Met and not expect—even promise—victory.

All the while Davey Johnson kicked back and smiled. This was exactly what he had wanted in spring training when he gazed into his crystal ball and saw *domination*. Great teams are allowed to talk smack, and the Mets were great. On his weekly radio show, Johnson himself took pride in teeing off on friends, foes, and especially the New York fans. "Sir," he liked to tell callers, "I don't think you have any idea what you're talking about." From his office atop Shea Stadium, Frank Cashen listened and cringed. *We're not winning with class*, he thought. He was equally troubled by Johnson's recently released book, *Bats*, a day-by-day chronicle of the '85 season. A local newspaper was running regular excerpts, and the passages were filled with strong opinions and shots at rival teams. In his defense Johnson says, "I never even read the book." (Peter Golenbock, his coauthor, did 100 percent of the writing.) "It pissed me off because there were things in there even I didn't want said." The excuse did nothing for Cashen. He spoke often with his manager about the team's overt obnoxiousness, but the complaints fell on deaf ears.

"Look, Davey," Cashen would say, "you've gotta put a lid on this. We're everyone's enemies."

Johnson could only laugh. "Frank, that's great," he'd say. "Nobody hates the shit teams."

In Johnson's opinion, cockiness made his club complete. It was the tenth man. He would look at struggling opponents like Atlanta or San Francisco, and the common trait was stoicism. "Without a strut it's hard to have the ruthlessness you need to win big," says Johnson. "It drives you to the next level."

Cashen was in his seventh year in New York. The ultimate rebuilding job was nearing fruition. Why couldn't Johnson and his guys win with humility? Win with respect? Win in peace?

Opponents started taking action. In a late-May game against the Dodgers at Shea, New York engaged in its first of four supersonic, no-holds-barred mega-brawls. It was a broiling spring evening, and patience was in short supply. Shortly before the first pitch, two Los Angeles players, first baseman Greg Brock and second baseman Steve Sax, faced off in an ugly shouting match in the visitors' dugout. By game time the Dodgers were in no mood for the Mets' in-your-face shenanigans. But that's what they got.

With the bases loaded and New York leading 3–1 in the sixth, Dodgers manager Tommy Lasorda pulled starter Bob Welch in favor of a right-handed reliever named Tom Niedenfuer, who came on to face George Foster. As always, New York's left fielder was greeted by the 35,643 fans with a chorus of angry boos, each one a needle in his spine. "It was never easy for me in that town," says Foster. "When you don't have the fans on your side, it's like having an extra opponent you have to face."

This time the Unloved One won them over. On Niedenfuer's second pitch, a meaty fastball over the corner of the plate, Foster whipped his black bat through the strike zone and hammered a grand slam 338 feet over the left field wall. As he slowly, deliberately rounded the bases, his chin tucked into his chest, Foster heard the unfamiliar sounds of clap-

ping. He was (gasp!) even called out for a curtain call. The Mets were up
7–1, another romp in what was turning into a romp-filled season.
Niedenfuer, meanwhile, was stewing. As soon as the ball was hit, he
stared directly at Ray Knight in the on-deck circle, eyebrows furrowed
in furor. "I walked to the plate, and I was thinking, 'Oh, shoot, don't
throw at me,'" says Knight. "But I knew he would."

Niedenfuer's next pitch—a 92-mph fastball—nailed the right-handed
Knight square on the left elbow. The third baseman slammed his bat and
helmet to the ground, took a step forward, and then—*whooooosh!*—
charged Niedenfuer like Mark Gastineau after a quarterback. "Had he not
stared me down, I probably would have accepted it," says Knight. "But I
never avoid a challenge." Both benches emptied, though except for a couple of shoves, some well-chosen curse words, and Kevin Mitchell yanking Brock by the right earlobe, there was minimal damage. No players
were ejected, and the Mets cruised, 8–1. The following evening Knight's
dinner companion was, of all people, Niedenfuer. The Los Angeles
pitcher wanted to make amends. "He was a good guy who was sorry
about the whole thing," says Knight. "He was getting hit all over the park,
and he just snapped. It happens."

As Bob Verdi wrote in *The Sporting News*, "Depending on whose brow
is furrowed or whose nose is out of joint, this gang of toughs from the
Big Apple is either arrogant, cocky, obnoxious, or, better yet, (D) all of
the above." Verdi forgot egotistical, holier-than-thou, truculent, and pig-
headed. The Mets were on top of the world, with a 28-11 record and an
overflowing goblet of confidence. In the win against the Dodgers, Hernandez hit a home run, returned to the dugout, and immediately lit a cigarette. He was fined $100 by NL president Chub Feeney, who said, "We
can't have that type of public display." The next afternoon Hernandez
was visibly puffing away again. It was a blinking SCREW YOU! sign lit up
for Feeney. Hernandez did not care about rules. None of the players did.
"We were just a nasty bunch of guys," says Ojeda. "We'd go into a town,
and we'd say, 'We're gonna drink their beer, we're gonna beat their team,
we're gonna kick their asses, and then we're gonna leave and do it to
someone else.'" They usually succeeded.

The Mets were, to quote Ojeda, "a bunch of assholes."

"Villains," says Hernandez.

"Bad, bad people," says Hearn.

"We weren't no choir boys," says Sisk.

"We wore the black hats," says pitcher Randy Niemann.

"We looked to fight," says Knight.

"We could be jerks," says shortstop Kevin Elster.

"We *were* jerks," adds Ojeda. "Big-time jerks."

Part of this was sheer personality. Much of this was chemical. A decade before it became common for baseball players to consume steroids and human growth hormones, many of the Mets were popping amphetamines as if they were Advils. While it was common for the 1980s ballplayer to abuse the drug, New York likely led the league. It was a matter of boasting a roster chock-full of on-the-edge, no-matter-what-it-takes, screw-my-health daredevils. Had they been deemed by a doctor to be overweight or suffering from narcolepsy, this might be okay. In the medical world, amphetamines were useful. But the Mets were looking for a boost, and the pills—also known as "speed," "up," "fast," "louee," "goey," "whiz," "pep pills," "uppers," and "greenies," and illegally distributed by an in-clubhouse employee of the club—did wonders. One New York pitcher says he was naïve to the world of the amphetamine until Hernandez ordered him to fetch a glass of milk. "I thought, *Milk*?" says the pitcher. "Then a week later Keith said, 'Go get me a beer.' See, he'd overdose on the greenies, and the milk would calm him down. Then he'd pound a beer to get it to kick in again."

To pop a greenie was to plug yourself into an electrical outlet. The charge was immediate, and just two or three tablets lasted nine innings. After a rough night on the town, a couple of greenies could revive even the most hungover player, turning what would have been a day on the bench into 3 for 4 with 2 stolen bases. But there were side effects. Amphetamines are addictive, and they sometimes cause violent, irrational outbursts, depressive disorders, and antisocial behavior. As Hunter S. Thompson once wrote of the user's experience, "Faster, faster, until the thrill of speed overcomes the fear of death." While McDowell describes the jolt as "like a Fropa Espresso from Starbucks," Howard Johnson says too many hits made him fidgety, restless, and agitated. "After more than two days I had to get myself to stop," he says. "They're easy to get hooked on."

The abusers were simple to spot.

- Anyone drinking a hot cup of coffee immediately before the game was doing so because the boiled water dissolved the capsule and the caffeine acted as a stimulus to kick off the impact.
- Anyone drinking countless cups of water was doing so to eradicate the cotton mouth caused by the pills.
- Anyone pacing back and forth, up and down the dugout for no known reason was high on speed.

"You'd see guys moving all over, screaming, 'I feel good! I feel really good!'" says Knight, who swears he took amphetamines no more than ten times in his career. "You don't have control over yourself, and you sort of act stupid, like there's no mute button." The Mets certainly acted stupid. Looking back, many of the players trace the clubhouse idiocy—meaningless fights, ludicrous arguments, banal shouting—to the drug. Plus it is completely unrealistic to load a bunch of amphetamine users onto an airplane for three hours and ask them to sit quietly. The buzz does not simply shut off once the game ends.

Dykstra, Backman, and Hernandez might have been the most prolific abusers of amphetamines, but nearly everyone—even Carter—gave them a whirl. Before his July 26 start at Atlanta, Gooden ingested greenies and then paid for it. "[I was] thinking I could throw even harder than I was already throwing," he writes in *Heat*, his autobiography. "What I didn't realize, however, was that amphetamines make a pitcher too jittery to focus. I was so out of control that when a ground ball was hit back to me, I saw three of them. Luckily I grabbed the one in the middle and made the play."

At the end of the inning Steve Garland, the Mets trainer, ordered Gooden to enter the clubhouse and drink a cup of milk. He allowed 3 runs and 10 hits over 7 innings in a 4–3 defeat. In a lifetime of questionable decisions, Gooden at least had the sense to make this the last time he pitched on speed.

On June 6, ten days after Niedenfuer-Knight I, the Pirates and Mets were booked to play a doubleheader at Three Rivers Stadium. The event was a matchup of baseball's best team and its worst, and en route to losing 98 games, the Pirates were clearly as putrid as they come.

But in the absence of skill, pride often flourishes. Just because Pittsburgh's starting shortstop was Rafael "I Hit .233" Belliard didn't mean the Bucs enjoyed getting harassed by the league's bullies. In the top of the fifth inning of Game 1, the Mets were doing their best Biff Tannen to baseball's Marty McFly.

Pitching for the Pirates was veteran right-hander Rick Rhoden, the team's ace and one of the sport's most notorious ball scuffers. During their four seasons as teammates with Pittsburgh in the late 1970s and early 1980s, Bill Robinson, the Mets' first-base coach, says Rhoden repeatedly cheated like a D student on a final exam. Years after the end of their careers, Carter says Rhoden even admitted doctoring to him. "He had a piece of sandpaper that was on his glove hand," says Carter. "With a little Super Glue, it's not hard to do."

With two outs and a three-balls, one-strike count on Carter, Robinson yelled toward home plate: "Hey, Kid, get the ump to check that baseball!" The ump, Billy Williams, simply tossed the ball out of play. Rhoden shoved a small object into the back pocket of his uniform pants. Annoyed more than concerned, Williams sauntered to the mound, gave Rhoden a perfunctory two-second examination, and resumed play.

As the inning ended, Robinson deliberately crossed paths with his old teammate. "Rick," he said, "you're way too good of a pitcher to cheat." Rhoden snapped: "Bill, fuck you! You guys are a bunch of fuckin' whiners!" Robinson shoved Rhoden in the chest, and in the four seconds it took for the dugouts to clear, the Mets' second rhubarb had begun.

Unlike the mild Dodger brouhaha, this one was a slugfest. Before he was restrained by four teammates, Strawberry had popped Pirate outfielder Lee Mazzilli (who before long would be acquired by the Mets) in the head with a right hook. Mets pitcher Ed Lynch grabbed Pirate manager Jim Leyland by the waist. Sid Bream, Pittsburgh's first baseman, jumped Robinson and broke his right pinky. In the middle of the scrum was Mitchell, contributing his ghetto-raw brand of aggressiveness.

Because he was a rookie, Mitchell had yet to learn the rules of baseball brawling. In the corner of his eye he saw Pittsburgh infielder Sammy Khalifa, a five-eleven, 170-pounder, charge Robinson from behind. Ever since spring training when "Uncle Bill" (as Mitchell affectionately called Robinson) took him under his wing, Mitchell considered it his duty to look out for the first-base coach. Thus, Mitchell blindsided Khalifa with a clothesline to the head, dropping the Pirate to the ground with an awesome thud. Mitchell proceeded to wrap his arm around Khalifa's throat and drag him facedown across the stadium's Astroturf surface. "White meat," says Mitchell, smiling. For the next ten seconds Mitchell held Khalifa in a headlock. As his face went from white to pink to red to a purplish blue, Khalifa gasped for air, his arms waving wildly. "I can't breathe! I can't breathe!" Finally, at the urging of several Mets, Mitchell let go. Khalifa crumpled.

"I would have killed him," says Mitchell. "It's the lion's den, and I was pissed because he was going at Uncle Bill from behind. If you're gonna do something like that, be a man and come from the front."

Pittsburgh won the game, 7–1. The Mets won the war.

"Two months later Rick Rhoden and I played golf," says Robinson. "No hard feelings. We were able to laugh about it."

On July 1, New York was 10 games ahead of second-place Montreal, which had as realistic a shot of winning the division as *Spies Like Us* did of taking home that year's Oscar for best picture. Instead of worrying about the NL East, the Mets found more trivial nuggets to ponder. Four starters—Gooden (9–3, 2.70 ERA), Darling (8–2, 3.19), Fernandez (9–2, 3.12), and Ojeda (9–2, 2.54)—were on course to win 20 games, an achievement last recorded by the 1971 Orioles of Dave McNally, Mike Cuellar, Jim Palmer, and Pat Dobson. As *The New York Times*'s Murray

Chass wrote, "If the Mets' first four starting pitchers were football players, they would be known as the Fearsome Foursome or the Purple People Eaters or the Steel Curtain. They are mere baseball players, though, so they are to be known simply as outstanding."

From Davey Johnson's perspective the breakout performer of the year was Darling. A graduate of Yale with a dual major in French and Southeast Asian history, the Honolulu-born right-hander boasted an intelligence and worldliness that belonged anywhere but in New York's boorish clubhouse. Before games he would sit in front of a TV with the equipment boys and rattle off *Jeopardy!* answers as if he and Alex Trebek were psychic friends. Darling was prepared to spend the forthcoming off-season studying Russian at New York University and, like Hernandez, was a regular book reader. By comparison, shortstop Rafael Santana entertained the nonliterate with an assortment of foreign films. "He'd bring in these crazy pornos and call us all over," says Vinny Greco. "I'd be like, 'Raffy, what the hell is that? A sheep with a one-legged woman?'"

Darling had none of that. In 1985, Darling would not listen to the advice of Davey Johnson, who agonized over his stubborn refusal to throw strikes. He was a nitpicker—low and outside here, high and inside there—and by the fifth or sixth inning of most games, his pitch count was one hundred plus, the Met position players were dying of boredom, and Johnson would be forced to use his bullpen. "He thought he was painting with a fine brush, but he was using a roll-on," says Johnson. "All he had to do was throw the ball over the plate, and his movement would take over. But he was just so goddamned intellectual, he thought he could figure everything out himself." Part of the problem was what Darling calls "pitching envy." As New York's number 2 starter after Gooden, he was responsible for charting most of Dr. K's starts. This meant paying attention to the details of the master. "I wanted to pitch as well as he did," says Darling. "But I didn't have his gifts, so I thought way too much." Darling won 16 games in 1985, but a National League–leading 114 walks severely diminished the impact. He was a 5-inning starter.

At the start of the '86 season, Johnson forbade Carter ever to call for an inside cut fastball when Darling was pitching. "You sit your ass right in the middle of the plate, and you make him throw the ball to you," Johnson said. "I'm tired of that son of a bitch having 110 pitches by the fourth inning. If he doesn't like it, blame me." Darling didn't like it, and the result was a season-long feud that resulted in manager and player duking it out in the press and avoiding each other like a bat does daylight. There was a logic to this: Darling and Johnson were both borderline brilliant and over-the-line stubborn. For Johnson there was no "*Maybe* I'm right." For Darling, there was no "*Perhaps* I should listen." Upset by his pitcher's lack of command in a May win at San Francisco, Johnson told the assembled media that Darling was "terrible." The remark stung. Revenge came in a *GQ* article that summer. Johnson, said Darling, "is threatened by me intellectually," and "[Johnson] doesn't believe in communicating with his players. Some players maybe, but not pitchers."

Somehow the bickering had positive results. In the Niedenfuer-Knight game against Los Angeles, Darling pitched a complete-game five hitter to set a team record with 6 straight wins to start the season. Darling's 12 strikeouts were a career high, and spurning the inside cutter, he managed to walk just two. It took ten starts for Darling to finally lose a game, and between June 11 and July 29 his record was 5–1, with a 1.50 ERA. "I didn't like being ripped in a magazine, and he was still stubborn," says Johnson. "But I think he was starting to listen."

Carter, meanwhile, was being hyped as the leading NL MVP candidate, both by the New York media and (surprise!) himself. Through July, The Kid ranked seventh in the NL with 17 homers and third with 73 RBIs. His numbers compared favorably with Philadelphia's Mike Schmidt (22 homers, 76 RBIs), the other front-runner. When a writer ambled by his locker to talk shop, Carter usually managed to drop some hints about his desire to be MVP. This rankled Schmidt, who reacted to the Mets catcher as most other major leaguers did—with contempt. "If I stop hitting, the Phillies go down the tubes," Schmidt told the *Post*. "In a one-on-one sense, I'm more valuable to the Phillies than Gary Carter is to the Mets." It all made for meaningless mid-season talk on a dominant team with little else to worry about.

From afar the Atlanta Braves seethed.

Manager Chuck Tanner's club was mired in what seemed like the organization's one hundredth straight lousy season, but unlike other going-nowhere teams that accepted their fate, the Braves were mad. They played in dumpy old Fulton County Stadium, home to 52,006 seats and four hundred fans. They had two stars—center fielder Dale Murphy and third baseman Bob Horner—and little else. Their powder-blue uniforms were the league's ugliest. Yet like the Mets, by and large, the Braves were a hard-edged, down-and-dirty group of grizzled veterans. Unlike the Mets, they took pride in professionalism. Atlanta's players looked at uppity New York and saw an organization that could use a few lessons in proper baseball decency. The Mets required an ass whuppin'.

Leading the way for the Braves was David Palmer, a starting pitcher with so-so stuff but an Incredible Hulk temper. Palmer had spent six years as Carter's teammate in Montreal, and he loathed the guy. The rah-rah garbage was hard enough to endure when Palmer benefited from Carter's production. But to see his former battery mate basking in the Big Apple spotlight, smiling like a buffoon for all of America to see, well, it ate Palmer up. On July 11 he took action.

As always, the Mets were beating Atlanta like an old bag of potatoes. In the bottom of the first, Palmer walked Dykstra and gave up a drag bunt single to Backman. After forcing Hernandez into a harmless groundout, he confronted the dreaded Kid. On the second pitch Carter launched Palmer's knee-high fastball over Shea Stadium's left field wall. As always, Carter jumped out of the dugout to take yet another curtain call. As always, Palmer seethed. His next pitch, another fastball, found the path to Strawberry's ribs. Palmer was six-foot-one and built like a professional bowler. Strawberry was six-six, 190 pounds. He was the wrong guy to hit.

Like Knight five weeks earlier, Strawberry flung down his bat and helmet and rushed the mound. All of a sudden Palmer wasn't quite so macho. He removed his glove from his left hand and flung it Strawberry's way. When that didn't work, he did the next best thing—he ran away. Braves catcher Ozzie Virgil tackled Strawberry before he could reach the pitcher, but that didn't stop brawl number three from unfolding. As the first Met to bolt from dugout to field, Hernandez made a beeline to the infield, plowing into Palmer and Virgil and driving them to the ground. With bodies piling on top of them, Hernandez turned to Palmer and in a calm tone asked a simple question: "Dave, why would you do that?"

Palmer yelled back: "Carter and all that bullshit! I hate that guy!"

Amid the mayhem Hernandez was unmoved. "Look, if you hate Gary, why hit Darryl?" he said, bodies flying left and right. "It's not right."

Palmer had to admit, the man had a point.

The next inning the gods of French-speaking catchers punished Palmer for his rashness. With the bases loaded, Carter again came to the plate and—*bam!*—crushed his second home run of the game. Palmer hung his head, cursed the world, and was pulled, trailing 7–0.

"They act as though they've won the seventh game of the World Series," he said afterward. "I don't mind if they hit 15 home runs off me, but don't show me up."

Once again the Mets had brawled to perfection. Following the game (an 11–0 trouncing), the beers were plentiful, the scars were minimal, and Carter was able to look into the myriad cameras and offer his brightest of grins.

Chapter 7

A LONELY TIME TO BE WHOLESOME

My wife wanted a big diamond.

**—MOOKIE WILSON on why
he was married on a baseball field**

THERE ARE THOSE who will read this book and say, "Why would any-one root for a team made up entirely of imbeciles?" They'd be right—almost.

Upon his activation in early May, Mookie Wilson quietly returned to the Shea Stadium clubhouse a forgotten man. In his absence Lenny Dykstra had hit .302 with 15 runs and a .398 on-base percentage as the sparkplug center fielder on an 18–4 team. And the new kid's emotional impact was even greater. With the fan-favorite Wilson rehabbing from his eye injury and shoulder surgery, Dykstra stepped into the spotlight and never let go. New York's hard-core baseball fans loved the way the scrappy, anvil-headed Dykstra slammed into walls and threw his body around the field like a kitten's play toy. Dykstra was always running hard, and unlike Wilson, his throws from the outfield didn't flutter and dove-tail after 10 feet. There was also the issue of race: Big Apple diehards always seemed to be searching for that next great white hope, the athlete with soulful style but pasty skin. Joe Namath had fit the bill with the Jets, Dave DeBusschere with the Knicks, and Joe Pepitone (among others) with the Yankees. Now there was Dykstra. *Naaaaiiilllls* had unseated *Moooookie* as Shea's favorite son, and almost any normal veteran ballplayer would have been bitter over the slight.

Wilson, however, was hardly a normal veteran ballplayer. As his reactivation date approached, he pulled Dykstra aside and complimented him on his play. "You're doing things the right way," Wilson said. "Keep working hard and with passion, and you'll go places." Sure, it hurt Wilson to slum in the shadows. This used to be a Mookie Wilson town, and now it wasn't. Yet on a team with many a selfish SOB, Wilson even took the unprecedented step of informing the press that Dykstra had earned the starting center field job fair and square. "Lenny deserves the chance," he told *Newsday*'s Marty Noble. "He gives the team a dimension I didn't even when I was healthy. I can't complain. I replaced somebody. Someone replaces me." Beginning with the days of Babe Ruth griping over Lou Gehrig's rise, the bonds of teammate sportsmanship had gone only so far in baseball. Yeah, you wanted your club to win, but were most ballplayers willing to sacrifice precious playing time in the name of triumph? "Mookie was a special person," says Dykstra. "He was nothing but helpful. I was a young guy, and I needed that." Would Dykstra have extended Wilson the same graciousness had the tables been turned? "Hell, no," Dykstra says. "I didn't have that much class."

The middle of Nancy and Jim Wilson's 11 children, Mookie knew from an early age that unless a miracle occurred, he was certain to follow his father into the thankless, demanding profession of sharecropping. Heck, he just had to look around: All of the Wilson kids were put to intensive labor. It is what the family had known for decades, dating back to the days of slavery: Wilsons worked the land, period. Throughout the long, hot falls in tiny Bamberg, South Carolina (population: 3,843), Mookie could always be found out in the fields, picking everything from watermelons to corn to beans. From dusk to dawn he counted the hours until he could crawl home, gorge down a hot meal, and collapse into bed. "We had nothin'," Wilson says. "I mean, we were poorer than poor. No hot water. No indoor plumbing. Hand-me-downs as clothing. We weren't a family you'd see and say, 'They've got it made.'" School and sports were mildly important to Jim Wilson, but not nearly as vital as a hard day of work in the fields. "If I had to miss a few days in class," Mookie says, "then I missed a few days. No discussion. There was a job to be done, and that was our priority."

Baseball was Wilson's outlet. He was the fastest kid in his family, the fastest in the neighborhood, and maybe the fastest in the state. "Man, could he fly," recalls Ed Lynch, Wilson's teammate with the Mets and at the University of South Carolina. "I mean, as explosive as you'll ever witness." He also happened to be an incredible ballplayer—a gifted merging of speed, power, and grace. In four years of varsity competition at Bamberg-Ehrhardt High School, Wilson emerged as one of South Carolina's top players, leading his team to a state championship as a senior. In fact, Wilson so loved the sport that on the day of high school graduation he was MIA. There was a summer league game, you see, a big one. "Pop, you have to let me go," Mookie told his father. "It's everything." It was around this time that Jim Wilson's son started to realize he didn't necessarily have to become Jim Wilson. Baseball equaled hope.

Mookie spent two years at tiny Spartanburg Junior College, so impressing the Los Angeles Dodgers that they picked him late in the 1976 draft. "It was an honor," he says, "but I had something else to do first." Determined to play at a higher amateur level, he accepted a scholarship offer to the University of South Carolina, where he thrived as the team's only black player before being selected by New York in the second round of the June 1977 amateur draft. (Wilson left school fifty-four credits short but graduated from Mercy College in 1996 with a degree in behavioral science.)

Now, nine years after leading the Gamecocks to the title game of the 1977 College World Series, here he was, a stranger in a familiar clubhouse. It was often assumed by New York's front-office types—most of whom were middle-aged whites—that black Mets stuck with black Mets; that whenever Mookie and George Foster spoke, Gooden,

Mitchell, and Strawberry were sure to listen. Like Foster, however, Wilson was not affiliated with blacks, whites, or anyone. Wilson knew all of his teammates, some of them fairly well, but he was a quiet man in a sea of wildness, more comfortable at a table for one than a bar for five hundred. To perfectly understand Wilson, drift back to 1981, when the players' union opted to strike in the middle of the season. While many of his peers flew first class to their expensive homes, Wilson did what all Wilsons did: He worked. Instead of heading back to South Carolina, Wilson took a gig at Joe Sea Food on Roosevelt Avenue in Queens. Did he need the money? Not desperately. Did he need to be productive? Without question. He was empty without it.

Simply put, here was a ballplayer that the average fan could root for and not worry about being let down. In his five previous years in New York, the center fielder's name never wound up on the police blotter, as too many of his teammates did. He was smart enough to know that people look at celebrities as targets. There was no evil in Mookie Wilson and no intentions, either. He recognized that many of his peers made a ritual of cheating on their wives, and he found it troublesome, to say the least. And naturally, Wilson was disturbed by the drinking and drug abuse that took place around him. It was a lonely time to be a wholesome Met, and while Wilson was not unduly mocked for his way of life, he certainly wasn't considered one of the guys. There were few off-the-cuff jokes between Wilson and the others, and bars were mostly off-limits. His on-the-road social life was a TV, room service, and a good book. Living a clean, wholesome, family-oriented life was the only way he knew.

During spring training Wilson often sent the batboys into the stands to fetch him a couple of snacks. Brian Cazeneuve, the onetime team batboy, recalls returning to the clubhouse with two footlong hot dogs for Wilson and then handing over the change. "What'd you get for yourself, kid?" Wilson asked. When Cazeneuve shook his head, indicating nothing, Wilson handed him one of his dogs. Upon learning the boy was a vegetarian, he said, "Then keep the change and buy yourself a pretzel."

"He was just a really good person to everyone," says Cazeneuve. "One of the best guys in baseball."

With a minimal amount of public hoopla, Wilson made his debut for the '86 Mets on May 9, grounding out as a pinch hitter in a 2–1 win over Cincinnati at Shea Stadium. While it was just another at-bat for most of those in attendance, the moment was hugely important to Davey Johnson's plan of mastering the baseball universe. With Wilson back, New York's bench now had everything: Mitchell and Howard Johnson supplied the pop, Teufel the infield depth, and Heep the pinch hitting extraordinaire. Speed was the latest ingredient.

Through his first 9 games Wilson struggled terribly, going 2 for 17 as a part-timer. Wilson's shoulder still needed time to regain full strength, but once it did, Davey Johnson made it clear that either he or Dykstra would start on a regular basis. As of mid-May, Dykstra was a .280-hitting whirling dervish with 12 stolen bases. Wilson was batting .188.

On May 18 fortunes started to change. In an 8–4 victory at Los Angeles, Wilson started in center and went 2 for 4, twice roping hard line drives into Dodger Stadium's vast outfield. Obscured by the performance of reliever Randy Niemann, who retired eleven of thirteen Dodgers for his first win as a Met, the pair of hits failed to make even the tiniest of media splashes. But they were significant. Wilson's success kicked off a 5-game hitting streak in which he went 10 for 22. Suddenly his average was up to .308, and Wilson was smoking balls all over the field. Most important, he was the Mook of old, an Amtrak express out of the batter's box—arms pumping and cheeks puffing. His confidence was sky high. So was his team's.

With right-hander LaMarr Hoyt starting for the Padres at San Diego on May 23, Davey Johnson penciled the switch-hitting Wilson into the leadoff slot for the third straight day. On the bench the left-handed Dykstra silently fumed, wondering what exactly he had done—besides hitting for a high average and providing tons of spunk—to land on the pine. That's one element of the Mets' greatness: Nobody wanted to sit, and anyone who did was certain it was a mistake. Wilson had 5 hits in 5 at-bats (the eighteenth 5-hit game in franchise history and the Mets' best individual offensive output of the season), and he nearly ended the night a hero. He led off the game with a double to right-center and scored two batters later on a groundout by Hernandez. He followed with three singles and then in the top of the seventh took an inside Hoyt fastball and lined it into the right field corner for a 2-run triple, tying the game at 7. It was his biggest hit since the return. To see Wilson fly around the bases like Seattle Slew, a cloud of dust rising under his heels, was a glorious vision of athletic perfection, and even the ultracompetitive, ultra-insecure Dykstra had to shake his head in admiration. Dykstra chugged. Wilson soared.

That the Mets wound up losing was no big deal. They were now 25–11, and their center fielder of the past was once again their center fielder of the future. At least one of two.

Chapter 8

COOTER'S-GATE

If you're a celebrity and especially a New York celebrity, people will try and find every way to take advantage. There's a bull's-eye on your back. I learned that the hard way.

—RICK AGUILERA, Mets pitcher

To BE A NEW YORK MET in 1986 was to go through life with a gigantic neon arrow floating above your head, the words LOOK WHO IT IS! flashing like a strobe for all the world to see. For good and for bad, nothing compares to athletic success in the Big Apple. You are a hero. A god. As the city's seventy-seven thousand homeless population struggles to wrestle away a bread crumb from a pigeon, any old baseball-playing millionaire can eat, see, and own whatever he likes, free of charge.

For example, Hernandez once had his agent call the Winter Garden Theatre to see if he could score a couple of tickets to the city's hottest production, *Cats*. Hernandez's wish wasn't just granted, he was provided six front-row center seats plus backstage passes for after the show. (The

Cats people were somewhat furious when six of Hernandez's friends—but *not* Hernandez—arrived for the performance.)

And it wasn't only the superstars. One could successfully argue that a monkey dressed in Mets duds would find himself besieged. MTV enlisted pitchers Bruce Berenyi and Ron Darling to serve as guest celebrity VJs on a Thursday night in May. The 2:36 P.M. Long Island Railroad train from Port Washington to Manhattan stopped at Shea on game days just so Roger McDowell didn't have to drive. Terry Leach was swarmed by autograph seekers while eating at the South Street Seaport. (Leach's response: "Are you sure you know who I am?") When Sid Fernandez and two friends purchased fourteen pieces of pizza from a restaurant in Queens, the *Post* reported it, noting that "each man averaged 4.66 slices."

Ed Hearn played a total of 49 games for the Mets that season, spending most of his time either polishing Carter's shinguards or slumming with Triple A Tidewater. But one night Hearn found himself stranded alone on a fishing boat in the Long Island Sound, gas tank on empty and too far from land to swim. Hearn turned to the boat's CB radio, desperately calling for assistance.

"Mayday! Mayday! I need help! I need help! My name is Ed Hearn! Mayday! May—"

Suddenly an answer: "Yeah, right. You're not Ed Hearn."

"Mayday! Mayday! I am Ed Hearn! Mayday! I play for the New York Mets! Mayday!"

"If you're Ed Hearn, what are you hitting this year, and who's your third-base coach?"

"Mayday! Mayday! .268! Mayday! And Bud Harrelson! Mayday!"

"How many home runs do you have?"

"Mayday! Two! Mayday! Now come get me! Mayday! Please!"

Within the hour Hearn was rescued by the Coast Guard. He signed autographs for the entire crew.

With each win the Mets' Q-rating soared like the mid-'90s NASDAQ. They were no longer just stars but icons. On a May visit to Manhattan, Ronald Reagan was greeted by three dozen picketers, marching in front of the Waldorf-Astoria with signs reading END WORLD HUNGER! U.S. OUT OF LIBYA! NO NUKES! and LET'S GO METS!

Once a Yankee town, New York was now largely blue and orange. So arrogant were the Mets that at the Yankee Stadium subway stop they posted BASEBALL LIKE IT OUGHTA BE advertisements. George Steinbrenner demanded that the signs be removed. "They stole the city," says Brad Arnsberg, a pitcher for the Bronx Bombers. "The Mets were the talk everywhere." The Mets drew a team record 2,762,417 fans for the season, an average of 34,104 per game. (The Yankees averaged 28,001.) It was all about pizzazz or, in the case of the Yankees, the lack thereof. The Mets would win big and then spend the nights prowling Manhattan's bars, clubs, and eateries. Unlike today's ballplayers who lock themselves in a hotel room with a PlayStation, a cell phone, and a couple of DVDs, the Mets were everywhere. If a fan wanted to get up close and personal, all he or she had to do was show up at Rusty's, the Upper East Side restaurant owned by Staub, and buy Ojeda or Dykstra a beer. The Yankees? They were a workmanlike 90-victory club, but their stars— especially the beloved Don Mattingly—were stay-at-home types of guys. "You couldn't find a Yankee fan," says Ojeda. "As unpleasant as we were and as obnoxious as we were, people took to us."

And it was no longer just a hometown thing. When the team traveled to Philadelphia, thousands of fans made the trek down I-95, camping outside the Hershey Hotel for autographs or, even better, a one-on-one chat with a star. "They had to rope the lobby off for us," says Samuels. "It was a zoo." Among the mobile loyalists was a gaggle of twenty-something groupies, always scantily dressed, always looking to bag a ballplayer. Like the Oakland A's of the mid-1970s, the Mets were as much of a draw drinking Coronas as they were slaughtering the Padres. "We were a traveling rock show," says Darling. "When we were coming into town, everywhere we went would be packed with girls. Word always got around: 'The Mets are here.'" In St. Louis the bar at the downtown Marriott was a buffet of large breasts and long legs. "Guys had their pick," says Darling, one of the twenty Mets who was married. "If you were a member of that team, you didn't want your wife or girlfriend to hear anything or see anything." Patterns developed. The tall brunette from Chicago would surprisingly show up in Atlanta. The perky blonde from Cincinnati would mysteriously appear in Pittsburgh. John Rufino, an assistant equipment manager, spent half the game running notes back and forth between player and hottie: "Meet me at the Hilton after the game" or "Be at the player's entrance in 10 minutes." "They'd fly to different cities just to be with us," says Aguilera. "They would conveniently be at the hotel bar as you walked by or near the rail as you came down to the pen."

Sisk, a struggling reliever who had enough trouble keeping his teammates' respect on the field, nearly lost it entirely when he brought his wife, Lisa, to a hotel bar soiree. There in the midst of beers passing hands and cigarettes burning, Mrs. Sisk could see four or five players, *married* players, wrapped around suspicious-looking women. "That," says one person close to the team, "was not good thinking."

Even Carter had his moment. While walking toward the hotel elevator in Los Angeles, he was approached by a voluptuous minx holding a drink and wearing a miniskirt the size of a catcher's mitt. "Gary," she said seductively, "are you here by yourself?"

Indeed he was. "Sorry, ma'am," Carter said. "I'm married."

From across the lobby his teammates hissed.

"Professional baseball is the world's biggest sweets shop," says Hearn. "It's very, very hard for a young man to go through that type of thing unscathed."

In the early to mid-1980s, Cooter's Executive Games and Burgers was not only the hottest nightspot in Houston but also one of the most talked-about clubs in the country. It was a place where on any given evening one was certain to see some of the brightest stars of the sporting world. If it wasn't Earl Campbell and Kenny Stabler downing beers at a corner table, it was Roger Clemens—in town during the off-season—partying with his friends. When baseball and football teams came to Houston, half the roster was guaranteed to wind up at Cooter's. Owner Rick McDowell drew the jocks by enforcing a simple rule: Athletes drink free.

When McDowell opened the club in 1978, the idea was to give white-collar Houstonites a centrally located, after-work social option that had nothing to do with cowboy hats, Wrangler's, or Hank Williams; an oasis among the country-and-western bars and mechanical bulls. All that had been fine back in the day, but as the city grew from hick emporium to up-and-coming metropolis, there was an entertainment void for the non-tobacco-chewing set.

Cooter's fit the bill perfectly. The music was strictly Top 40, with six bar stations, a dance floor, a pool table, and multiple stools, chairs, and televisions covering 2,100 square feet. There was even a dress code that in the beginning was strictly NO JEANS ALLOWED. ("And this was *Texas*," says one former bouncer. "Can you imagine?") Gradually, as hotter women began stopping by, so did the athletes. (If "free stuff" is a baseball player's favorite phrase, then "smokin' ass" is a close second.) At first it was primarily Astros like Cesar Cedeño and Joe Niekro hanging out after victories, but in time the out-of-towners came to consider Cooter's a home away from home. "Once we had the entire San Francisco Giants roster pull up in limos," says Sam Sansone, the bar's manager from 1981 to 1984. "That wasn't really out of the ordinary." It didn't hurt that the neighbor of Cooter's was Baby O's (now the infamous Men's Club), the city's Number 1 strip joint.

By 1986 there was no other place in Houston like Cooter's. McDowell loved the idea that common folk and superstars mingled together over beers and wings. Yes, there was some special treatment. But if you went to Cooter's after nine hours of taking dictation or filling molars, odds were that you'd hang with royalty. Maybe even snag an autograph. "You knew you could come to Cooter's and be with the guys you see on TV," says McDowell. "That was our appeal."

And to some degree its trap. For every hundred fans who get goose bumps buying Wayne Krenchicki a Michelob, there will always be one or two who would like nothing more than to see rich athletes bleed. It has something to do with the mixture of testosterone and hops, augmented by a drunken friend screaming, "Hey, Wayne—you suck! My retarded brother Rufus coulda caught that ball!" While Cooter's was often able to maintain the peace, there were occasional flare-ups. "You had to watch out because people look to make names for themselves," says Sansone.

To Tim Teufel a bar was a bar was a bar. He could have headed to the Golden Stein, Remington's, Confetti, Cody's, or any of a hundred other Houston establishments and been perfectly content. Truth be told, all he wanted to do was go out with a couple of teammates after the Mets-Astros game, down some cold suds, and celebrate the recent birth of Shawn Michael Teufel (8 pounds, 10 ounces), his first child. Anywhere would suffice.

In his fourth month with the team, Teufel was still struggling to find his niche. In Minnesota his quiet, respectful manner was perfect. But these were the Mets, where the strong survived and the weak were mocked. Thus far Teufel was weak.

Unlike most major-leaguers whose résumés included baseball domination from the age of three, Teufel had always been a good, not great player. He was the youngest of three sons of a hard-drinking, heavy-smoking carpenter, and Teufel insists that a childhood lesson sank in. "One day a doctor told him that if he didn't quit drinking and smoking, they'd both kill him," Teufel says. "So he stopped on the spot, pure willpower." It was a powerful example of personal strength overcoming human weakness. Teufel might have had a gawky build, small muscles, and average athleticism, but he loved the game and believed in himself. After growing up without distinction in the ranks of the Greenwich, Connecticut, Little League system, Teufel walked on at St. Petersburg (Florida) Junior College, where he garnered playing time only after injuries shelved the two third basemen in front of him.

Teufel turned down an offer to sign with the Brewers, instead accepting a scholarship to play second base at Clemson University. He maintained a sense of humility that would stay with him into the pros. In other words, he was unlike almost all of his arrogant, often obnoxious Met teammates.

"It was difficult for Teuf because every team has one guy who's the foil for a lot of jokes, and he was it," says Darling. "That's not easy for the new guy." It didn't help that Teufel was brought in to serve as a right-handed platoon at second base, thus taking away at-bats from the beloved Wally Backman. "Everyone was a Wally fan," says Ed Lynch, the right-handed pitcher. "He had this spark that lit us all." Still, Teufel made an effort. He worked hard at becoming a part of the team's social fabric, sometimes going out with the boys when he preferred to stay in. And although he was not a heavy drinker, Teufel would consume a beer or two for solidarity's sake.

"I heard about this bar, Cooter's . . ."

Eighteen years later the words still haunt. They emerged from the mouth of one Robert Michael Ojeda, a man whose good intentions had mixed results. Throughout the decades there have been few baseball players with such terrible luck as the big-hearted left-hander whom teammates affectionately called "Bobby O." In 1988, Ojeda sliced off the tip of his left index finger with an electric hedge-cutter in the backyard of his Port Washington, New York, home. Five years later he narrowly escaped death while attending spring training with the Cleveland Indians, when a boat he was on crashed into a dock. Two teammates, pitchers Tim Crews and Steve Olin, were killed. Ojeda had surgery for severe head lacerations and returned to the sport. For some reason a great guy was handed horrific twists of fate.

Yet that was all in the future. On this night Ojeda was doing the right thing—picking a bar with loud music and hot chicks, a place where Teufel and the boys could relax and drink for free. Earlier in the evening Houston catcher Alan Ashby hit a 2-run, game-winning single off Ron Darling in the bottom of the seventh to beat the Mets 3–0 at the Astrodome. Under normal circumstances the loss would have been a rough one for New York. But the Mets were in good spirits. Even with two straight defeats to the Astros, Davey Johnson's club was a league-best 60–27, 12 games in front of the fading Expos.

"I heard about this bar, Cooter's . . ."

Doug Sisk heard Ojeda first. *Cooter's?* he thought. *Don't be friggin' stupid.* It was just two years earlier that he and a teammate joined the Houston Police Department's Cooter's hit list. On that night, following a couple of beers, Sisk says, he excused himself to go to the bathroom. When he returned, two police officers slammed him against the wall, wrapped his wrists in cuffs, and took him to the station. He was charged with simple assault and public intoxication. He's still shocked. "I can honestly say that I did nothing—*nothing!*—to get arrested or even draw police attention," says Sisk. "That bar had a history of bad relations with athletes." With the memory still fresh, Sisk stopped Ojeda and issued a stern warning: "Don't go there," he said. "It's trouble waiting to happen." The words went unheeded.

Had Sisk not had relatives from nearby Del Rio, Texas, in town for the Astros series, he says he would have tagged along as a sort of watchdog for fishy bouncers and jock-sniffing troublemakers. Instead he and the family went out for a late steak dinner. With the hard-living Sisk in tow, would "Cooter's-gate" (as the incident was called) have transpired? "Honestly," says Sisk, "I don't think so. I'd have directed them to another place."

Without Sisk the Mets were unprepared for an attack. Five men— Teufel, Ojeda, Aguilera, Darling, and Strawberry—took the fifteen-minute taxi ride out to the nightspot. There was no one there to warn them that Cooter's was crawling with vicious athlete envy. There was no one there to warn them that they would be watched like ring-card girls at a boxing match. Worst of all, there was no one there to warn them that in Houston police officers wouldn't roll over because—*Oh, my God!*— Ron Darling was on TV hours ago. Just the opposite, actually.

Strawberry was bored, and who could blame him? Cooter's was packed, and the music was loud and the drinks were cold, but except for the beer, it wasn't his type of place. The faces were mostly white, and the tunes were cheesy. Plus everywhere he stepped, stares followed. Strawberry ordered a beer, and people watched and whispered. Undeniably, part of it was celebrity: When baseball's most prodigious young power hitter cruises the town (any town), heads spin. But Strawberry had been around enough to know when an out-of-town brother wasn't exactly welcome with open arms.

At approximately 11:20 P.M., Strawberry said, "Teuf, I'm taking off. Congrats, man."

Teufel nodded good-bye, then returned to his shot—his fourth or fifth, depending on who's counting. On a team that drank by the keg, Teufel was a lightweight. Five shots was a year, not an evening. "He was the most innocent guy on our club," says Ojeda. "If you picked one guy *not* to get in a bar fight, it would be Timmy—easy. He was just a laid-back, mild-mannered person." Even here at Cooter's, surrounded by friends and wasted, Teufel surely felt mildly uncomfortable. Around him, women were seductively brushing by, clearly aware that fame was in the house. While his last name translates to "devil" in German, Teufel wasn't the average baseball-playing hound. By all accounts he was 100 percent loyal to Valerie, his wife.

Locals don't differentiate between saintly baseball players and sinister ones—especially male locals in the south, the type still seething with anti-Yankee rage. As a growing number of Cooter's patrons became aware that the four loudmouths drawing all the women (and being served for free) were members of the Mets, a growing number of these patrons started grumbling. "Here they hate people from New York—absolutely hate 'em," says Lisa Calvin, a Cooter's waitress from 1986 to 1991. "New York is not popular because it's so big, and big is everything here. Plus, New York teams traditionally beat the crap out of us. Houston men don't like that."

While accounts of what exactly transpired differ, we know that over the next couple of hours the four remaining Mets ordered more and more shots, drew the attention of more and more cowgirls, and infuriated more and more male customers. Nothing about their obnoxiousness was intentional. They were by nature loud, drunk athletes celebrating the new son of a (surprisingly) loud, drunk teammate. They were having fun.

Nobody is quite sure which of the four baseball players uttered the most asinine sentence in Houston saloon history, but it was undeniably uttered.

At 1:45 A.M. a Cooter's bartender announced the last call for alcohol.

At 1:59 A.M. approximately 2,996 of Cooter's approximately 3,000 patrons that night had left the building.

At 2 A.M. a Cooter's waitress asked the four remaining Mets to leave. The response: "We're the fuckin' New York Mets, and we'll leave when we want to."

Imagine being the staff of Cooter's. You have spent the past three hours pouring shot after shot for four bigmouthed members of an arrogant out-of-town baseball team from, of all places, New York City. You have received nary a thank-you, nary a dime in tips. You have worked all night, your hair smells like cigarette smoke, and all you want to do is close up shop and head home to your bed. Instead you get this: "We're the fuckin' New York Mets, and we'll leave when we want to." How do you react?

To their credit the employees did very little. But as the Mets continued to linger inside the bar, not a care in the world as they casually polished off their drinks, some workers began to wonder if they would ever depart. Finally, thirty-five minutes past closing time, Officers Dale Bristley and Randy Gresham, the two Houston policemen hired by Cooter's that night to work security detail, were asked to leave their posts out front, enter the bar, and help out. (Under one of Texas's countless ill-conceived state laws, fully uniformed but off-duty police officers were permitted to accept private money to work as security guards. On a nightly basis Cooter's had a pair of rent-a-cops stationed outside.) It wasn't pretty. As soon as the four players saw the uniformed officers approach, all good spirits turned dark. "We had heard complaints about their behavior all night from some of the waitresses," says Bristley. "When we encountered them, they started throwing the F-word at both of us. We went in there with the idea of just having them exit the bar and everything working out peacefully. That didn't quite happen."

As Darling and Aguilera went to use the men's room a final time, Teufel and Ojeda exited through the front door, chatting away as if they were in the Shea clubhouse. Ojeda had his right arm wrapped around

Teufel's shoulder. With his left arm he hailed a cab parked in front of the bar.

"Hey! Hey! What are you doing?" The voice belonged to Bristley, who had returned to the front of the bar.

"What do you mean, 'What are we doing'?" Ojeda replied. "We're leaving."

"No way! I don't think so!" Bristley said.

Bristley pointed to Teufel, who was holding a half-consumed Heineken in his right hand. Under Texas law no opened alcoholic beverages are allowed in public. Traditionally, police officers treat offenders with kid gloves. Few look the other way entirely, but if the drinker is willing to return to the bar and rid himself of the beverage, no harm, no foul, no ugly moments.

Here, such was not the case. "You can't just leave with that beer!" Bristley yelled. "It's the law!"

Depending on whom you speak with, Teufel gave one of two responses:

- "Fuck off!"

or . . .

- "You can't do anything to us. We'll buy this damn club!"

Either way, Bristley snapped. He reached for the beer, which caused the out-of-his-head Teufel to cock back his right fist and lunge toward the officer. Even at his most muscular the second baseman had as much business throwing a punch as Kurt Waldheim did joining B'nai B'rith. Teufel was a softie, and softies do not engage in barroom brawls with cops. The doormen on duty, Sandy Hooper and Nate Wishnow, grabbed him by the arms and waist and pulled him away from Bristley. Wishnow came from behind and right-jabbed twice at Teufel's stomach, sending him stumbling to the ground. Although he had no experience as a professional boxer, WWF superstar, or ultimate fighting champion,

Wishnow felt a rush of adrenaline that equaled a thousand black coffees. At five-foot-ten and 175 pounds, this was the twenty-eight-year-old doorman's first celebrity fight, and he milked the moment for all its value. Standing atop the fallen Teufel, he looked down and said, "You know, for an athlete you're a pretty big wimp." Teufel, battered and drunk, could only sigh.

When Darling exited Cooter's at the end of the battle, he was shocked to see Teufel pinned on top of a box of plants, his hands cuffed and Bristley holding him down with a knee to his back. "Break his arm!" someone yelled. "Break the guy's arm!"

"When I heard that," says Darling, "I got involved." Instead of helping Teufel, though, Darling found himself on the receiving end of an old-fashioned smack-down. According to police reports, when Bristley called for Gresham to help restrain Teufel, Darling charged Gresham and hit him in the throat. "Was Tim wrong to leave the bar with a beer?" says Darling. "Yes, no question. But did the officers take things a little too far? Yes." During the altercation Darling was pushed into a glass-encased sign outside the club, which splintered into dozens of shards. Gresham cuffed Darling and sat him on the pavement. "They put him on the glass by accident," says Hooper. "He asked me politely to clean the glass so he wouldn't damage his pitching hand. I understood."

As the mayhem erupted around them, Aguilera and Ojeda did their ineffective best to keep the peace. Aguilera tried to hold Darling back from Gresham, and Ojeda begged Bristley to give Teufel a break. "Look, he's a good guy," Ojeda said. "His son was just born, and he drank a little too much. This stuff happens." There was no sympathy. Teufel and Darling were led back into the bar to be formally charged with aggravated assault of a police officer. Meanwhile, Aguilera and Ojeda sat on the curb, anxiously trying to think of a way out of the mess. "If nothing else, we'll at least follow 'em to the jail and bail 'em out," said Ojeda. "We've just gotta keep this quiet." Aguilera nodded and looked up. A police officer was requesting their presence inside the bar.

Upon reentering Cooter's, Aguilera and Ojeda were cuffed and charged with hindering an arrest. "Are you fuckin' kidding me?" yelled

Ojeda. "We didn't do anything. What the hell did we do?" There was no answer. The four Mets were packed into police cars and shipped off to the Houston City Jail.

As the Mets filed into the building, something strange happened. Aguilera, the first one to be fingerprinted and photographed, was accidentally shuffled off into the general clink where the jail's main population was housed. The three other Mets were put in a private holding cell. For two hours a petrified Aguilera found himself surrounded by inept car jackers, pickpockets, convenience-store crooks, and purse snatchers. "It was like a scene from *Stir Crazy*," says Aguilera. "I'm walking around the cell, trying to act all tough. *I'm bad. I'm bad.* They eventually got me out of there, but at that moment I wanted to cry."

So did Teufel, who was both humiliated and—after too much booze—sick. Throughout the Mets' first twenty-five years, players had been traded, released, booed, cheered, honored, and arrested. Teufel was the first to puke his guts out into a prison toilet.

At age twenty-eight, Ojeda was the oldest of the group and, with a couple of bar fights under his belt, seasoned enough to laugh at the predicament. The holding cell was in the jail's main corridor, so whenever a new inmate arrived, he would be dragged past the four Mets, who spent most of the night leaning against the bars in disbelief. From surrounding cells there were screams of agony, unintelligible curses, mindless rants, and maniacal laughs. Says Ojeda: "I just turned to Ronnie at one point, smiled, and was like, 'Man, is this shit really happening?'"

One of the players listed Charlie Samuels, the team's equipment manager, as a primary contact, and a sheriff placed a call. Samuels hurried to the station with a wad of cash but was told that office hours were 10 A.M. to 7 P.M. He spent the night asleep outside on the jailhouse steps.

At 2:20 A.M. Ojeda was allowed his one phone call. He reached Arthur Richman, the travel secretary, asleep in his hotel room. "For now you guys are stuck," said Richman, "but let me do some things." Richman had an in. Back in the mid-1940s, Frank Mancuso was a weak-hitting backup catcher for the old St. Louis Browns, and Arthur and his big brother, Milton, were huge baseball fans. Every time the Browns came to New York, the two Richman boys would stand outside the team hotel and hunt for autographs. After enough go-arounds, Mancuso started looking for Richman's pug face. Now, forty years later, Mancuso was Houston's vice mayor, and the pug needed help. "My phone rang while I was eating breakfast," says Mancuso. "I said, 'Art, what the hell is going on?'" He pulled a few strings, and two hours before official release time, Aguilera, Darling, Ojeda, and Teufel exited the Houston City Jail. Samuels, curled up on a step, was there to greet them.

To the players' relief there were no TV cameras waiting to capture the humiliation. The inevitable New York headlines, however, were plentiful, and plenty harsh:

A FINE DAY FOR METS BASEBRAWL SUPERSTARS!

SLAP-HAPPY METS!

THE BOYS OF SLAMMER!

Even David Letterman got in a jab. "I contacted Met management," he said in a monologue, "and they told me that was the most solid contact Teufel has made all year."

Jay Horwitz, one of the game's top PR gurus, couldn't put a muzzle on the public record. Any cop reporter knows that the first thing you do each morning is head down to the station and examine the previous night's arrest log. In this case, listed were the names of four prominent figures on baseball's most prominent team. "What made it worse is that at the time very little was happening in the news," says Horwitz. "We were the news."

At 11 A.M. the four Mets arrived at the Astrodome for the third game of the four-game series. They had:

A. spent a night in jail.
B. gotten zero hours of sleep.
C. been berated by Cashen, McIlvaine, and Richman.

Before his chums arrived, Roger McDowell, the Mets' wacky reliever, thought up "how to screw with my teammates idea number 12,471." In his two seasons with New York, McDowell had thrived not only on baffling opposing hitters but on transforming shaving cream, chewing gum, dirt, paint, ink, sunflower seeds, and dozens of other objects into weapons of mass destruction. This time he grabbed a roll of white tape from the training room, painted it black, and lined the lockers of Aguilera, Darling, Ojeda, and Teufel with mock prison bars. McDowell placed a bar of soap, a razor, and a piece of bread on each stool. Atop the stalls Hearn, McDowell's assistant, taped inmate identification numbers. A scrap of paper reading MACHO CAMACHO covered Teufel's nameplate.

Aguilera and Darling were the first to notice the props, and both laughed. When Ojeda saw it, he sighed, shrugged, and chuckled. But Teufel, with a welt on his upper right arm and a King Kong Bundy–sized hangover, was in no mood for a reminder. He swatted the items off his stool and sat down. "Yeah, that's pretty fuckin' funny!" he yelled. "Pretty fuckin' funny!"

For a moment there was silence. That turned into laughter. And more laughter. "It's how we handled things," says McDowell. "When everybody's laughing and one guy's pissed, you have a choice: Either join in, or we'll keep laughing because you're pissed."

Finally, Teufel turned around and joined the hysterics. It wasn't quite the way he had wanted to celebrate the birth of his new son, but at least he could laugh.

In February 1987, after numerous hearings and depositions, a Harris County District Court sentenced Darling and Teufel to one year's probation and a $200 fine, and dismissed all charges against Aguilera and Ojeda. The Mets had been wise: The lawyer they hired was Dick DeGuerin, an up-and-coming legal star who seven years later would gain fame by representing David Koresh in his standoff against the FBI and ATF at Waco, Texas. DeGuerin's case—that the Mets were victims of celebrity, abused by over-the-line cops anxious to pound some famous folk—was smoothly delivered. It was an easy win.

But with their egos bruised, the two officers let greed take over. In August they filed suit against the Mets for $10.2 million. "The allegations that we beat them just were not true," says Bristley. "What about our reputations? We had to protect ourselves."

They hired an overmatched local attorney named A. Lee McLain who made statements to the press like "I just really feel like these officers have been victimized by prima donnas" and "This is a stigma they've had to live with, and it's just gotten worse."

Luckily for McLain and his clients, Cashen wanted Cooter's-gate to disappear, and the Mets settled for $5,000. The most disappointed person was DeGuerin, who says he was armed with oodles of anticop material. In addition, according to the *Post*, the A.C.L.U. had recently filed a lawsuit against the Houston Police Department for—in the words of lawyer Bruce Griffiths—a policy of "covering your butt charges" in which the cops frequently file charges to cover up the fact that they mishandled a prisoner.

A week after the Cooter's incident, a Houston police officer printed up T-shirts that read: HOUSTON POLICE 4, METS 0. As dozens of cops wore the shirts, dozens of cops looked like buffoons.

The only winner was Cooter's. Instead of stopping in to see Earl Campbell drinking a beer, patrons wanted to stand in the exact spot where Tim Teufel took a pounding. "I hate to say this, but it wasn't like anyone got killed," says Rick McDowell. "Business skyrocketed, and we even got on the front page of *USA Today*. What more could you ask for?"

Sadly, Cooter's never recaptured the excitement of July 19, 1986. It closed five years later.

Chapter 9

DOC AND DARRYL

There is no greater place to be a star than New York. You want to run a little wild. But, when you do that, you're gonna stub your toe in unknown waters.

—REGGIE JACKSON

IN A STRANGE WAY the melee at Cooter's helped the Mets organization more than it hurt. Yes, Cashen hated his recurring mental image of four orange-and-blue Mets hats bobbing up and down behind prison bars. And, yes, it led to countless comparisons to a humiliating event that took place twenty-nine years earlier when Mickey Mantle, Billy Martin, Whitey Ford, and four other Yankees engaged in a skirmish at the famed Copacabana. And, yes, it would forever be glued to Aguilera, Darling, Ojeda, and Teufel like a bug to flypaper.

But as New York's daily newspapers were focusing all their energy and manpower on the night in Houston and its aftershocks, it drew attention away from the team's two largest headliners, Dwight Gooden and Darryl Strawberry.

Even without the distraction of Cooter's, it would have been easy for an unfocused observer to miss the decline of the Mets' newest problem children. After all, both men were heavily endorsed, heavily hyped wunderkinds, seen everywhere from TV to newspapers to advertisements for Diet Pepsi and Nike and Kellogg's Corn Flakes. Just four days earlier Gooden and Strawberry had joined Hernandez and Carter as National League starters at the All-Star Game (held, of all places, at the Astrodome). At ages twenty-one and twenty-four, respectively, they were at the top of the baseball world.

But beyond the resplendent glow there was a reality at hand. A major league–high 1,619,511 fans voted for Strawberry to start in right field, which meant 1,619,511 fans had no clue what was going on in the sport. Strawberry was in the midst of his worst season in four years, hitting .292 but with just 13 homers and 45 RBIs. Most troubling for the Mets was his remarkable lack of interest in becoming an all-around team player. Strawberry was a lazy fielder who too often loafed after line drives into the gap. When he wanted to perform, he brought to bear a nearly unstoppable constellation of skills. (In the All-Star Game Home Run Contest, he joined Mike Schmidt as the only men in history to ever hit one of the Astrodome's ceiling PA speakers. "I don't usually swing like that," he said afterward. "But when I put my mind to something, good things happen.") When he wanted to daydream, he was worthless. "There were times when Darryl would go nonchalantly after balls, and guys would turn singles into doubles," says Sid Fernandez. "If you're a pitcher, that can kill you."

As for Gooden, NL manager Whitey Herzog named him the All-Star Game starter based more on hype than success. Because he stood out as the darling of the New York media and the reigning Cy Young Award winner, it was easy to forget that with a 10–4 record and a 2.77 ERA, Gooden was just another very good but not great hard-throwing right-handed pitcher. Truth be told, no fewer than six National Leaguers were more deserving of the starting nod, including Fernandez (12–2, 2.67), Ojeda (10–2, 2.24), and—based on a red-hot July—Darling (9–2, 2.84). But like the twenty-five-story mural of Gooden painted on the side of a Manhattan building, the young phenom's image was larger than life.

Just take a look at the way ABC and Major League Baseball hyped the All-Star Game. Unlike in past years, where advertisements featured an array of stars, this game was about (cue stirring music and deep-voiced announcer) *"the clash of baseball's premier young guns!"* It was Gooden starting against Boston's twenty-three-year-old Roger Clemens, and unless you lived in a cave on Pluto, it was impossible to ignore. The Red Sox right-hander was 15–2 with a 2.48 ERA. If a Cy Young Award had ever been locked up by July, here was Exhibit A.

Mike Schmidt? Ho-hum. Tim Raines? Big whoops. This was Gooden versus Clemens. Clemens versus Gooden. They were two hard-throwing, steel-jawed superstars who, one assumed, would rule the game for the next decade. It was a marketing executive's dream come true, and baseball milked it for everything it was worth.

Oddly, the head honchos of MLB forgot to mention one thing: Gooden, they believed, was on drugs.

On the night of April 17, 1986, Ray Knight and his wife, golf star Nancy Lopez, attended a black-tie gala at Manhattan's Marriott Marquis Hotel. The event was the fourteenth annual New York City Multiple Sclerosis Dinner of Champions, a $500-per-plate affair. For Knight, a legitimately charitable guy who spent most of his career in the under-the-radar outposts of Cincinnati and Houston, the event was an eye-popper of celebrity who's who. *Isn't that Gardner Dickinson one table over, chatting away with Benny Parsons? Look, it's Vijay and Anand Amritraj! And Alex Webster! Holy cow, is that . . . Deborah Carthy-Deu, the reigning Miss Universe!*

Okay, so the stars were C list. That didn't stop Knight and Lopez from having a blast, taking in the orchestra music (but no dancing—Lopez was eight months pregnant with the couple's third child), posing for pictures, and chatting away over rubber chicken and defrosted cheesecake. In the midst of a detailed chitchat with his spouse, the Mets third baseman felt a tap on his shoulder.

"Ray, do you have a minute?"

Standing before Knight and Lopez was Peter Ueberroth, baseball's second-year commissioner and one of the sporting world's most powerful figures. Just two years earlier Ueberroth had run the Los Angeles

Olympic Games, producing arguably the most successful edition in the event's eighty-eight-year history. Now as a reward he was being paid $200,000 annually to disperse the dark cloud engulfing the game of Ruth and Gehrig, Mantle and Mays. To lead baseball back to prominence was to wipe out drugs. It was that simple.

Knight rose and snapped to attention. He had met the commissioner once before, but there was still the discomfort of being confronted by a superior. So at the same time actor James Garner was at the podium accepting an award, Knight followed Ueberroth into a hallway, curious about what was so urgent that he had to miss a speech. It didn't take long to find out.

"Look, Ray, I'll get right to the point here," Ueberroth said. "I wouldn't feel comfortable telling you the name of the player, but you have a young black superstar on the Mets whom we're investigating in the commissioner's office."

Knight was confused. "Investigating?" he said. "For what?"

The commissioner was getting to that. "We think he's doing drugs, Ray. Actually, we're pretty positive of it."

There were five African Americans listed on the Mets' roster: Kevin Mitchell was young but not a superstar. George Foster and Mookie Wilson could theoretically be considered stars, but they were squeaky clean and veterans. Dwight Gooden was young, black, and a star, but he was way too wholesome to be involved in such troubles. That left one man: Strawberry.

"It's not that Darryl had too many inconsistencies," says Knight, "but he did brood sometimes and he was a bit moody."

With drug abuse poisoning the league's image, the last thing Ueberroth needed was the arrest/suspension/ejection of an up-and-coming all-star on the game's best team (which happened to play in the media capital of the world, no less). The commissioner's message to Knight had a simplicity that belied its urgent nature. "If there's any way you can get this thing settled or calmed down, we'd all really appreciate it," Ueberroth said. "We'd like to have this taken care of in the easiest way possible."

There was a reason (besides convenience) that Ueberroth turned to Knight. From the time he had entered the league twelve years earlier, New York's third baseman had earned a reputation as an honest, well-intentioned man whose integrity was rock-solid. "Ray is unmatched in character," says Carter. "What he says is what he'll do. He's a true giant."

What Knight was facing was the potential destruction of a baseball team. Surviving the Hernandez drug fiasco was hard enough, but this cut to the heart of the Mets—the young, awe-inspiring superstar who drew millions of fans to the stadium. Without Strawberry, New York's swaggering giant of a baseball team was mortal. "Of all the tough times, this one was the worst," Knight says. "I didn't know much about drug use, but I knew it could ruin a person, not to mention our team."

The following afternoon Knight arrived unusually early at Shea Stadium for the evening game against the Phillies. He sat quietly by his locker and waited for Strawberry—generally one of the last to enter the clubhouse—to show up, the minutes feeling like days. Unlike most of the veterans on the Mets, Knight had an odd fondness for the young right fielder. Where others saw arrogance, Knight saw immaturity. Where others saw laziness, Knight saw confusion. He, too, had once been an up-and-coming star, sometimes unsure which side of the right-wrong line was proper turf. "I love Darryl," says Knight. "He's always been very misunderstood. He has a heart as big as anyone I've ever known."

Finally, Strawberry entered the room. Knight immediately pulled him aside. "Darryl, I've gotta ask you something, and I want you to be honest with me," he said. Strawberry stared blankly at Knight. "I talked to a high-ranking official in the commissioner's office last night at this banquet, and he said there's a young black superstar around here who he thinks has drug problems. And I, umm . . ."

On the awkward silence scale, this one was a ten. Strawberry knew exactly what Knight was implying. Knight thought he knew exactly what Strawberry was thinking. *(Damn, I'm busted.)* But then in a moment Knight will never forget, Strawberry pulled his sunglasses to the edge of his nose, looked Knight square in the eyes, and with no emotion uttered a single word: "Doc."

Doc?

Knight felt the air rush from his stomach as if someone had slugged him in the gut. Dwight Gooden on drugs? The idea was ridiculous. Heck, Gooden was anything but a drug user. Just look at his background. Unlike many of the African American athletes Knight had played with whose stories of conquering ghetto life and overcoming the obstacles numbed the ears, Gooden was the product of a wholesome upbringing. His folks, Dan and Ella Mae, raised their son with loving discipline, making certain Dwight's homework and chores came before balls and strikes. It might not have been Mayberry, but it was darn close.

Little did Knight know that during spring training Ueberroth had received some troubling pieces of information. According to *Sports Illustrated*, in December 1985, sheriff's deputies, acting on an informant's tip, pulled over Gooden's car and conducted a search. They found a holstered pistol on the floor of the front passenger's seat, $4,000 in cash, and a bag of baking soda. Herman Cousin, Gooden's friend, was riding along that night. He explained away the gun as "protection" and the money as nothing unusual for a wealthy baseball player. But when it came to the baking soda, often used to cut cocaine and as an agent in freebasing, Cousin was speechless.

Knight wasn't best friends with Gooden, but from across the clubhouse he greatly admired the young pitcher's placid demeanor, a calmness that made you think he was a ten-year vet, not a twenty-one-year-old kid. While Strawberry would stroll into the stadium ten or fifteen minutes late, Gooden was always on time, always flashing his boyish grin and gold front tooth. He was a Boy Scout. What was it a spokesman at Gooden's favorite New York bar, Shout!, had told the *Daily News*? "He doesn't even drink beer here. All he has is carrot juice, which we stock mainly for him." Gooden? Drugs? No way.

"Darryl, are you sure about this?" Knight said, unconvinced. "You're not the one involved in this stuff?"

With that Strawberry let Knight in on a little secret. On June 14, 1985, Gooden was scheduled to pitch against the Expos in Montreal.

Generally, a starting pitcher is one of the first players to arrive at the stadium—a final opportunity to review scouting reports and watch some tape. Carter, the cagey catcher, made a point of meeting one-on-one with the starter for a final checklist of the opposing lineup.

Three hours before the game at Olympic Stadium, no Gooden. Two hours, no Gooden. One hour, no Gooden. With thirty-five minutes until the first pitch, Gooden burst through the clubhouse doors. At the time nobody thought much of the misstep. Sure, it was one of the Doctor's worst starts of the season—8 innings, 6 hits, 3 runs, and a no-decision in a 5–4 Mets loss—but he still struck out 11, and his bad outings were like anyone else's best. Hell, Gooden was perfect. He was probably stuck in traffic.

But now Strawberry was telling Knight a different version. "Remember that night, Ray?" he said. "Doc was late because he was up on an all-night cocaine binge the night before. He was out of control." The exchange with Knight revealed as much about Strawberry's character as Gooden's. What type of friend (and despite occasional reports to the contrary, Gooden and Strawberry were close chums) snitches with such easy indifference? There was no arm twisting here, no job threats. Strawberry found himself confronted with a serious charge, and he took the easy way out: He ratted on Gooden. It was a transgression few of his teammates would ever forget.

As soon as he and Strawberry parted ways, Knight relayed the story as well as Ueberroth's warning to Davey Johnson, who promised he would handle the crisis. Later that afternoon, as the team took BP, Johnson spoke with Gooden and Strawberry in the outfield. One imagines the line of communication went something like this:

JOHNSON: "There's a rumor that you guys might be doing some things you shouldn't be involved with. Is that true?"
GOODEN: "No."
STRAWBERRY: "No."
JOHNSON: "Okay. Just checking."

"I saw Davey talking to Dwight and Darryl in the outfield, but I don't think anything happened," Knight says. "Davey didn't believe Dwight was using, either. I don't think many of us did."

If there was one person who had no business squealing on Dwight Gooden, it was Darryl Strawberry. The right fielder was as wholesome as a Nevada brothel, and whether it was coke or rum or beer or just plain ol' cigarettes, no Met beat on his body more.

Although the twenty-four-year-old Strawberry was sculpted in the mold of Adonis, the abuse seemed to be taking a toll on his success as a baseball player. Johnson repeatedly fined the right fielder for arriving late to the ballpark, and if the slumped shoulders and dragging feet didn't tell the previous night's story, then Strawberry's reddened eyes certainly did. Tired of repeated lackluster efforts, Johnson initiated the Darryl Strawberry Rule. "I told Darryl, 'I won't fine you for not running out a ground ball,'" says Johnson, "'But if a fielder bobbles it and you should have been safe if you had been running hard, you owe me $500.'" Johnson donated all of Strawberry's fine money to a Catholic orphanage in Queens. He does not recall the year-end total, but says with a laugh, "Let's just say Darryl supported the place."

Even in his worst states, Strawberry evoked fear in rival pitchers. In batting practice, teammates and opponents would gather around the cage to watch him crush baseballs that, in McDowell's words, "traveled to distant planets we've never heard of." Yet by the summer's dog days, Strawberry was in the worst funk of his career. Within a span of two months he suffered through an 0-for-24 slump, followed by an 0-for-21 lag, and at one point he was 0 for 47 at Shea Stadium. In an August 30 home game against the Dodgers, Strawberry was repeatedly heckled with a viciousness usually reserved for Foster and Sisk. When he misplayed a ball in right field, the sound was that of 50,000 angry ghosts: *booooooooooo!*

"I've just got to learn to suck it up and put my time in and not get frustrated," he told *The New York Times* afterward. "The trouble is, people read stories in the papers and I get labeled and the fans get down on me. Maybe it's time to be somewhere else if I'm not wanted. There are a lot of places where you could be happy." When Johnson read such quotes in the paper, the frustration took over. Countless times he had urged Strawberry to go easy on his body, to stop staying out so late, to work a little harder on the fundamentals. "Darryl, you don't just struggle for no reason," he told him. "God gave you a strong physique, and you have to take care of it."

Did such talks work? "Darryl would listen for a day or two," says Johnson, "and then he'd be showing up at the park bleary-eyed again." Even his party-minded teammates encouraged him to slow down.

Strawberry's first experience with cocaine came in 1983, shortly after he was promoted to the major leagues. While he had long been a beer drinker, it was not until his debut season that Strawberry came face-to-face with a powder that two decades later would leave him broke, imprisoned, and abandoned. According to *Sports Illustrated*, some veteran Mets teammates asked the rookie outfielder to try something new and exciting. "There's a couple of lines in the bathroom for you, kid," Strawberry recalled the veterans saying. "This is the big leagues. This is what you do in the big leagues. Go ahead. It's good for you."

Strawberry awkwardly snorted the coke. It was love at first sniff.

"With Straw there were a lot of signs," says one former team employee. "I'd go so far as to say that the front office knew the deal. They called him upstairs a couple of times, and they asked him—not asked but *told* him—they knew the company he was keeping and the things he was rumored to be doing." (Cashen denies that management had any knowledge of Strawberry's abuse at the time.)

Adds Hernandez, a reformed cocaine user: "I had a hunch about Darryl. I pretty much knew he was not taking care of himself."

Hard drugs or no hard drugs, if there was a bus to ride on, a plane to fly on, a room to sit in, a restaurant to eat in, a speech to listen to, Strawberry always made certain to bring along alcohol. In his autobiography, *Darryl*, Strawberry looked back at '86 and wrote, "I drank at parties, I drank at clubs, I drank on the bus, I drank on the planes, I drank alone." On the Mets heavy boozing did not make Strawberry especially unique. His inability to handle it, however, did. Whereas a player like Hernandez could stay out until the wee hours and then show up at the stadium and go 3 for 4 with two doubles, Strawberry's stomach was soft and his tolerance low. Many were the times that he would ask Davey Johnson for the afternoon off, citing a phantom tight muscle. Nearly as numerous were the times that Johnson—furious at his star's lack of dedication—would ignore such requests and stick him in the lineup.

"We always had to worry about whether Darryl was going to play and what kind of mood he would be in," says Hernandez. "He was basically up all the time." It got to the point that behind his back teammates would mock Strawberry anytime he was spotted in the trainer's room. "Skip, I've got a bad back," they'd say, laughing. "Those shot glasses are really heavy."

Strawberry did much of his damage at Finn MacCool's, a tavern in Port Washington where many of the Mets hung out. One night Henry Downing, the bar's manager, concocted a drink for the Mets that he named The Nervous Breakdown. It was a potent combination of vodka, cranberry juice, tequila, and schnapps, and the twelve Mets sitting around the table eagerly devoured pitcher after pitcher. Among the participants were Ojeda, Mitchell, Dykstra, and Backman—guys who could hold their own. Yet the one who drank the most was Strawberry. "I remember he really took to that," says Connie O'Reilly, MacCool's owner. "I guess he liked the taste."

As Strawberry guzzled away, he got louder and louder. Then he started stumbling around. By the time he took a taxi home, it was 2 A.M. Strawberry was wasted.

"The next afternoon we were watching the game from the bar, and the broadcaster said Darryl wasn't playing," O'Reilly says. "They showed him sitting on the bench . . . something about a twenty-four-hour virus."

Whether or not they ever snorted cocaine, several Mets had at least been around the scene or, if nothing else, were familiar with the odd behavioral patterns of those who were chemically altered. In the late 1970s and early 1980s, one could walk into the bathroom of a nightclub in most American cities and spot someone sniffing powder off a mirror. In an era virtually fueled by coke, its users weren't exactly covert.

Those who knew Gooden well were baffled by his actions. As Strawberry writes in *Darryl*: "There were times when some of the players would be getting ready to go out after a game or go to dinner and Doc would have to go back to his hotel room and get something. He would tell us he'd meet us at the restaurant, but then sometimes he'd not show up at all. This wasn't what you'd call 'aberrant' behavior or anything, but it was inconsistent." Away from the field, his reliability deteriorated as the season progressed. Gooden started showing up ten minutes late. Or twenty. Or he would simply never arrive.

From the shadows of his self-imposed seclusion in the corner of the clubhouse, Foster watched with sad eyes as Gooden's persona morphed from innocence and joy to ornery and disturbed. He saw a once-dynamic assortment of pitches begin to turn flat. And as an eighteen-year veteran who had experienced everything a career could offer, he seemed to know: *This kid's got issues.*

In April 1987, seven months after his last game with the Mets, Foster was asked by the *Post* whether he had suspected Gooden's drug abuse during the '86 season. "When you're around individuals who've been into drugs, you notice they start acting differently," he said. "You observe that and think of things it might be. . . . He wasn't as poised or relaxed as he was before. I could see chemical reactions of the body."

Foster was not alone. Backman, one of the club's heavy-duty night stalkers, says: "Shit, I think just about everybody on the team knew something was going on. If guys were honest with themselves, they knew. But as long as any users kept performing on the field, no one was going to say anything."

That's the rub: Gooden's record was 10–4 at the All-Star break, so other players' concerns were kept private. But his season was a roller coaster: two good starts, one terrible; one dominant, three sloppy; four great, two miserable. In spring training when some began to question his off-the-field missteps, Gooden was battered by opposing hitters like a soggy piñata. Still it was just the exhibition season, when it was easy for the team to dismiss it as rust or indifference. But for a guy who absolutely dominated baseball in 1985, the output was puzzling. "I'm not concerned," Gooden told the daily writers. "When it counts, I'll turn it on."

Briefly, he did. Gooden kicked off the season by going 5–0 with a 1.04 ERA through early May, and talk of a second straight Cy Young Award abounded. After Gooden's fifth victory, a 4–0 two-hit shutout of Houston on May 6, *Newsday*'s Steve Marcus wrote, "It is always a special night when Dwight Gooden is on the mound for the Mets. He presents a long list of possibilities. The question always is: What can he do this time?"

But now the question changed: What's wrong with Dwight Gooden?

In his next nine decisions Gooden went 5–4. His ERA during that span was a mediocre 4.02. In a 3–2 loss to the Reds on May 11, Gooden had a one-ball, two-strikes count on Ron Oester, Cincy's light-hitting second baseman. Instead of blowing Oester away with vibrating heat, Gooden's fastball glided over the heart of the plate. Oester singled. "I knew something was wrong right there," Strawberry said after the game. "When he gets 2 strikes on someone like Oester, he usually buries him." This was less a dig at an opponent than a simple fact: Guys like Ron Oester don't touch Dwight Gooden. At least they never had before.

What truly told the story was the increasingly common sight of a once indomitable force standing beside the mound, head down, hands on his hips, as average players like Dane Iorg and Rick Schu circled the bases after slugging home runs. On May 22 at San Francisco, Gooden experienced a head-scratching low: a 4-inning, 9-hit, 6-run pounding at the hands of the terrible Giants. Teammates were mystified. "He hasn't had the extra five miles per hour on his fastball," said Hernandez, offering his best attempt at an explanation.

The most vivid portrait of the new Gooden was painted on June 18 in Montreal. It was an ideal night for baseball—not only the matchup of the NL East's top two teams, but Gooden's first start against his old high school friend and teammate, twenty-two-year-old right-hander Floyd Youmans. Their dream of teaming up in the majors nearly came true in

1982 when, after selecting Gooden in the first round of the amateur draft, the Mets took Youmans as their second pick. But then Youmans was sent to Canada as part of the Carter deal. The dream was dead. "Dwight was the best prime-time pitcher in baseball," says Backman. "If there was anything on the line and Doc was pitching, we knew it was wrapped up."

This time the Expos beat up Gooden, crushing him for 7 runs in 6⅓ innings in a 7–4 victory. Third baseman Tim Wallach, 1 for 19 with 11 strikeouts lifetime against Gooden, hit 2 home runs. It was the eleventh time in fourteen starts that he failed to record double-figure strikeout totals. "It was," Gooden said afterward, "embarrassing."

On the morning of his start against the Expos in late June, Bruce Berenyi stopped off at a shoe warehouse near Shea Stadium. Even though he was nothing more than a journeyman, Berenyi was fortunate enough to have an endorsement contract with Adidas, which meant he was entitled to snag his fair share of free product. On this day Berenyi was inspired by a pair of Big Bird–yellow patent leather Adidas hightops. "I took them because they were totally different," says Berenyi. "Not cool, just different." When he arrived at the ballpark, Berenyi showed the shoes to a couple of teammates, laughing at their outrageous gaudiness. "Sure, I'll wear 'em—at the next Halloween party."

After a few minutes Strawberry, whose locker was next to Berenyi's, entered the room.

"Hey," he said, "you gonna give those to me?"

Berenyi, who found Strawberry as charming as a starved pit bull, ignored the right fielder.

"Really," he said again, "gimme the shoes."

For the next three minutes Strawberry berated Berenyi for having the audacity not to gift him with a pair of Big Bird-yellow patent leather Adidas hightops. Repeatedly and with increasing volume he wondered how a scrub like Berenyi could ignore longball royalty, and he made certain everybody in the clubhouse heard him. "You're never gonna wear 'em anyway!" he said. "You're not fly enough."

"Darryl thought he was a big man, and he wanted you to know it," says Berenyi, who kept his sneakers. "If he wasn't a young star, he would never get away with that junk. He just wasn't a very nice person."

This was the story of Strawberry '86: great player turned bad human being. It was distressing to watch because, like Gooden, Strawberry displayed flashes of a surprisingly compassionate heart. Bud Harrelson, the team's third-base coach, remembers being on the telephone with a dying pediatric patient in a nearby hospital, trying to pep the boy up on one of his last remaining days. "Darryl walks by, so I asked him to talk to the child," recalls Harrelson. "Well, ten minutes later he's still on the phone. Thirty minutes later he's still on the phone. He made that kid's day. Darryl would do things like that, and you'd think, 'Wow, here's someone who really cares.'"

Sadly, it was a side of the man that was rarely seen. Strawberry's head was as large as the Goodyear Blimp, and with each magazine cover story and frenzied autograph request it only grew. Ed Hearn, the backup catcher, calls Strawberry "as big an asshole as I've ever met.

"I'd like to say there were moments that season when I liked Darryl," says Hearn, "but I didn't. He was selfish and vicious, and he took a lot of pride in making people feel crappy. People went to him when Doc was in trouble, and Darryl's response was 'Oh, no. I would never do drugs.' Okay, whatever, Darryl. Whatever."

What some failed to see was the hurt inside Strawberry, the immature adolescent from south central Los Angeles who never grew up and never truly learned how to deal with other adults in a mature manner. Unlike Gooden, whose father was always available with a bit of sound advice, Strawberry went through life never knowing the unconditional love of a male role model. His father, Henry Strawberry, physically abused his five children before walking out on the family when Darryl, the middle child, was twelve. "It starts with abuse: verbal and physical abuse," Strawberry told *Sports Illustrated* in 1995. "It leaves scars you carry to adulthood." While Strawberry said his mother, Ruby, was equal parts mom and dad, there was always an unsatisfied need in her son that screamed for attention and affection. Perhaps that's why he married his first wife, Lisa Strawberry, against the wishes of every breathing humanoid who had seen the couple together. By '86, Darryl and Lisa would have made fantastic material for Friday Night Fights. If it wasn't yelling, it was cursing. If it wasn't cursing, it was slapping. Once, riding with Gooden to Shea Stadium from their homes on Long Island, Strawberry—still fuming from a fight with Lisa and wanting the last word—demanded that Doc turn the car around. They were half a mile from the park. "I knew there was no dissuading him," Gooden writes in his autobiography, *Heat*. "So I said, 'Listen, man, I'm going into the clubhouse. You want to go home, I'll give you the car. You drive yourself back.'"

At that moment Dwight Gooden wanted nothing to do with Darryl Strawberry. It was hard to blame him.

Chapter 10

OUT OF LEFT FIELD

George Foster was a weird guy.

—**WALLY BACKMAN,**
Mets second baseman

IT WAS NOT EASY to be an outcast on the 1986 New York Mets. From jerks like Strawberry to introspective loners like Mookie Wilson, everyone on the roster found his niche and played his role, and everyone at one point or another was mercilessly made fun of to his face. There was no exception.

Well, there was *one* exception. Dating back to his arrival in New York four seasons earlier, George Foster fit the Mets like a mitten on a porcupine. It was with good intentions that Cashen sent three players to Cincinnati for Foster in 1982, and even better intentions that he signed Foster to a five-year, $10 million contract. "It was a message to baseball and to our fans that we were in it to win," says Cashen, recalling the franchise's dark days. "From here on out we would do whatever it takes."

This seemed to be a great start. At age thirty-three, Foster was still in the prime of his career as one of the game's most intimidating and accomplished power hitters. For six straight years he had hit at least 22 homers and driven in more than 90 runs. In 1977, the season that established him as an elite player, Foster's .320 average, 52 homers, and 149 RBIs made him the easy choice for NL Most Valuable Player. With his muscular forearms, lambchop sideburns and 35-ounce black bat twirling above his shoulders, Foster could be downright scary. Or, as Met pitcher Terry Leach says, "George was the guy you never, ever, *ever* wanted to face."

Foster's talent was matched by a curious lack of self-awareness. In his first season with the club, Foster traveled to Shea Stadium from his Greenwich, Connecticut, home not by taxi or bus or commuter rail but in a long gray limousine driven by a chauffeur. Each time that New York's most rabid fans—the ones who stood outside Shea's player entrance waiting for autographs three hours before game time—saw Foster step from his limo and ignore the masses, they had yet another reason to detest the new star in town. His teammates didn't much like the act, either. It didn't help things that Foster could be found on page one of the *Book of Busts*. His first season was an unmitigated disaster: 13 homers, 70 RBIs, and a .247 average.

Foster did not fit in in New York. He was a quietly religious guy with a strange sense of humor. In an early effort to blend with his new surroundings, Foster would kid teammates by making sarcastic wisecracks that came off more cruel than lighthearted. It was not uncommon for him to pick out someone's weakness—a speech impediment, a mediocre arm, an ugly child—and turn it into an uncomfortable punch line. "He had a funny way of saying some things," says Knight, Foster's teammate for six seasons in Cincinnati. "He would say something playfully, and it would come across as sarcastic. I knew it was playful and George knew it was playful. But no one else did." The result was isolation.

As Foster's production decreased from 1983 (.241, 28 homers, 90 RBIs) to 1984 (.269, 24, and 86) to '85 (.263, 21, and 77), the rabbit ears protruding from the side of his head grew exponentially. During his time at Shea, no Met (with the exception of Doug Sisk) endured even one-sixteenth of the abuse delivered to Foster, whose name changed from "George Foster" to "George Foster, the $10 million bum." By 1986, Foster was a dead man walking. The Mets possessed the option to re-sign him for '87, but unless every other member of the team was abducted by aliens or rendered clinically blind, he was gone. Foster was especially disliked by Davey Johnson, who considered him everything a manager *didn't* want in a player. Foster wasn't a leader. Foster struck out too often (more than one hundred times a season for three straight years). Foster was slow. Foster brooded. During spring training in 1985, Foster, citing a clause in his contract, reported six days after Johnson's required date. The manager let him have it, yelling at Foster behind a closed door: "Do you think $2 million means you don't have to earn your time? Because it doesn't!"

With few exceptions Foster was ignored in a clubhouse where teammates frowned at his jokes and tired of his selfishness. No matter how many times Knight explained that his friend was "a really good fella who you're misunderstanding," no one bought in. Had he been hitting .300 with 30 homers, it might be tolerated. But in May, Foster had yet to hit his first home run. Defensively, his three-legged-dog pursuit of line drives into the gap incensed Met pitchers.

"I liked Dykstra diving, I liked Mookie crashing into walls," says Leach. "I had to have outfielders like that, or I wasn't very good. And George wasn't like that. He knew there was a chance of getting hurt if he went diving into stuff, so he avoided that type of play. I understood his way of thinking, but that doesn't make you too popular."

By late May he was playing less, surrendering some of his left field duties to Danny Heep and Kevin Mitchell. Foster's initial signing might have symbolized the start of a turnaround for the Mets, but he wouldn't stick around for the fruition.

Although the rumble at Cooter's goes down as the Mets' most publicized brawl, it was not by any means the most thrilling. The real pugilistic highlight took place on July 22, when New York, cruising along at 12½ games in front of the Expos, was in Cincinnati for an otherwise nondescript 3-game series against the Reds. Ever since the All-Star break 7 days earlier, the Mets had struggled, losing 3 out of 4 games to Houston and suffering through the humiliation of Cooter's and its legal aftermath. Still, they were the kings of the NL East. There was no panic.

The Reds, on the other hand, were just plain pissed. It had been an up-and-down season for player-manager Pete Rose's club, which despite high expectations trailed Houston by 6 games in the NL West. Cincinnati's roster was stuffed with veterans, many of whom had grumbled from afar at the Mets' countless displays of arrogance. It was not uncommon for Dave Parker, the Reds' outfielder and a man who described himself as filled with "old-school baseball respect" to walk past a TV showing New York highlights and scream out, "Fuck the Mets!" The feeling was hardly limited to one man.

"They walk around like their stuff don't stink," snarled Reds closer John Franco. "If that's not cocky, what is?"

In the bottom of the tenth inning of a seesaw 3–3 game, Rose called on Eric Davis, a third-year outfielder, to trot out to second base as a pinch runner. Five pitches later Mets reliever Jesse Orosco threw strike three past Eddie Milner for out number two. On the delivery Davis broke for third, slid, and as he beat Carter's throw, inadvertently popped straight up into Knight, the Mets' third baseman. This was a bad idea.

After playing eight seasons in Cincinnati, Knight now was part of an enemy, and he spent the series hearing his old fans boo his every move. It was not only irritating but hurtful. Knight, a former Golden Gloves boxer, was not one to hurt.

Knight shoved Davis, who shoved back. Then—*pop!* Knight uncorked a right hook straight out of Mike Tyson 101, twisting Davis's head like a screw-off soda cap. The punch was so impressive that later in the season Tyson attended a game at Shea just to meet Knight, his new hero. "It looked like the mouthpiece had come out of Eric's mouth," recalls Mitchell admiringly, "but it was spit." As soon as the punch was thrown, both dugouts emptied, and for the next fifteen minutes utter mayhem broke out. Fans along the third base line threw coins at the New York players. Milner charged toward Orosco from home plate. Carter lunged toward Davis and yanked him away from Knight. Mookie Wilson, peaceful ambassador 364 days of the year, slugged pitcher Bill Gullickson. Reds pitcher John Denny, who had a black belt in karate, executed the move of the year, placing two fingers atop Carter's shoulder blade (a.k.a. the Vulcan Death Grip) to freeze the catcher as if he had been taxidermied. "I remember Bill Robinson yelling, 'No, John! No, John!'" says Reds pitcher Tom Browning. "But it was too late—Carter was finished." (Mets players had a field day with Carter the next afternoon when the *Cincinnati Enquirer* reported that he had been "pummeled.") Parker, a six-foot-five, 230-pound barrel-chested mound of muscle, tossed Mets left and right in search of Mitchell. The violence-loving rookie, meanwhile, was making a beeline toward Parker when Gullickson and Mario Soto, Cincinnati's ace pitcher, grabbed him around the neck from behind. Bad move. Mitchell shoved Gullickson away like a pillow, then reached back, took Soto by the shoulders, and flung him through the air. Browning tried to help his teammates but only succeeded in ripping off Mitchell's gold chain.

"I have three guys on me, people are trying to kill each other, it's all-out mayhem," says Mitchell. "And one guy is on the pine, watching it all happen."

When Mitchell retells the story, there is no anger, no hostility, not even an ounce of resentment. But at the time, as he and the other twenty-two members of the New York Mets returned to their dugout, they could not believe what awaited them: George Foster sitting on the bench with his arms folded. Not only did he not partake in the brawl, but he hadn't even stepped on the field. This did not go over well.

"Hell, even Vern was out there," said one anonymous player to *Newsday*, referring to Vern Hoscheit, the sixty-four-year-old bullpen coach. "And George was right where you'd expect him—sitting."

Foster's excuse—"What kind of a message are we sending to kids?"—was summarily rejected by teammates, and especially by Davey Johnson, who had thrived for thirteen years as a major league second baseman by exercising toughness and an even-if-I-must-die bravado. One of Johnson's first rules for success was that a team stuck together as a team, in good situations and bad.

When he took the job as Mets general manager in 1980, Frank Cashen (here with Cardinals manager Whitey Herzog) was handed the keys to the worst organization in baseball. Within four years, he built the Amazin's into a contender. Almost as quickly, he allowed the franchise to crumble. *(Chuck Solomon/Sports Illustrated)*

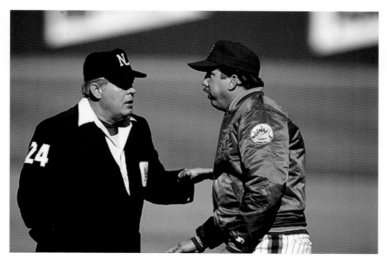

Though manager Davey Johnson never shied away from an on-field confrontation with an umpire, he felt most comfortable in front of a computer screen. Johnson was one of baseball's first skippers to rely on technology to analyze matchups and determine lineups. *(Jerry Wachter/Sports Illustrated)*

The fightin' Mets engaged in four on-field brawls in 1986, including this one against the Dodgers after third baseman Ray Knight charged the mound. Later in the season, an impressed Mike Tyson visited Shea just to meet Knight, a former Golden Gloves champion.
(Walter Iooss/Sports Illustrated)

Otherwise best known for his role in *The House on Sorority Row*, B-movie actor Michael Sergio made a huge splash when he parachuted into Shea Stadium during the sixth game of the World Series. He was later sentenced to twenty-one days in jail. *(John Iacono/Sports Illustrated)*

Always a spark plug, Mookie Wilson does it again, dodging a wild pitch from Boston's Bob Stanley in the bottom of the 10th inning of Game 6. Kevin Mitchell charged home with the tying run, and the Mets won on Wilson's roller seconds later. To this day, fans still call Wilson "Mookie '86." *(John Iacono/Sports Illustrated)*

Though he retired with 2,715 hits and borderline Hall of Fame credentials, Bill Buckner will always be remembered as the man who lost the
World Series. In reality, Boston manager John McNamara deserves most
of the blame. *(John Iacono/Sports Illustrated)*

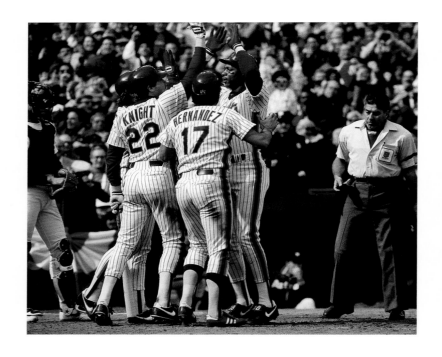

At his best, Darryl Strawberry, here being congratulated by Gary Carter, Ray Knight, and Keith Hernandez after a homer, was the most complete player in baseball, an unrivaled combination of power and speed. *(John Iacono/Sports Illustrated)*

At his worst, Strawberry *(right)*, here chatting with Dykstra *(left)* and Hernandez *(center)*, was useless—a moody, arrogant man despised by many teammates. Catcher Ed Hearn said, "Darryl made you feel like a ball of crud." *(Ronald C. Modra/Sports Illustrated)*

Ron Darling, Dwight Gooden, Bobby Ojeda, and Sid Fernandez gave the Mets four aces with four very disparate personas. Darling's haughty attitude drove manager Davey Johnson crazy. Gooden was battling inner demons. Ojeda was the cool, cocksure veteran. Fernandez refused to believe the WWF wasn't real. *(Joe McNally/Sports Illustrated)*

Despite Gooden's winning the Cy Young Award in 1985, Mets pitching coach Mel Stottlemyre *(with hand to face)* thought improvements needed to be made. His insistence on teaching Gooden a changeup resulted in the pitcher's erratic mechanics and inconsistent performance.
(V. J. Lovero / Sports Illustrated)

George Foster arrived in 1982 with a $2 million contract and grandiose predictions. Yet the 1977 National League MVP, who once hit 52 homers in a season, never produced, and became a toxic influence in the clubhouse. Foster was released in August after accusing the club of racism. He was replaced on the roster by Lee Mazzilli, a white outfielder. *(Ronald C. Modra/Sports Illustrated)*

Hailed as the future of the franchise when he first arrived at Shea in 1976, Brooklyn-born Mazzilli turned out to be little more than a decent major league player. After four years away, his return to the team in August was a feel-good story. Mazzilli proved his mettle as a pinch hitter. *(Heinz Kluetmeier/Sports Illustrated)*

Nicknamed "World B. Free" for his willingness and ability to play any position, rookie Kevin Mitchell was invaluable to the Mets. Yet when the front office began disassembling the team, Mitchell—thought to be a bad influence on Dwight Gooden and Darryl Strawberry—was first to go. "I'm not the one who went out there and sucked up some lines, like Dwight Gooden did," says Mitchell. "I'm a decent guy." *(David Walberg/Sports Illustrated)*

Beginning with his days in Montreal, Gary Carter was mocked by teammates, who considered his over-the-top aggressiveness a triumph of style over substance. Yet Carter, here being bowled over by Reds outfielder Eddie Milner, was a fantastic defensive catcher who blocked the plate better than anyone else in the league. *(Chuck Solomon/Sports Illustrated)*

When he was with the Cardinals, Keith Hernandez was ridiculed by manager Whitey Herzog for his pregame ritual of cigarettes and crossword puzzles. In New York, however, Davey Johnson appreciated his first baseman's sangfroid. Though not as flashy as Carter, Hernandez was the undisputed leader of the Mets. *(Ronald C. Modra/Sports Illustrated)*

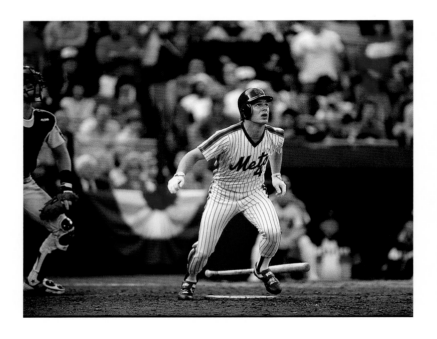

Lenny Dykstra watches his game-winning homer leave Shea in the 9th inning of the NLCS against Houston. Manager Davey Johnson usually bemoaned the diminutive center fielder's obsession with power, but in this case, there was no complaining. *(John Iacono/Sports Illustrated)*

Pitchers Jesse Orosco and Bobby Ojeda are doused with champagne following the exhausting 16-inning triumph over Houston in Game 6 of the NLCS. The clubhouse celebration was a tea party compared to the all-out melee that broke out on the charter flight back to New York.
(Peter Read Miller/Sports Illustrated)

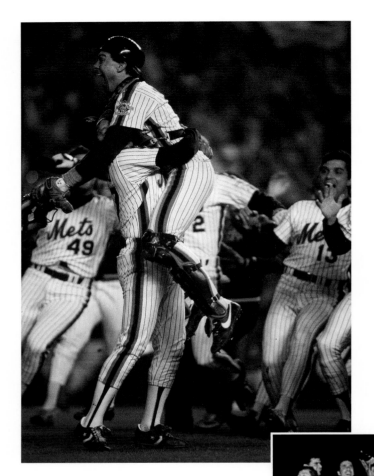

Gary Carter leaps into the arms of
Jesse Orosco after the final out of the
World Series. With a deep pitching staff, a
potent lineup, and a loaded farm system, the
Mets were supposed to dominate for the next
ten years. Instead, management, uncom-
fortable with the hell-raising antics of the
Wild Bunch *(right, holding an unofficial postgame
celebration on the mound)*, split up the team.
They have yet to win another Fall Classic.
(John Iacono/Sports Illustrated)

*(Ronald C. Modra/
Sports Illustrated)*

Later, the Foster-light brawl would overshadow what turned into one of the stranger games of the season. In fact, the fight never would have occurred had not the bumbling Parker, with the Reds leading 3–1 in the ninth, dropped a routine fly ball in right field that allowed 2 runs to score. "I went back and stumbled a little bit, but I regained my balance," he said afterward. "Then it hit the top of my glove. Would you believe some jerk in the stands yelled, 'Use two hands'?" When the inning finally ended, Franco walked toward the Cincinnati dugout from the mound, removed the mitt from his hand, and promptly slung it against the wall. The night would get worse.

With Strawberry ejected in the sixth for arguing a strike call, and Knight and Mitchell booted after the fight, the Mets had no more position players. Davey Johnson was forced to use his (rather large) noodle. For the next 3 innings Ed Hearn caught, Carter played third base (a position he had not manned since 1975), and the lefty Orosco and right-handed Roger McDowell alternated between the pitcher's mound and right field, depending on whether a right-handed or left-handed hitter was at the plate. In the thirteenth, McDowell and left-fielder Mookie Wilson even swapped positions once to defend against the left-handed-hitting Parker. The first time Johnson returned Orosco to the mound from the outfield, umpire Gerry Davis decided to allow eight warm-up pitches, which sent Rose into a hissy fit. His argument, that a pitcher doesn't get the standard number of warm-up pitches if he is already in the game, was a sound one. Davis forced Orosco to start pitching. "That game is definitely one of the strange memories from my career," says Orosco. "It was exciting. It was neat. I remember catching my one ball in the outfield. I squeezed it so hard, the stuffing could've come out."

The battle finally ended in the fourteenth when Howard Johnson hit a 3-run homer over the right field fence for a 6–3 win. But instead of popping open beers and boyishly reliving the brouhaha, most of the Mets steamed over Foster. It was one thing to keep to yourself and tell stupid jokes and brood over this and that. It was another to refuse to defend your teammates.

"I don't know if that was the end of Foster with us," says one Met, "but it was definitely the beginning of his end." Coincidentally or not, the following afternoon Davey Johnson summoned Foster into his office to inform him that Mitchell and Heep would be the new left-field platoon.

Foster did not handle his demotion well. New York won 8 of its next 12 with either Mitchell or Heep in left field, and the man Cashen once assured the press would "lead by his tremendous example" spent most of the game either in the clubhouse or on the bench, sulking. Part of it was boredom. But another part was understandable jealousy. On August 1 the Mets signed free-agent outfielder Lee Mazzilli to a minor league contract and assigned him to Triple A Tidewater. At the time Cashen downplayed the acquisition, explaining to the press that Mazzilli—who had been released by Pittsburgh in late July—"might" be able to help the club down the road.

But to Foster, Mazzilli represented his demise (which was ironic considering that four years earlier Foster's signing made Mazzilli expendable). "I know something is brewing," he said. "I don't think a guy would opt to go to Triple A if something wasn't promised." Foster was right. Even though Cashen denied it to the press, he had signed Mazzilli with the idea that he was a better fit than Foster. He even told Tidewater manager Sam Perlozzo that Mazzilli would be down "only for about a week. Then we'll get him." Mazzilli was eager to return. Since the day he had been traded to Texas for Darling and Walt Terrell four years earlier, his career had taken a remarkable downturn. He went from all-star to journeyman parttimer to—as a Pirate—pinch hitter. "I never wanted to leave the Mets," Mazzilli says. "Shea Stadium was my home."

Foster became even moodier and more disconnected. He arrived later and later at the stadium, and on August 4 at Wrigley Field, he entered the visitors' clubhouse five minutes before he was to take BP. An anonymous player spouted off to the *Post*. "What, he's too good for us? And he's supposed to be one of our leaders? Ha!"

The following afternoon, in a pregame interview with Jim Corbett of the *Gannett Westchester-Rockland* newspaper, Foster predicted his imminent release and blamed the move on race. "I'm not saying it's a racial thing," he said, "but it seems to be the case in sports these days. When a ballclub can, they replace a George Foster or a Mookie Wilson with a more popular player." He went on to tell two writers that the Mets "would rather promote a Gary Carter or a Keith Hernandez to the fans, so parents who want to can point to them as role models for their children rather than a Darryl Strawberry or a Dwight Gooden or a George Foster. The kids don't see color."

The accusations were unfounded. Not only was Foster benched for another African American (Mitchell), but the Mets on the most magazine covers and television commercials were not Carter and Hernandez but Strawberry and Gooden.

The comments did not go over well. He had put the other African American Mets on the spot: Either agree with Foster and bash the organization, or disagree and look like a sellout. It was thankless. Foster and his moody eccentricities had been tolerated for four and a half seasons, but now everyone agreed the cancer had to be expunged.

Johnson was told of the remarks after the 8–5 loss to the Cubs, and he confronted Foster outside the team hotel later that afternoon. "George, do you really believe the reasons I play guys are racially motivated!?" he said, his voice rising with each word. "Is that what you genuinely believe?"

Johnson was prepared for an argument. He wanted one. He wanted Foster to say to his face that he was a racist manager. *Bring it on, George. Bring it on.* Instead, Foster meekly explained that his quotes had been taken out of context. While with the Reds, Foster accused team management of promoting whites over blacks to *Newsday* and *Sport* in two separate interviews. Now he was trying to save face. Johnson knew Foster was full of it. So did Cashen, who finally agreed to swallow $1.7 million ($1 million in buyout options, $700,000 in remaining salary) and dump the former star.

"George accused me of being a racist in front of the whole team," says Johnson. "I had to release him, and I'm glad Frank Cashen let me. Otherwise, I would have lost credibility with the club."

Before the guillotine was dropped, Foster had to face his teammates one final time. He tiptoed into the Mets clubhouse the next afternoon to gather his belongings, twenty-three pairs of eyes following his every move. With the entire team present, Foster stood in front of the room and asked for everyone's attention. There was complete silence. In his high-pitched cackle, Foster spoke, looking at the floor the entire time. "I just want to say . . . if I've caused any problems, if I've hurt some of you, I'm sorry. I apologize." Foster took a deep swallow and retreated to his corner locker. Knight, the only player with any remaining sympathy, walked over and put his arm around Foster. "I went over because I cared about George, and I wanted to talk to him and make sure he was okay," says Knight. "In that clubhouse nobody cared that he was gone. Well, I did. I knew he said something he shouldn't have. But George is a good man. A very good man."

On the day the Mets finally decided to part ways with the out-of-favor Foster, Mazzilli was in Tidewater, Virginia, playing left field for the Tides in a game against Maine. In the top of the sixth inning a message flashed on the stadium's scoreboard: THE METS HAVE JUST RELEASED GEORGE FOSTER. Mazzilli looked up and read the news, and at the end of the inning he walked toward Sam Perlozzo in the dugout. "Am I outta here?" he asked.

Perlozzo, who had received a phone call from Cashen minutes earlier, smiled and nodded. "I told him he was free but that I'd appreciate it if he could play a couple more innings for us that afternoon," says Perlozzo. "He did. I think about that—if he'd gotten hurt at that point, I would have been in serious trouble."

When Mazzilli joined the Mets in Chicago, it felt as if he had stepped through a time warp. Ten years earlier Mazzilli had made his major league debut against the Cubs at Wrigley Field. The date was September 8, 1976, and he was called upon to pinch-hit for shortstop Bud Harrelson. "I'm kneeling in the on-deck circle, and someone taps me on the shoulder," recalls Harrelson, the Mets third-base coach in '86. "I look up and it's Maz. He says, 'Buddy, they want me to pinch-hit for you. Can I use your bat?'" Moments later Mazzilli turned on a fastball from left-hander Darold Knowles and hit it out of the park for a home run.

This time around, Mazzilli was thirty-one years old and had had a rocky career. One of the first men to greet Mazzilli was Gooden. During his original tour with New York, Mazzilli wore number 16, which now belonged to Dr. K. In an act of kindness Mazzilli still remembers fondly, Gooden offered to hand over the digits. "I told him that he'd done number 16 very proud and that he deserved to keep it," says Mazzilli. "I took 13 and was fine with that."

With New York a season-high 17½ games ahead of second-place Montreal, Mazzilli became the feel-good story that a somewhat bored press corps cried for. Not only was he a once-upon-a-time Met from the bad old days, but he was as New York as a Dr. Brown's Cel-Ray soda. Although he was no longer as fast as the kid who stole a career-high 41 bases in 1980, Mazzilli proved to be a perfect addition. Stripped of his egocentric ways, he was perfectly happy to pinch-hit or enter as a late-game defensive sub. Mazzilli batted .276 as a Met, with a couple of home runs to boot. He led the league with thirteen walks as a pinch hitter.

Best of all, he was *not* George Foster.

Chapter 11

HOT STUFF

What do I have to say about Roger McDowell? How 'bout this—the man was insane.

—KEVIN MITCHELL, Mets outfielder

BY THE TIME mid-August rolled around, New York led the pack by 18 games, which meant the pennant race was transformed into a pennant snore. Even Expos manager Buck Rodgers, as driven a competitor as the sport knew, acknowledged reality. On August 2, with 63 games still remaining but his club 17½ out, he officially conceded. "Realistically, we have no chance of first place," Rodgers told the press. "If we compete and finish a strong second, that would be a good season." (An injury-plagued second half dropped the Expos to fourth place, with 78 wins, 83 losses, and 29½ games out of first.)

But instead of coasting, the Mets continued to play hard, winning 41 of their final 62 games. This was a team that, for all its night activities, possessed tremendous pride. There was still one thing more important than guzzling beer and meeting chicks: winning. From Dykstra to Ojeda to Hernandez to Hojo, the perfect way to ruin an evening of big plans was to come up on the short end of the scoreboard. On the night of Rodgers's white flag, the Mets beat Montreal 3–1 behind a vintage 5-inning, 7-strikeout breezer for Gooden. The next morning's *Newsday* headline was CUE THE FAT LADY!

Still, hard play alone was not enough to keep twenty-four young men occupied. In the dog days of August (and September), the New York Mets turned to mischief. Oh, maybe it wasn't quite that dramatic. Sure, the 1986 Mets had spent nearly the entire season farting, burping, pie slamming, and insult slinging like no other club in modern history. But with boredom—often combined with a couple of rum and Cokes—came a new level of devilish deeds. And the team's head jester was Roger McDowell.

Only one year earlier, McDowell was a soft-spoken rookie relief pitcher, happy to be in the majors and even a bit nervous surrounded by the larger-than-life personas of Hernandez, Carter, Knight, and Foster. Unlike the bonus babies who made up much of the roster, McDowell was an average guy who had to go about things the hard way. He was undrafted out of Cincinnati's Colerain High, then accepted a partial athletic scholarship to attend Bowling Green, where he studied commercial art before being selected by New York in the third round of the '82 draft. McDowell did not throw especially hard, and his athleticism was nothing to ring the cowbell about. But his ball moved, and that was enough. "I was good," he says, "but underwhelming." In 1983, while starting for Double A Jackson, McDowell felt a sharp pain in his right elbow. Despite two months of rest, the throbbing continued, and in January 1984 he had a dozen bone chips and three spurs removed from his elbow. His career was on life support.

As McDowell recovered, he watched teammate Rick O'Keefe, a left-handed starter, struggle to return from the exact same operation. Start after start, O'Keefe's normally tricky assortment of pitches went flat and soft. After two weeks of frustration, O'Keefe retired. "I thought about that a lot," says McDowell. "I made up my mind not to give in. I would fight."

And reinvent. When he returned to the mound that August, McDowell found that his already outstanding sinker had mysteriously acquired the drop of the Coney Island Cyclone. It was a magical, career-altering discovery caused primarily by a slight decrease in arm angle. "It made him very, very tough to hit," says Greg Pavlick, Jackson's pitching coach at the time. "He was nasty."

Although he had pitched only $7\frac{1}{3}$ innings of minor league ball in '84, McDowell reported to spring training the following season and blew Davey Johnson away. Here was a fearless kid with the perfect temperament for New York. The Mets' two-headed bullpen monster of Orosco and Sisk required another neck. On April 1, Johnson called McDowell into his office and congratulated him on making the club. Four days later, however, he was dealt a horrible blow. Hanging from his locker was the clipped headline from a story in that week's edition of *The Sporting News*. It read MCDOWELL TO BE SENT TO MINORS. "I got the grapefruit in my throat," he recalls. "I started having tears. It was very discouraging." Behind him the room erupted in laughter. The subject of the article was *Oddibe* McDowell, a Texas Rangers outfielder. Roger McDowell was safe.

The spirit of the prank—pulled by pitcher Ed Lynch—stuck with the rookie, who in hindsight found it wonderfully wicked. Always a fan of high jinks and magic tricks, McDowell gradually emerged from his shell like a Gremlin from the cocoon. By the time the '85 season had ended and McDowell could proudly look back at his 17 saves and 2.83 ERA, he was a different man. Confident. Secure. Proud.

Warped.

McDowell had the innocent, aw-shucks looks of a young Jimmy Stewart and the "What happens if I press *this* button?" mischievousness of a four-year-old. In 1986, at ease as a fixture in the bullpen, he let his creative side take over. "All of a sudden I had a little money to get some things," he says. "So I did." McDowell, affectionately nicknamed "Skeeter" by teammates after the *Muppet Show* character, arrived at the stadium in a myriad of costumes, from a rubber Richard Nixon mask (says McDowell, "Hey, he was a big fan of ours") to an orange afro clown wig. Before a game at Philadelphia he purchased a pair of roller skates at a sporting goods store. "Their field was Astroturf, so I thought it'd be cool," he says. McDowell painted the skates blue and put orange Met emblems on the side. As he rolled through the dugout toward the field-level steps, he passed Davey Johnson, who nearly swallowed his tobacco juice. "No! No! No! Take 'em off!" he yelled. "If you twist an ankle, it's my ass!"

This was just a temporary setback. And besides, roller skates were kids' stuff. McDowell had a higher calling where footwear was concerned. During a May game at Cincinnati, McDowell pulled off one of the great stunts in the history of baseball antics, officially guaranteeing himself a special place in the team's Hall of Hysteria.

In the bottom of the second inning of a scoreless contest, Bill Robinson, the team's first-base coach, was sitting by himself at the end of the Mets' bench, slowly making his way through a bag of sunflower seeds. With the blessing of his teammates (but without Davey Johnson's knowledge), McDowell climbed under the bench and on elbows and knees crawled the 20 feet to Robinson's dangling cleats. In one fist McDowell held a single Marlboro cigarette and a roll of gaffer's tape. In the other he had a fully loaded book of matches. Exercising the dexterity of Spider-Man, McDowell, lying at Robinson's feet, removed the staple from the matchbook, wrapped the book around the cigarette, and taped the two together. Then softly and gently he stuck the device on Robinson's left cleat. As soon as the inning ended, McDowell lit the cigarette and crawled back to the other end of the dugout.

"There are a lot of complications," McDowell says. "You have to time the cigarette, and you also have to make sure there's enough air between the match and the cigarette so it doesn't die out. It's pretty intense."

Usually when a hotfoot ignites, it takes anywhere from twenty to thirty seconds, and the result is a burning sensation and a small, manageable flame. This was no ordinary hotfoot. Robinson left the bench, took his post next to first base, watched the pitcher warm up, traded a few words with a fan, and clapped and yelled encouragement to Darryl Strawberry. As Gary Carter, the next hitter, stepped into the box, Reds manager Pete Rose noticed the smoke oozing from Robinson's foot. Unable to contain his laughter, he called his entire bench to join him at the end of the dugout. On the Mets' side, McDowell told Bill Webb, the director of WWOR's televised broadcast, to keep a camera on first base. The count was 1 ball, 1 strike on Carter. Suddenly *whooooooosh!* An inferno exploded and flames shot up Robinson's leg as if he were the guest of honor at a Hawaiian pig roast. Robinson began jumping up and down, screaming in pain. For McDowell it was perfection.

"It was like NASA just launched something," he says. "The greatest hotfoot ever. And Bill, to his credit, never got mad. He just said, 'You won't get me anymore. I'm done with that.' To me that was like when you're a kid and someone says, 'Don't call me that!' What are you supposed to do?"

The answer was obvious. McDowell, along with partner and technical adviser Howard Johnson, lit Robinson's shoe no fewer than fifteen more times that season, including seven or eight in August and September alone. At season's end Jay Horwitz, the Mets PR whiz, incorporated a section on hotfoots into the team highlight video, including McDowell and Hojo demonstrating their step-by-step approach.

Before a game against the Cardinals on August 17, Robinson was sleeping on a couch in the Shea Stadium clubhouse when he felt yet another burning sensation. This time Johnson and McDowell were especially ambitious—both of Robinson's shoes were ablaze. "I grabbed the shoes to get 'em off me," says Robinson, "and the plastic from the laces burned the shit out of my hand." Robinson took his ashen right shoe and flung it at McDowell's head, missing by a couple of inches.

Tired of repeatedly abusing such an easy target, McDowell diversified. Against the Dodgers eleven days later, Pavlick, now an assistant pitching coach, was sitting on a wooden chair in the bullpen, mindlessly watching the on-field action. With his teammates egging him on, McDowell lit a piece of paper with a match, placed it beneath Pavlick's seat, and as nonchalant as a bus driver, returned to his regular position. "I look down because I smell smoke," says Pavlick. "The chair I'm sitting on is on fire, smoking."

With only meaningless wins for the press to write about, McDowell's zaniness became a matter of public record. He endeared himself to Met historians on "Thanks Rusty Day," July 13, when he purchased twenty electric-orange wigs for his teammates to wear in honor of Le Grand Orange. McDowell was a guy who, after giving up the winning run in a game that broke the Cubs' 13-game losing streak, reported the following afternoon with a paper bag over his head. Who threw firecrackers into occupied bathroom stalls. Who, before Game 1 of the upcoming National League Championship Series, wrote the names of his parents and two college roommates on a piece of duct tape and stuck it on his head in anticipation of televised player introductions. (McDowell was bummed when NBC showed only the starting lineups.) Who, when Jay Horwitz returned to the clubhouse after a weeklong bout with chicken pox, greeted him in a doctor's gown.

McDowell was not the only prankster in the clubhouse. Although most lacked his creativity, many of the veteran Mets were routinely on the lookout for beating boys—young players with lives perfectly suited to be ruined. The targets couldn't be boring stiffs like Hearn or Dave Magadan. They had to have style. Flair. Goofiness. They had to be like Kevin Mitchell.

Mitchell's status as the club's top rookie made him an obvious end-of-the-season target. If Mitchell had been another run-of-the-mill first-year plebe, keeping his head down and his eyes in his glove, perhaps McDowell and the crew would have ignored him. But the gang lifestyle and tough image and gunshot wound and wardrobe (baggy velour sweat suits, thick chains, and gold Gazelle sunglasses) were just too tempting a target. Mitchell *had* to be picked on. He was asking for it.

Plus, for all his street smarts, Mitchell was naïve—not as bad as Sid Fernandez, but close. On July 4, Mitchell and Charlie Samuels, the equipment manager, were watching the New York City fireworks celebration on a TV in Davey Johnson's office. Something caught his eye.

"What is that thing?" he asked Samuels.

The clubhouse manager was perplexed. "You mean the Statue of Liberty?"

shit!" Mitchell screamed. "You mean to tell me the Statue of
here in New York? I've gotta call my brother and tell him!"

Early on, after the last game of a 3-game series at San Diego in May,
Mitchell learned his place. He entered the clubhouse to find that Ron
Darling and Bobby Ojeda had snuck into his locker and cut the pant legs
and sleeves off his suit. Mitchell fumed and became even more angry
when he was forced to wear the garment on the five-and-a-half-hour flight
home. Things only got worse. Much worse. In early August, Mitchell was
sitting on the bench in Montreal's Olympic Stadium when Ojeda approached from behind and set his hat on fire. (Said Mitchell: "Don't you
guys know I've got a Jheri curl! This shit will flame up!") During a trip to
Chicago that month, a crew of veterans coerced Mitchell into drinking to
the point of blindness, then heading downtown in the middle of the
night and painting the (rather large) testicles of a prominent horse sculp-
ture in Met orange and blue. "Painting nuts ain't fun," says Mitchell.
"Now, because of us, they have a fence around the stupid thing."

The definitive Mitchell moment came at Montreal in the season's
final week when Hernandez hosted a team fiesta at Sergio's, an upscale
downtown restaurant. Veterans handed the rookie tequila shot after
tequila shot until Mitchell was stumbling around with a napkin atop his
head. Finally, Hernandez wrapped his arm around Mitchell's broad
shoulders and said, "Mitch, you probably should stop now." To the
rookie who survived a lifetime of violence, this sounded like a challenge.
Mitchell *loved* challenges. He reached toward the bar, grabbed another
shot, guzzled it down, and—*pop!* The five-foot-eleven, 210-pound behe-
moth fell back off his stool and slammed headfirst into the floor. Six teammates acted as mock pallbearers, lifting Mitchell up, lugging him outside,
and resting him on a bench. They proceeded to retreat inside for more
merriment. At 3 A.M., with Mitchell still out cold, the Mets finally returned to the hotel.

The next morning Mitchell woke up in the hallway near his room—
barefoot. A teammate had stolen his shoes and socks.

When he arrived at the ballpark that afternoon, Mitchell was bleary-
eyed, hung over, and frightened to learn that he was starting at third

base. Between innings he retreated to the clubhouse bathroom with a bag of soup crackers and a glass of water. "Kept throwing 'em right back up," he says. "Those guys corrupted me."

Yet of all the Mets, no player was more out of control—in the literal (non-cocaine snorting) sense of the phrase—than Lenny Dykstra. Unlike McDowell, the gritty center fielder wasn't one for harmless little pranks. Dykstra was a twenty-four-hour-a-day Porsche traveling at two hundred miles per hour.

Upon reaching the majors, Dykstra refused to hold back. No dare was too bold, no drink too strong, no car too fast, no poker hand too big. On his first day with the team in 1985, he yelled to a batboy, "Kid, how 'bout lacing my shoes!" That didn't sit well with the veterans, and Darling immediately walked to the rookie's locker, cut his laces in half, and ridiculed the white *Miami Vice* wannabe blazer he was wearing. But thanks to an endearing naïveté, soon enough Dykstra was one of the guys. Dykstra spoke in an unintelligible southern California–inspired dialect that, coupled with a thick lisp and raspy voice, made verbal communication futile. His favorite words included "Dude," "Sweet," and "Bitchin'." Dykstra could even use them all in a single sentence: "Dude, that babe is bitchin' sweet."

"You couldn't help but like him," says Ed Hearn. "He was so stupid, so stupidly funny." Once, a bunch of the Mets spent a couple of hours at a collectibles show in New Jersey. Dykstra signed hundreds of items, rarely glancing up from beneath his sunglasses. Near the end of the session a Roseanne Barr look-alike handed him a baseball. Dykstra snapped. "Lady," he said, "you are too fuckin' fat for me to sign this thing for you!" Security was called in to escort Dykstra to his car.

During the September doldrums Dykstra was as reckless as ever. In the era immediately before HIV, media circuses, and O. J. Simpson, you could be an athlete, go crazy, and *not* get caught. In fact, getting nailed never entered the center fielder's mind. He was iron-coated and indestructible. One night in Montreal, John Rufino, an assistant equipment manager, was returning to the hotel after he and Howard Johnson had spent an evening at the racetrack. It was approximately 2:30 A.M., and as he walked down the street, Rufino bumped into Dykstra. "C'mon, dude, let's go!" said Dykstra. "I know this great club!"

"Lenny, it's almost 3 A.M.!"

"No, dude, they're open till 6 o'clock. If you don't wanna come, I'll just go myself."

Rufino tagged along, afraid Dykstra might be found the next morning:

A. naked and penniless or
B. married to a transvestite stripper or
C. dead.

The two walked and walked until they arrived forty-five minutes later at a dingy, hole-in-the-wall card club. Although many of the Mets engaged in serious, oft-heated airplane poker games, Dykstra was at a different level. He was a competition fiend, from cards to golf to Ping-Pong to video games to basketball. It was what made an otherwise ordinary-looking physical specimen into the ultimate overachiever. Dykstra bet himself—as well as anyone who dared think otherwise—that he would be a major league star. He did not want to win. He *needed* to win. At anything.

"Lenny, how much money do you have on you?" asked Rufino.

Dykstra: "I ain't got much, dude. We won't be long."

Rufino: "Seriously, Lenny, how much you got?"

Dykstra: "Only about $2,000. Nothing."

Two thousand dollars! Rufino wanted to run away. "I'm thinking, 'We're dead . . . we're dead,'" he says. "'We're not coming out of this place alive, and they'll never find us. Never."

They entered the club and slowly walked up the creaky wooden steps and through the door.

"Yo, Lenny!"

"Hey, Lenny boy!"

"What's up, Lenny!"

Said Rufino, "You know these people?"

Dykstra: "Yeah, dude, relax. It's all good. Relax. You're nervous."

For the next two hours Dykstra played poker, smoked cigarettes, and downed beers with a cast of characters straight out of *The Dirty Dozen*. When the two finally left, it was sunny outside. That night Dykstra walked, singled, stole a base, and scored 2 runs in an 8–2 victory at Olympic Stadium. Rufino, meanwhile, could barely keep his eyes open.

"Lenny was just bored," says Rufino. "Baseball came easy for him, and we were up by twenty games. You needed diversions. He was just able to find some really interesting ones."

For example, on the morning of September 8, hours before he had to report for that night's game against the Expos at Shea, Dykstra picked up Connie O'Reilly, the owner of Finn MacCool's. The two were scheduled to play a round of golf at the nearby North Hempstead Country Club. While driving his red Camaro down Port Washington Boulevard at what O'Reilly calls "frightening speed," Dykstra began to make a sudden U-turn, one illegal in all worlds except Planet Dykstra. At the same time a silver Mercedes approached from the opposite direction. Without looking, Dykstra continued his U-turn, smacking into the oncoming car's front fender. "Lenny was so wrong, it wasn't even close," says O'Reilly. Dykstra leapt from his vehicle and ran toward the other driver, who had every right to strangle the obnoxious Met. "Did you not see me?" Dykstra screamed. "I'm in a fuckin' hurry here to play fuckin' golf! What the hell are you doing?"

O'Reilly was aghast. Dykstra would be going to jail—no question. He had made an illegal turn, ruined a man's fancy automobile, and screamed in his face. It was hopeless, completely, 100 percent hopeless.

"Holy cow!" the Mercedes owner yelped. "You're Lenny Dykstra!" And that was the end of that. "Screw the car," the man said. "Just gimme your autograph, and I'll be happy."

"Lenny was dangerous," says O'Reilly. "From turning a car right in the middle of a boulevard or walking into a bar someplace and having ten of the biggest guys wanting to hang him, it wouldn't matter to him. He just wanted excitement."

When Dykstra wasn't driving at lunatic velocity, he could often be found on the golf course, wagering large amounts of money on a game he played with skills inversely proportionate to his baseball abilities.

Dykstra was not a horrible golfer, but he was very bad. "Out of pride he always refused to take strokes," says O'Reilly. "And he got beat *a lot.*" Upon learning of the center fielder's trade to Philadelphia in 1989, Davey Johnson's first thought had nothing to do with baseball. "It was a gigantic pay cut for me," says Johnson. "I made a couple of thousand dollars off Lenny in golf every year." To Dykstra, betting $500 per hole was no big deal as long as—win or lose—he was allowed to talk trash. Oftentimes he and Aguilera would play at Plandome, a well-known Long Island country club. Every time Aguilera took a good swing, Dykstra responded with a scoff. "Don't show me that shit!" he'd yell. "Is that all you got? You come at me with that shit?"

Dykstra's most egregious moment in golf took place in July 1986 when O'Reilly invited him as a guest at the pristine Nassau Country Club. After playing eighteen holes, O'Reilly and Dykstra entered the clubhouse where a group of twenty priests were toweling off after a shower. Without so much as an "excuse me," Dykstra lifted his left leg and let fly the loudest, stinkiest, deadliest fart since the days of Genghis Khan.

Nobody said, "Amen."

On the night of August 30, the Mets were able to sum up their season-long arrogance, bravado, childishness, and, yes, *skill* with the Shea Stadium Diamond Vision debut of a smoothly produced four-minute music video that became the trademark of baseball's most dominant team. Many Mets fans look back at '86 and recall Mookie Wilson hitting the grounder between Bill Buckner's legs. Some Mets fans remember Darryl Strawberry's monstrous Game 7 World Series homer. A couple even recall the presence of nonentities like Tim Corcoran and Stanley Jefferson.

Every Met fan knows "Let's Go Mets!"—the song that defined a team.

It is funny, in more than one way, that the same franchise which vehemently refused to allow Foster's *Get Metsmerized* to be sold anywhere near Shea Stadium now had a song and video of its own. But it is not ironic. As soon as Foster approached the Mets with his *Get Metsmerized* idea, the club followed the lead of most other powerful, greedy American corporations: They stole it.

With the aid of Della Femina, Travisano & Partners, the Mets set out to produce a package that would blow away the Chicago Bears' multi-platinum *Superbowl Shuffle* of 1985. Della Femina's concept was to create a thirty-minute film on the "Making of the Mets Music Video" that would mimic the hugely popular "The Making of Michael Jackson's Thriller." It would sell for $24.99 all over New York, and anyone with the slightest bit of team allegiance would buy it. "A great marketing idea," says Drew Sheinman, the team's director of marketing. "Brilliant." There was one problem: to have a "Making of the Mets Music Video," the team was required to have an actual music video.

Della Femina was quick to call every hot musical star they could think of, from Billy Joel to Elton John to Stevie Wonder, pitching what they believed to be a historic, no-brainer, one-of-a-kind pop culture opportunity. When nobody showed an iota of interest, the company turned to Shelton Leigh Palmer, one of America's up-and-coming commercial music stars. Only thirty-one, Palmer had already written jingles for the likes of Meow Mix and Six Flags Great Adventure. He also happened to be a native Long Islander and die-hard Mets fan. It was a perfect match.

Within a month Palmer and his team of songwriters, musicians, and producers had penned the lyrics to "Let's Go Mets!," a catchy, Dr. Pepper commercial of a tune with the memorable hook, "We've got the teamwork to make the dream work." After auditioning a half-dozen studio singers (including a young long-haired nobody named Michael Bolton; "He was okay," says Palmer, "but I heard better"), the job went to Tommy Bernfeld, a scratchy-voiced demo veteran who had gained some notoriety as a background singer on Eric Clapton's seminal 1974 album, *461 Ocean Boulevard.*

Cashen and the other members of the front office went gaga over the idea of the video *Let's Go Mets!*, and filming was to commence in late July. Palmer remembers meeting with the players in the clubhouse before a game in Philadelphia and nervously playing a cassette of the tune to a roomful of smirks and awkward laughs. With the exception of

Carter, who grinned and nodded to the beat, the reaction was a restrained yet universal "You must be kidding me." For a team that considered itself ultra-cool, *Let's Go Mets!* was nerd central.

And yet one of the beautiful things about the '86 Mets was a unique open-mindedness to the bizarre. No, the players didn't really dig the song. But hell, all they had to do was lip-synch and—*cha-ching!*—the riches would pile up. Indeed, on the night of July 25, less than twelve hours before Palmer was supposed to begin his first day of shooting, he received an unexpected phone call at his Manhattan apartment from Hernandez, the team's unofficial spokesman.

HERNANDEZ: "Shell, how's it going?"

PALMER: "Good, Keith. It's interesting to hear from you tonight. What's up?"

HERNANDEZ: "Well, you know, not only am I captain of the team, but I also happen to be our major league baseball player representative for the union."

PALMER: "That's good to know. Thanks, Keith."

HERNANDEZ: "I just wanted to tell you that the players aren't coming tomorrow."

PALMER: "What!?"

HERNANDEZ: "Hey, don't take it personally. We all like you. But the Mets didn't include us in the negotiations."

PALMER: "Umm . . ."

In a panic, Palmer called the assistant GM, Al Harazin, who confirmed that (*oops*) the team had forgotten that when more than three players were to appear in uniform for a nonplaying purpose, union approval was required. At six the next morning Palmer and his crew arrived at Shea Stadium, hoping for the best. They got the worst. Not one New York Mets player was around.

By day's end a settlement was reached. For their participation each Met would be paid $1,000 and given a VCR and a copy of the videotape *Dick Clark's Best of Bandstand* (supplied by Vestron, the company that financed the project). Palmer breathed a deep sigh of relief. But over the course of the next five days, he received one ludicrous request after another. The self-importance of professional athletes is generally off the charts, but this was insane. The Mets wanted everything. E-v-e-r-y-t-h-i-n-g. Upon asking a star to, say, film a sequence of mock home run swings, Palmer was met with "Oh, he needs to do that? Okay, but a $2,000 donation to his foundation would really make him happy" or "Sure, he'll pitch for ten minutes, but he'd be happier doing so if there were some new LPs in it for him." Things reached a truly ridiculous apex when a team representative told Palmer that a player's cooperation hinged on whether the production company would buy him a new Cadillac Coupe de Ville. "It was like some of these guys lived in an imaginary world where money falls off trees and someone is always there to kiss their feet," says Palmer. "Anyhow, my budget couldn't support it."

Even though the filming of *Let's Go Mets!* failed to add much to the players' riches, money alone does not buy happiness. Palmer's crew was composed primarily of recent college graduates, several of whom were attractive females. Some members of the team couldn't help themselves. A woman would walk by, maybe smile, and it was all over. "Hey, baby girl, whatcha doin' later tonight? You like steak?" They were putty. "Let's just say," says one person involved with the project, "many of them can identify the Mets by markings on their penises."

According to Palmer, Strawberry—who was in his second year of marriage at the time—indulged in the most overt extracurricular affair, a behind-the-scenes sexual relationship with one of the women on the crew. Instead of keeping it hush-hush, players joked about it aloud, making comments in front of both Strawberry and the woman. "I knew what was going on," says Palmer. "It was what it was. As long as it didn't affect the video—and it didn't—I didn't care."

The final product is a jovial, highlight-packed music video that exceeded all expectations by going triple platinum and receiving substantial radio and MTV airplay. The only flaw that troubled Palmer is something he had no control over. Jon Peisinger, the president of Vestron, thought it wise to include as many local celebrities as possible.

To Palmer this meant Mayor Ed Koch, Woody Allen, and Billy Joel. "Prime-timers," says Palmer. "Strictly top names." Peisinger's vision was, ahem, different. If the video featured New York disc jockeys, he believed, the song would receive more airtime. No star was too small. As a result the last twenty seconds of the video is an embarrassing nod to such not-so-luminary luminaries as J. J. Kennedy, Melba Moore, Soupy Sales, Chuck Leonard, Mark McEwen, two schlubs from Twisted Sister (neither of whom is named Dee Snider), a no-hit-wonder R&B trio named Cameo, and Dr. Joyce Brothers. "She was the weirdest of all," says Palmer. "You could pose for a picture with her, but she wouldn't let you put an arm around her. One time I said, 'Maybe you should see someone for that.'" Brothers didn't laugh.

The Mets ran large newspaper advertisements hyping *Let's Go Mets!*, which would make its world debut minutes before the August 30 game against the Dodgers at Shea Stadium. It was to be a blockbuster event highlighted by an invitation-only premiere party hosted by Cashen at the upscale Diamond Club. On the eve, Harazin called Palmer to congratulate him on the finished product. Palmer was touched. "It means a lot," he told Harazin. "And I just want you to know, I really wish we didn't go $100,000 over budget like it did. But we worked real hard, and everything came out great and . . ."

"Hello?

"Hello?"

There was silence. *One hundred thousand dollars* over budget? Was Harazin hearing this right?

"Shelly," he said, "you must be kidding me. The deal was $163,000. We're not paying an extra $100,000. Where'd that even come from?"

Palmer explained that New York's players were always late, be it ten minutes for Mookie Wilson to shower or two hours for Strawberry to chase tail. That added up to crew members sitting around the Shea Stadium infield, watching their days waste away. Anyhow, Jeff Peisch, the liaison between Vestron and the Mets, had signed off on every billing. It was all kosher.

"Well," said Harazin, "there's no way we're paying that. We didn't approve any of it."

Palmer—though short, balding, a bit chunky, and only a few years out of N.Y.U. Film School—was not one to be intimidated. "You know what's interesting about that?" he told Harazin. "I seem to have lost the master, and I'm not 100 percent sure if I know where the rest of the tapes are. Okay, I guess I'll see you down the road. Bye." Click.

Fifteen seconds later the phone rang. It was Harazin. "What do you mean you don't have the master?"

Palmer's testicles grew by the minute. "Look," he said, "if I don't have a certified check for $263,000 in my hand at 9:30 tomorrow morning, you guys can take over the production, and what you'll find are some empty film canisters. That'll probably make it tough to show a video tomorrow night, though. Don't you think?"

The next morning a check for $263,000 arrived. It got there by eight o'clock.

Chapter 12

PLEASE STAY OFF THE FIELD

We must keep our playing field intact, so any celebrating of a division clinching cannot be done on the field. If you're a real Met fan, you'll certainly understand this. If not—if your sole purpose of being at the ballpark is to vandalize the field—we must inform you that any violators are subject to arrest and prosecution.

—FRANK CASHEN in a prerecorded message to fans played on September 17, 1986.

ON SEPTEMBER 12, 1986, the New York Mets traveled to Philadelphia for a 3-game series against the Phillies. They needed just two more wins to clinch the NL East, which meant that the clubhouse equipment staff not only had to worry about the usual crates of bats and helmets but also the dozen cases of carefully packed Andre champagne that had been purchased in New York a few days earlier.

Of course, it would be just a matter of hours. The Mets were the best team in baseball. The Phillies were fighting to stay above .500. In the New York clubhouse the talk was of *when* they would win, not *if*.

In the first game the Phillies won, 6–3.

No biggie. We'll get the next one!

In the second game the Phillies won, 6–5.

So what? There's always tomorrow!

In the third game the Phillies won, 6–0.

Umm . . .

Finally, after splitting a pair with the Cardinals, the inevitable occurred. On the evening of September 17, 1986, a near-capacity Shea Stadium crowd of 47,823 watched as Dwight Gooden threw a complete-game 6 hitter in New York's 4–2 win over the Cubs. The hero was a rookie September call-up named Dave Magadan. In his first career start he hit three singles and drove in two runs while replacing a flu-ridden Hernandez at first base. (Desperate to be on the field when the Mets clinched, Hernandez played the final 2 innings.)

The NL East title, the Mets' first in thirteen years, was sealed.

Alas, keeping with the rest of a turbulent season, nothing went entirely smoothly. As it became more and more apparent that New York would defeat lowly Chicago, Shea Stadium turned from baseball stadium to potential war zone. In the top of the ninth, fans began spilling out of the bleachers and into the photographer wells beside the dugout. Security guards lined the warning track. In the Mets' dugout, players, coaches, batboys, front-office officials, and police stood packed like sardines.

As soon as Wally Backman fielded Chico Walker's grounder and threw to Hernandez for the final out, a terrifying wave of blue-and-orange-coated humanity engulfed the Shea playing field. Backman darted toward the dugout, and fans pulled the hat off his head and the glove off his hand. Carter lost his mask and helmet. Gooden, the team's brightest icon since Tom Seaver, was swallowed by a cloud of arms and legs. For five minutes he was at the bottom of a rapidly growing pile until Hernandez, Kevin Mitchell, and three police officers began screaming at the rowdies. "Don't you know who's down there?" Hernandez yelled. "That's Dwight Gooden . . . and you're killing him!" Meanwhile, players dashed for safety, running for their lives as if they were on the streets of Pamplona. Rick

Aguilera, the number 5 starter, was exiting the dugout for the field when a fan jumped on his back and dislocated his left shoulder. "I was in the shower after the game, and I couldn't lift my arm to shampoo my hair," says Aguilera. "I was lucky it wasn't my pitching arm."

All the while, five gigantic words flashed from the Diamond Vision screen: PLEASE STAY OFF THE FIELD!

Even when all the Mets had retreated to the clubhouse, the fans continued to act like water buffalos on a plush marsh. "We're hoping everyone here has a wonderful time," said Rusty Staub, who was announcing the game for WWOR. "We're also hoping that Shea Stadium survives." It would, but not unscathed. The bases were ripped from their hinges and lugged away. So was the pitching rubber. Huge chunks of grass and dirt were dug from the ground and brought home as keepsakes. "Big craters the size of boulders were all over the place," says Bob Mandt, the director of stadium operations. "And it looked as if moths had gotten at the infield." When things began to die down, the police officers—holding clubs and decked out in riot gear—formed a line across the backstop and gradually walked from the infield to the outfield, pushing the masses toward the right field stadium exit. Only two fans were arrested—one for stealing a seat, another for assaulting a cop in the parking lot.

Although most team officials were able to laugh off the mayhem as "typical New York," those seated near Cashen were shocked to see steam rising from his ears. Yes, he was pleased with the clinching. But this was his stadium—his beautiful stadium. Where was the restrained joy? The simple happiness? And who the hell were these morons trampling his grass? The GM ordered Mandt to publicly condemn the celebration, and when that was met with a stern refusal ("Frank," Mandt said, "I live in New York, I love New York, and I understand what happened"), the general manager did so himself. "My emotions have ranged from incensed to disgusted," he told the New York media. "I don't understand why New York fans feel they have the birthright to tear up the field. It does a disservice to the real fans and the players. Once the mob psychology takes over, you have no chance. It was vandalism and destruction, pure and simple. It was a disgrace."

Cashen's patronizing words were ignored by almost everyone, beginning with his players. As soon as the Mets escaped the war zone that was the Shea Stadium infield, they were greeted by a clubhouse stocked with beer and the dusty bottles of champagne. Darryl Strawberry soaked Mayor Ed Koch in Andre. Darling, Aguilera, and Ojeda were lathered in shaving cream from forehead to waist. McDowell cruised the room wearing nothing but a garbage bag and a headset. Davey Johnson, the manager who specialized in letting his players be themselves, was roughed up the most. First Darling and three others walked into his office and showered him with beer. Then McDowell arrived and poured a bucket of ice down his back. After that, Strawberry and Aguilera smothered his face with a tray of shaving cream. Finally, six players carried the fully uniformed Johnson into the shower, plopped him down, and blasted the freezing water. Afterward, as usual, the Mets dove into an all-night booze bonanza at Finn MacCool's.

Yet as the players who contributed to the team's startling success bathed themselves in glory, one stood far to the side, mixed in his emotions but saddened by his position as an outsider.

To this day Ed Lynch still cherishes his role on the 1986 New York Mets; still proudly wears his World Series ring. But he also cringes at the memory of September 17 when he was forced to endure a ballplayer's darkest moment.

Through much of the early '80s, Lynch was not just a loyal mainstay on what was for most of his time one of baseball's lowliest teams. He was *the* mainstay: the only member of the Mets staff in town long enough to gain wisdom from an in-his-prime Craig Swan and then turn around years later and impart it to Gooden, Darling, Fernandez, and Aguilera. Never a great pitcher, Lynch was called up in 1980 on the basis of guile and smarts and a whole lot of guts. Opposing batters used to hate Lynch because instead of challenging with heat, he would peck the corners. "I had no choice," he says, chuckling. "I had no fastball."

From 1982 to 1985, Lynch led the Mets in games pitched. His thirty-eight career wins ranked ninth in franchise history. But by '86 the team was overstocked with young, hard-throwing phenoms, and the need for a thirty-year-old soft-toss spot starter making $530,000 was limited. New York did everything it could to trade Lynch during spring training, but any potential deals were squashed when the pitcher tore cartilage in his left knee. As it swelled to the size of a pumpkin, the Mets placed the veteran on the disabled list, where he remained for more than two months. "I'm finally on the best team of my career," he says, "and I'm not even playing. I was really bumming." Lynch made four rehabilitation starts for Triple A Tidewater, and on July 1 he was scheduled to return to New York to rejoin the Mets. It was a thrilling time to be Ed Lynch, a man with enough memories of bleak Shea Stadium summer nights to salivate at the idea of a pennant race. Lynch pictured himself on the mound, the World Series title hanging in the balance with each pitch, the fans behind him chanting, "Ed-die! Ed-die! Ed-die!"

Pop!

On June 30, Lynch was sitting in the lobby of a hotel in Norfolk, Virginia, when he opened to the sports pages of *The New York Times*. There in cruel black and white was the small headline LYNCH TRADE IS EXPECTED. The article began:

> Ed Lynch, who has thrived during five years as the "odd man" of the Mets' pitching staff, will end a 20-day medical rehabilitation tour in the minor leagues Monday and is expected to be traded rather than restored to the staff.

It was the first concrete word he'd heard about a possible deal since spring training, and it made his hands shake and his belly ache. Lynch returned to his room, and Harazin soon called to deliver the blow: Lynch had been dealt to the last-place Chicago Cubs for pitcher Dave Lenderman and catcher David Liddell, two minor-leaguers he had never heard of. Lynch sat on his bed and cried.

"It was like living with a family the whole year and getting thrown out of the house on Christmas Eve," he says. "I was devastated. I had never been on a winner. When I was in college at South Carolina, we lost the national championship game twice. I was never on any kind of play-off team in the minors, and this was my one shot to get to a World Series. It would have meant so much to me."

Although he went 7–5 with a 3.79 ERA in twenty-three games with the Cubs, Lynch earned the World Series ring that still rests on his right ring finger, both in service time and immediate contributions. Besides appearing in one April game for the Mets (he pitched in ⅔ of an inning), Lynch was responsible for his old club's one-hundredth victory when he permitted 2 runs in 1 ⅓ innings in a 6–5 Cubs loss at Wrigley Field on September 25. After allowing Hernandez to score, Lynch peered into the New York dugout and saw his old first baseman pointing and snickering at him.

So now here was Lynch on September 17, standing next to Lee Smith in the Shea Stadium visitors' bullpen, watching the top of the ninth inning unfold and wondering just what god he had angered to reach this point. As Hernandez clutched the ball for the final out, Lynch stared out at the mayhem, a stranger in a strange land. "We're behind this Plexiglas shield, and it was like watching a show on wild animals," he says. "I remember some knucklehead had ripped home plate out of the ground, and he ran with it to the left field corner. Guys were kicking him, trying to take it away. It was scary."

After retreating to the clubhouse to shower and change into street clothes, Lynch walked through the stadium's concrete bowels, which after several hundred yards led to the Cubs' bus. The path went past the Mets' clubhouse. As he made the final turn, Lynch could hear the whooping and hollering from his former teammates. "There was probably some temptation to go in," he says, "but it was no longer my place." Years later Lynch is left with a memory that would keep lesser men up at night: "There's Randy Myers, who had been with the team about a week, and he's got his arm around two gals, and he's got a bottle of champagne in each hand," says Lynch of the rookie reliever who appeared in 10 games that season. "I remember just looking at him and thinking, 'Where's a grenade when you need one?'"

———

As soon as they clinched the NL East, New York's stars treated the remainder of the season as if they were second-semester high school seniors. Sure, they showed up at the stadium and played. But even though the Mets won 13 of their final 17 contests to finish with 108 victories (making them one of nine clubs to ever reach that total), it was not accomplished passionately. With Davey Johnson's blessing, veterans arrived a little later to the park. Youngsters like Dave Magadan, Stanley Jefferson, Kevin Elster, and John Gibbons were granted extended playing time. It was the good life at Shea Stadium.

But approximately sixteen hundred miles away, the Mets' rivals were hardly quivering with fear. On September 25, eight days after the Mets won the NL East, the Houston Astros clinched the NL West with a 2–0 triumph over the San Francisco Giants at the Astrodome. If any of the Mets happened to catch the highlights, they would have witnessed a chilling sight: Mike Scott, Houston's six-foot-three, 215-pound fire balling right-hander, was no-hitting the Giants with a buffet of untouchable splitters. It wasn't simply that Scott struck out thirteen while becoming the first man to hurl a no-hitter in a pennant-clinching situation. It was the way he struck out thirteen. In a game of incredible magnitude, Scott's split-fingered fastball hypnotized opposing batters. Watch ball. Swing at ball. Miss ball.

Although the Astros entered the National League Championship Series with 12 fewer regular season victories than New York, they had a real chance of knocking off the favorites. Like the Mets, Houston boasted a deep bench and bullpen; a dominant, middle-of-the-order power threat (first baseman Glenn Davis had 31 home runs and 101 RBIs); grizzled veterans who had already experienced the playoffs (Davey Lopes and Jose Cruz); a hard-nosed defensive catcher (Alan Ashby); pesky, aggressive baserunners; and a similarly unyielding belief in inevitable victory. The Astros might not have had the outward swagger of their New York rivals, but there was enough sass in the Houston clubhouse to go around. This was a team that, just like the Mets, had come from behind to win 39 games in 1986. For the first time in a season filled with romps, the Mets were about to face a club that wasn't intimidated. In fact, the Astros saw themselves as the intimidators. The Mets? Just another bump in their path. "Oh, we knew we were the best team in baseball," says Billy Hatcher, the team's brash center fielder. "I guess the Mets were considered the team to beat. But in our hearts we were going to win the World Series."

Most important, manager Hal Lanier's club was armed with starting pitching. Lots and lots of starting pitching. Scott, the year's NL Cy Young Award winner with an 18–10 record and 2.22 ERA, was the headliner, but he was hardly a solo act. The Astros' number 2 starter was Nolan Ryan, the ageless thirty-nine-year-old flamethrower who had 194 strikeouts in 178 innings pitched. Unlike the members of New York's rotation—none of whom had any postseason experience—Ryan had been to the playoffs four times, highlighted by a spot on the roster of the world champion '69 Mets. And while the Astros' number 3 man, left-hander Bob Knepper, had won only once from August 15 through the season's end, three of his career-high 17 victories that season had been taken from the Mets. Plus, following the 90-mph heat of Scott and Ryan, Knepper's assortment of curves, sliders, and change-ups drove hitters batty. Heck, Lanier probably wouldn't even need rookie left-hander Jim Deshaies, who went *only* 12–5 and set a major league record by striking out the first eight batters he faced in a September start against the Dodgers.

During the season's final 12 games, Houston's starters combined for a 1.34 ERA. They were four big, nasty, poised, intelligent pitchers who had done a number on the National League. Little did the Mets know that it would take only one of them to nearly end their magical run.

Chapter 13

GREAT SCOTT

The idea that a guy can blatantly cheat and be allowed to get away with it because of who he is disgusts me. What are we teaching the kids about sportsmanship?

—RUSTY STAUB, former Mets outfielder

THE TRADE WASN'T CRITICIZED. The trade wasn't praised. The trade was a bip.

In the world of sports journalism, a bip is what newspapers resort to when there's news to report, only it's news that nobody—except for the craziest of sports crazies—could possibly care about. It's the New England Patriots releasing their fifth-round draft pick out of the University of Delaware. It's the hiring of Bucknell University's assistant women's volleyball coach.

On December 11, 1982, the bip—appearing in the transactions listings of sports sections around the country—was this: "Houston Astros obtain Mike Scott, pitcher, from New York Mets in exchange for Danny Heep, outfielder/first baseman."

In parts of four seasons with the Mets, the right-hander was one of the least imposing pitchers in the National League. In 1982, his final year with the Mets, Scott went 7–13 with an NL high 5.14 ERA. In 147 innings he allowed 185 hits, while striking out just 63. Batters hit .321 against him, and he was unbearably inconsistent—a fastball with electric movement, followed by an 82-mph meatball.

"Sometimes his confidence wavered, and sometimes his command of pitches wasn't very great," says Roger Jongewaard, a scout for the Mets at the time. "I think the Mets probably thought he was too nice."

By 1982, Scott was an official bust, owner of a 14–27 major league record and a likely future of selling preowned cars or life insurance. He remembers being in his house in Chandler, Arizona, on that December day, picking up the phone, and learning that the only organization he had ever known was dumping him.

Scott was thrilled. For much of the '82 season he had complained to the Mets about a sore right shoulder that had reduced the velocity of his fastball from 94 to 83 mph. Scott says the Mets medical staff looked at his arm, but not with enough rigor to term it an examination. "The coaches were frustrated," he says. "They would say, 'Throw with some velocity! Show me something!' I was throwing as hard as I could." Much of the blame goes to manager George Bamberger. Because his club's pitching was so thin, Bamberger thought it a fine idea to operate the majors' only four-man starting rotation. Scott collapsed after seven starts. "It was a terrible idea," says Rusty Staub, an outfielder on the club. "The body couldn't handle the strain." Unbeknownst to those involved, Scott was suffering from tendinitis. He was not just ineffective but damaged.

Scott was never one for the New York experience anyway. Shea Stadium was a charmless dump, the fans showed up only on Hat Day, the early-season weather was too cold, and the press wanted to know what color underwear you were wearing. Worst of all, he was surrounded by disinterested, worn-down veterans. Every spring Scott would show up thinking this could be the year for the Mets. Then he'd watch players like Ellis Valentine and Dave Kingman jog through training camp as if it were a Club Med getaway. "I was young and naïve," he says. "We'd be 30 games out by May." When a players' strike began on June 12, 1981,

Scott—who was making $32,500—could barely afford a plane ticket home to Arizona. "With New York housing prices, food, transportation—you can't be poor in that city," he says. "I was ready to leave."

Houston wasn't exactly frenzied over its newest addition. When Alan Ashby, the club's longtime starting catcher, learned of Heep-for-Scott, his first thought was *Why?* "Danny Heep was an extremely talented-looking hitter with a bright future," says Ashby. "And Mike Scott was ordinary." Scott spent the first month of the 1983 season on the disabled list with a weak rotator cuff, then returned to pitch relatively well as Houston's number 5 starter. But when he reverted to his old form the next season (5–11, 4.68 ERA), Scott could sense the major league grim reaper looming. "I didn't know if my career was done," he says, "but I knew it wasn't going very well."

That off-season Scott attended the Astros' annual postseason golf holiday, which owner John McMullen hosted at the Pine Valley Country Club in Clementine, New Jersey. One night during the vacation several Astros were sitting together in the dining room, chatting about family and baseball. That's when Enos Cabell, Houston's third baseman, approached Scott and changed his life.

In 1982 and 1983, Cabell had played for the Detroit Tigers where pitching coach Roger Craig was on staff. For most of his career Craig's claim to fame was starting the final game in Brooklyn Dodgers history. Though no Cy Young on the mound, Craig was something of a guru off it. In 1980, while working as an instructor at the San Diego School of Baseball, Craig was frustrated over his efforts to find a breaking pitch that wouldn't hurt the arms of his teenage protégés. One day in an attempt to discover the perfect, arm-safe solution, Craig started experimenting with the forkball, which he had thrown with some success near the end of his career. Now, however, he gripped the ball farther from the palm and threw it with a fastball motion. In the words of a 1986 *Sports Illustrated* story, "Wonderful things happened." An innocent-looking fastball approached the plate and then—*whoosh!*—dropped dramatically from the batter's elbow to his toes. It was the unhittable pitch. Now you see it, now you don't. The split-finger fast-ball was born.

Upon being hired to manage the Tigers in the winter of 1979, Sparky Anderson offered the pitching coach job to Craig, his longtime chum. When Detroit won the World Series in '84, starters Jack Morris, Dan Petry, and Milt Wilcox—practitioners of the magical pitch—all had at least seventeen victories. The onetime journeyman was the most rev-olutionary pitching coach in baseball.

Craig resigned after the World Series and retired to his ranch in San Diego. (Ten months later he would be hired to manage the San Francisco Giants.) Meanwhile, thousands of miles away in Clementine, New Jersey, Cabell was raving to Scott about this crafty old wizard. McMullen, who overheard the conversation, mentioned the idea of a Scott-Craig pairing to GM Al Rosen and Astros manager Bob Lillis. The reactions were iden-tical: *Mike Scott is almost out of baseball. What do we have to lose?*

A few days later Scott flew to San Diego. Over the next 8 days Craig worked on breaking Scott down and building him up again. Almost immediately Scott was a new pitcher. His large hands were perfect to grip the splitter. His velocity, still in the low to mid-90s, was above aver-age. "To this day people ask me how to throw it," says Scott. "They say, 'Do you snap your wrist? Do you have a funky grip?' And the truth is, it takes nothing. I just spread my fingers and throw a fastball."

Scott reported to spring training that February atop a tidal wave of confidence. On the first day of workouts, Lillis issued an order: Throw only fastballs and splitters. This made Scott smile. He still remembers his debut start that spring, a four-inning, one-hit performance against the Cardinals. "It was an eye-opener," he says. "The swings and the misses, the called strike threes, the ground balls. I knew right then—Roger Craig had saved my career."

In 1985, Scott went from a mediocre nobody to an 18-game winner. His ERA dropped from 4.68 to 3.29. Thanks to his breakout season, Scott was rewarded with a new three-year, $2 million contract. Mean-while, opposing hitters and managers began grumbling about the suspi-cious movement of his splitter. It came to a head on May 26, 1985, in the

Cubs' 10–8 win over Scott at Wrigley Field when Chicago first baseman Leon (Bull) Durham found a scrap of sandpaper near the mound between innings. "It was brand-new, cut in a circle, and just big enough for him to hide it in his glove," Durham told the *Chicago Tribune*. Chicago manager Jim Frey sent the sandpaper to the office of NL president Chub Feeney, but no action was taken. Scott dismissed the incident as sour grapes.

The next season, 1986, Scott edged out Los Angeles' Fernando Valenzuela for the NL Cy Young Award, posting an 18–10 record and leading the league with a 2.22 ERA, 306 strikeouts, 275⅓ innings pitched, and 5 shutouts. This was not just a pitcher on a very good ride; Scott had become a master. Before 1986 he had never struck out more than eight batters in a game. That season, he fanned nine-plus nineteen times. "When Scottie was out there, we knew we'd win," says Matt Galante, the Astros' third-base coach at the time. "It was visible intimidation."

His rivals insisted it was also visible cheating. Scott, they alleged, was marking up the baseball. At the time Tom Browning was a second-year left-hander with the Reds who, as a rookie, had come out of nowhere to win 20 games. Browning remembers pitching against Scott on September 9, 1986, at the Astrodome. He remembers the fear of facing the game's newest ace. He remembers the pressure to keep his team in the game. And he remembers *the baseball.*

"Mike Scott had left a marked ball on the mound between innings," recalls Browning. "It had a big ol' scuff mark on it, as clear as a quarter on a piece of paper. This wasn't an accidental scuff from contact." Instead of requesting a new ball for his warmup pitches, Browning threw Scott's scuffer to catcher Bo Diaz. "I held the ball one way, and it moved to the left," recalls Browning. "Then I held the ball on the other side, and it moved to the left again. I tried throwing it one more way, and again it went left." Browning finally tossed the ball to the home plate umpire and requested a new one. Cincinnati manager Pete Rose was incensed. "What'd you throw it away for?" he yelled. "That was our evidence!"

In a game at Houston on June 13, Craig—who had initially warned Scott that there would be nonbelievers—asked the umpires to check his former student's baseball three different times. "How can a pitcher be this good?" Craig whined. "Nobody is this good." Scott, who felt as though he and Craig had formed a kinship, was hurt. What he didn't know was that, in the same game, a member of the Giants' front office had a cameraman film Scott the entire afternoon. The goal was simple: Catch him in the act and send the tape to the commissioner's office.

Then it happened. In the third inning, two San Francisco players said they watched Scott remove something from his glove and drop it down his shirt. After the game, the Giants anxiously viewed the tape and found *nothing*. As Scott was supposedly disposing of the sandpaper, the cameraman was shooting Craig barking at an umpire. The footage was useless. The cameraman was axed. Scott was safe.

On September 25, Scott again faced the Giants at the Astrodome. Houston needed one win to clinch its first NL West crown in six years. Scott proceeded to throw a 2–0 no-hitter. Afterward, Craig accepted his team's fate and tipped his cap to Scott. "Why did it have to be me," he sighed, "who taught him that damn pitch?"

Years after the fact, those close to Scott are willing to admit that his mastery had something to do with a sleight of hand. Was Mike Scott cheating?

Steve Smith, a former Pepperdine teammate and recent third-base coach for the Texas Rangers: "We've talked about it, and I know the truth. It's his secret, and it's a good one. I'll just say this: When he threw that pitch, the ball looked like a Wiffle Ball."

Galante: "Oh, I don't know about, umm . . . Well, it's a tough question, a tough question. But, uh, if I were, umm, on the other team, I'd, umm, I'd have been concerned."

Ashby: "Well, umm, ha, hmmmmm, well, I think I'll, ummm . . . Well, let's just say that Mike was doing everything he could to win ball games. What Mike did I probably wouldn't, ah, comment any further. Well, what did Mike say?"

Great question. At age forty-nine, Scott lives in Aliso Viejo, California, with his wife and two children. He plays golf several times a week and is happy to be out of the spotlight. A couple of years ago his golden

Cy Young Award trophy began turning green. It rests comfortably in a closet.

Although he enjoyed three more seasons of 14-plus wins, Scott never recaptured the dominance. But in 1986 everything went right. His fastball snapped. His splitter split.

So years after the fact, will Mike Scott finally admit to scuffing?

"That'll be in my book," he says. "I promise."

When is Scott planning on writing a book?

"I'm not."

Chapter 14

"IT DOESN'T GET ANY BETTER THAN THIS"

The Houston Astros should have been in the 1986 World Series. I still believe that.

—CHARLIE KERFELD, Astros reliever

LIKE ALL OF THEIR NATIONAL LEAGUE PEERS, the twenty-four men who made up the active roster of the Houston Astros loathed the New York Mets. It was bad enough that 108-win New York was a heavy favorite to wipe out the out-of-nowhere Astros and their merry band of nobodies. But what really irked Houston's players was the attitude. The Astros took pride in winning the right way, with humility and class and a silent dignity. They were a veteran team of hustlers and scrappers, many of whom attended chapel every Sunday morning.

The Mets were Satan.

The Astros had paid close attention to New York for much of the season, knowing that if they won the NL West, a playoff clash was inevitable. They saw the music videos, the curtain calls, the high-fives, the sixty-minute home run trots, the endorsements—and they snarled.

"To me the Mets were Gary Carter," says Charlie Kerfeld, Houston's eccentric reliever. "I'd never seen a guy who looks for the camera so often, and that team followed his lead. They were *so* cocky."

Leading up to Game 1 of the National League Championship Series, the Mets made very little effort to conceal their lack of respect for the Astros. Hanging above the locker of Houston closer Dave Smith was a clip from the *Daily News* in which several New York players dismissed the Astros bullpen. Two days before the beginning of the series, Darryl Strawberry was asked by the *Daily News* in what areas the Mets held an edge over Houston. "Where do we have the edge?" Strawberry replied. "The team." The sentiment was backed up by Wally Backman. "Put it this way," he told the *Post*. "We play the way we're capable, and I love us in the playoffs. Houston's got a good club, but we're deep."

To the Astros, the disrespect hit closest to home on the eve of Game 1, when several New York players accused Scott of defacing baseballs. It wasn't so much that the Mets were wrong. They weren't—and every Astro knew it. (Manager Hal Lanier's response to whether Scott was legal: "I haven't seen Mike Scott get caught. If they can get away with it, let them get away with it.") But the Houston coaching staff, equally convinced that Howard Johnson was corking his bat, had taken the high road and, lacking physical proof, said nothing.

Scott's biggest critic was Carter, who was armed with firsthand experience. During the All-Star Game that July, he spent an inning catching Scott. With Toronto outfielder Jesse Barfield at the plate, Scott threw a ball that snapped inside and broke three feet. "I checked the ball, and it was scratched," said Carter. "I mean, scratched big-time." The veteran catcher knew whereof he spoke. From 1978 to 1980 in Montreal, Carter was regularly behind the plate for left-handed starter Ross Grimsley, a man who lathered his ball with so much Vaseline that in between pitches, The Kid ran his fingers through the dirt to wipe off any lingering grease. If anyone recognized a dirty ball, it was Gary Carter.

Yet as his teammates cursed the opposition, Scott became more and more confident. Not only was he the possessor of a magical pitch, but he was as powerful with the mind as he was with the baseball. Though openly brash and obnoxious, New York's hitters quivered at the prospect of Scott's unhittable splitter.

The Astros had another huge advantage as well: home cooking. The National League determined home-field advantage by alternating years between the two divisions, and since the Dodgers had hosted the Cardinals for Game 1 in the 1985 NLCS, Shea Stadium was supposed to be the location this year. Unfortunately for the Mets, a scheduling conflict with the NFL left the Astrodome unavailable for Games 3, 4, and 5. League president Chub Feeney did the only thing he could: He announced that the series would open in Texas.

Ever since July 19 when Aguilera, Darling, Ojeda, and Teufel were arrested in the Cooter's melee, New York had soared past the Dodgers, Reds, and Giants to the top of Houston's hate list. To the city's residents it wasn't just baseball, it was personal. How else to explain the HOUSTON POLICE 4, METS 0 T-shirts that continued to sell two and a half months later like cowboy boots? Davey Johnson did his team no favors in a taped interview that aired during the ABC pregame show when he answered a puff question about Houston's running game by dumping on the so-so arm of Ashby, the Astros' beloved catcher. "No doubt [Houston will] be aggressive on the bases," he said. "But Gary's really better than Alan Ashby. I like Gary's chances better than I do Ashby's."

The pitch that officially turned Game 1 of the National League Championship Series into something more than just another battle was thrown at 8:17 P.M. Central time on October 8. It was, naturally, a split-fingered fastball from the right hand of Mike Scott delivered to Gary Carter, and as it crossed the plate, the ball literally dove two feet, then took a physics-defying twist to the right. Physically, it is possible for a baseball to curve, rise, and drop, but *twist?*

Following a vicious yet fruitless swing of his bat, Carter turned toward home plate umpire Doug Harvey. It was only four batters into the first inning, but Harvey would have had to be blind not to feel the furor in Carter's glare. The veteran umpire immediately stuck out his hand, took the ball from Ashby, and looked it over. He found nothing. (Eight years earlier Harvey had been threatened with a lawsuit by Don Sutton after ejecting the Dodgers pitcher from a game in St. Louis for throwing a defaced baseball. It was suggested by the Mets that Harvey was gun-shy of repeating such an event.) Seconds later Scott threw yet another nasty split, striking Carter out on three pitches and sending the Astrodome into an ear-bursting frenzy. For New York it was the beginning of the end—a gigantic psych-out.

Over the ensuing 8 innings Scott reduced New York's potent lineup—one that led the NL in runs, hits, and batting average—to baseball's answer to the Keystone Kops. With each of Scott's playoff-record 14 strikeouts, a Met player would inevitably moan, scream, or complain in agony on his return trip to the dugout.

With Gooden on the mound in the bottom of the second, Houston first baseman Glenn Davis took a letters-high fastball and sent it 399 feet above the center field wall, handing his team a 1-0 lead that, with Scott buzzing along, felt like 100-0. In the top of the sixth, Dykstra became the first Met to successfully lead off an inning, walking on seven pitches. After Backman flied out, up came Hernandez, the one New York player who seemed to understand Scott and, with a fourth-inning single, the first to register a hit in Game 1. Entering the NLCS, Hernandez boasted a career .377 average against the Houston superstar. "Carter was whining all the time," says Hernandez. "It was cheating, and we knew it. But you've still got to throw the ball over the plate." With the count full and Dykstra running, Scott unleashed a splitter that started down the middle and then—snap!—broke way outside. As the Mets captain gestured toward first, Harvey bellowed a loud, late *strike three!*

Hernandez flipped. For the next ten seconds he positioned his face two inches from Harvey's and screamed away: "That was a fuckin' ball! You can't be serious! Did you see how outside that was!? Just terrible! Terrible . . . terrible!" Hernandez pounded his bat into the ground. He paced and pouted. He cursed some more. In the end it was all for naught. Carter followed with his third straight strikeout, and the inning was over. New York would challenge once more in the eighth, but with runners on first and second and two outs, Hernandez swung through a high, inside fastball to end the threat.

For the Mets, Game 1 was a wipeout. A dispiriting 1–0 wipeout.

"That may have been the first time all year I'd seen our team not believe in itself," says Ray Knight, who went 0 for 4 with 2 strikeouts. "I'd seen teams say, 'We can't beat this guy.' But not our team. Not until that night."

Most upsetting to the New Yorkers was that proof was so close, yet so far. Each time a ball was fouled off or tossed out of play by the umpire, Houston's batboy would sprint out, pick it up, and return it to the Astros' dugout. There was nothing sketchy about the routine; all home teams were responsible for the retrieval and collection of baseballs. But in the conspiracy-addled minds of the Mets, every Scott baseball was a scuffed baseball. If only they could prove it . . .

Considering the outcome of Game 1, the Mets retained a shocking reserve of chutzpah. On the bus ride back to the hotel, Hernandez made an announcement: "I don't want anybody to go back to his room! We're all going downstairs to the bar!" For the next hour Hernandez bought his teammates beers and pepped them up for the following night. Sure, Scott was Christy Mathewson and Don Drysdale rolled into one, but he was also a cheater on a once-in-a-lifetime roll. In Game 2 the opposing pitcher would be thirty-nine-year-old Nolan Ryan.

To most of baseball Ryan was as intimidating as he was old. If it wasn't the heat emanating from his pitches, it was the serial killer glare, peeking out from under a tucked-down Astros cap. New York didn't care. "The only guy who has a chance to beat us is Scott," Dykstra said before Game 2. In his mind the reasons were plentiful. Ryan was born during the Civil War. His 3.34 ERA was his second worst in six years. He had spent a month and a half that season on the disabled list with a sprained medial collateral ligament in his pitching elbow. Best of all, he wasn't Mike Scott.

While it remained in vogue to call Gooden the Mets' ace, Bobby Ojeda was the starter who over the course of the season both led the club in wins and inspired the most confidence in his teammates. There was just something reassuring about the man, a sanguine air that made up for less-than-dominant stuff. Compared with the eyebrow-searing heat of Gooden, Darling, Fernandez, and Aguilera, Ojeda's slow-motion assortment of change-ups and curves appeared as threatening as a doe at a rifle club. He was deceptive enough that Carter nicknamed his ever-sinking off-speed pitch "The Dead Fish." Whether he was facing Dale Murphy with the bases loaded or sitting in a Houston jail cell at 3 A.M., Ojeda had an easygoing demeanor. "Bobby was as cool as could be," says Roger McDowell. "He was a perfect guy for pressure baseball because he didn't feel it."

For the first 3 innings, neither did Ryan. He was The Express of old, mowing down five of the first nine Mets and, in the top of the third, whiffing Knight, Rafael Santana, and Ojeda on 14 pitches. In the fourth, New York rallied. With Hernandez on first and Backman on second, Carter ripped a double off the wall in right center field, driving in the Mets' first run of the NLCS. One batter later, Strawberry's sacrifice fly to left made the score 2–0. It was all a huge relief to New York and specifically to Carter, who had missed two weeks late in the season with a partial ligament tear in his left thumb. The Mets compiled an 11–3 record in his absence, and nobody could blame The Kid for feeling a bit unwanted.

New York struck again the following inning and in the process sent a powerful message. Even though the Astros found Carter an aggravating, buffoonish cheerleader, many of the players reserved their greatest contempt for Dykstra. It wasn't enough for the Met center fielder to walk up to the plate and swing away. No, he had to strut, with his chin held high and his chest protruding and little wads of tobacco sliding off his tongue. So with Ojeda on first following a failed sacrifice bunt, Ryan did something about it. After his first pitch was fouled off deep into the right field corner, Ryan threw a 94-mph fastball that, had he not ducked out of the way, would have transformed Dykstra's head into a dish of mashed potatoes.

Instead of cowering, Dykstra got mad. He popped up from the ground and stared menacingly at the six-foot-two, 195-pound legend.

On the next pitch, another heater, Dykstra lashed a single to left field. "Lenny wasn't one to take any shit," says Backman. Ryan didn't just agitate one player. He woke up an entire team. Backman followed Dykstra with a single, scoring Ojeda for a 3–0 advantage. Hernandez then turned on a waist-high fastball and roped it to the outfield. Billy Hatcher, Houston's speedy center fielder, dove, missed, and watched the baseball roll all the way to the wall. Two more runs scored, and the Mets held a 5–0 lead. Ojeda went 9 innings for the 5–1 victory. The series was even.

When a man like Bob Knepper comes along in the relatively blah world of major league baseball, a light goes on and the siren blares. Entering Game 3 of the NLCS, Knepper was not just the left-handed starter entrusted with the responsibility of guiding his underdog club to a 2–1 series lead. No, unlike the cardboard personas of Scott and Ryan, Knepper was an attraction. Among other things, he collected Mario Lanza records, foreign coins, historical biographies, and John Wayne artifacts. At home on his thirteen-hundred-acre cattle ranch in Wilbur, Oregon, Knepper subscribed to nineteen publications (approximately nineteen more than the average big leaguer), including *National Cattleman, Beef, Evangelist*, and the newsletter of the National Federation for Moral Decency. That last periodical was in large part a result of a 1978 religious experience that resulted in:

A. Knepper handing over his life to a man named Jesus Christ.
B. Knepper becoming something of a kook.

At least that was the view shared by more than a few Houston Astros who often wondered aloud whether their number 3 starter really needed all thirty of his handguns, rifles, and shotguns. "Knep was the oddest of birds," says Ashby. "Mike [Scott] and Knep would ride to the park together, and when Knep was pitching, he'd say to Scottie, 'Who are we playing tonight?'"

By starting Knepper, Houston manager Hal Lanier made New York field a less threatening lineup. Instead of leading off with the left-handed-hitting Lenny Dykstra and the switch-hitting Wally Backman (who batted .340 versus right handers but only .192 versus lefties), Davey Johnson shifted Mookie Wilson from left to center and hit him first, followed by the right-handed left fielder Kevin Mitchell. Tim Teufel, a good-hitting, so-so-fielding second baseman, hit seventh. Just like that, New York's feared one-two speed punch was glued to the bench, replaced by a pair of free swingers and a mediocre middle infielder. "Lenny and Wally could've been the MVPs of our team," says Knight. "Without them we were much less dangerous."

Like Knepper, Mets starter Ron Darling—Yale alum and *Jeopardy!* star—also had very little in common with the average ballplayer. Unlike the countless Mets who had married either their high school sweetheart or the hot chick working behind the bar in some minor league dive of a saloon, Darling's bride was Toni O'Reilly, a twenty-seven-year-old Dublin-born model/actress with long legs and sparkling eyes. (Darling did well with women, once even going on a date with Madonna.) That's why when it came to fitting the pitcher with a nickname, Carter had no struggles. "Mr. P—for Mr. Perfect," says Carter. "Not a speck of dirt, not a problem in the world. Ronnie was perfect in every way."

Like much of what Carter says, there is a bit of dry sarcasm here. The Mets loved to bust on Darling, especially the way—on days between starts—he never, ever wore his hat. The reason? Perfect dark hair, nary a strand out of place. Yet Darling was not perfect. Far from it. Despite Davey Johnson's insistence that Darling had grown as a pitcher in '86, he still managed to irk his catchers. "Ronnie thought he was a lot smarter than he really was," says Ed Hearn. "He was a shaker-offer, like he was looking down at you as a catcher. I was like, 'C'mon, man! Throw the pitch!'"

Of the Mets' four All-Star-caliber starters, Darling was most likely to bounce a ball in front of the plate, to the right of the plate, to the left of the plate, or into Carter's groin. Against plodding teams like Atlanta or San Diego, that was fine. But Houston's offense was built on speed. Lanier's game plan was to run like crazy.

With one out in the top of the first, Hatcher singled up the middle;

then, with Denny Walling at the plate, he took a lead the size of a grand piano. After a foul ball and one throw to first, Hatcher took off, barely sliding under Santana's late tag. Walling singled to right on the next pitch, driving in Hatcher with the first run. Davis, the powerful first baseman, followed, and after a Darling wild pitch moved Walling to second, he was plunked by a fastball. When Jose Cruz's single scored Walling, the Astros were up 2–0.

Throughout the year Darling and Davey Johnson had bickered like two rival rappers, and here was a prime example why. Most of Darling's strikes were coming off fouls, and his balls were bouncing inches in front of the plate. It was the type of thing that drove managers to chew Rolaid after Rolaid, and Johnson had downed his fair share. *Dammit,* he often thought to himself, *just throw strikes!* In the second inning Darling again forced the first out, then allowed a base runner, walking Craig Reynolds on 5 pitches. Second baseman Bill Doran followed by hitting a fastball above the right field wall. Darling watched the flight of the ball, turned back toward Carter, and bowed his head. Not only did Houston end the inning with a 4–0 lead, but Knepper was cruising.

"Because we're human, there naturally comes a point in a baseball game when you start thinking about consequences," says Knight. "You're in the playoffs, you're losing by a couple of runs, and you think, 'What happens if we lose this game? What if we go back to Houston in a big hole?' But then you remember the heart of the team you're on. We weren't prepared to lose."

In the bottom of the sixth, with the score still 4–0 and the only noise coming from the passing airplanes, the Mets' fortunes changed. On the fifth pitch of the inning, Mitchell hit a soft chopper that bounced over the head of a leaping Walling at third base. For the first time New York had its leadoff man aboard. The crowd, desperate for any flicker of hope, began to stir. When Hernandez followed with a blooper to center and Carter nubbed an awkward dribbler under the glove of Reynolds at short (driving in Mitchell), Shea Stadium came alive.

Luckily for Knepper, the inning looked as if it was about to become easier. Up to the plate strolled Strawberry, "the black Ted Williams" to many but "the black Paul Zuvella" to Knepper. In his first three years in the league, Strawberry had faced Knepper twenty times, and the results were awful: 2 hits, 9 strikeouts, and just 1 home run. Knepper's method for handling the Straw? Throw offspeed pitch after offspeed pitch. Throw low and inside. Employ long, rhythm-killing delays between pitches. Never, ever throw fastballs over the plate.

Knepper and Strawberry had already squared off twice in Game 3, and twice the slugger had looked impotent, striking out and slapping a soft roller in front of home plate. As he prepared to leave the dugout for his third at-bat, Strawberry was approached by Dykstra, who patted his teammate on the butt and barked, with typical Lenny bluntness, "We need a fuckin' homer, Straw!" That was enough. Knepper's first pitch was an inside fastball that tailed over the plate, and as he cocked, stepped, and swung, Strawberry, along with 55,052 fans, knew the 85-mph pitch would travel a long way. "Sometimes," Strawberry said, "you can just feel it on impact." Unlike most of his 27 homers of the season—routinely mammoth shots that cleared three or four boroughs—this was a line drive over the auxiliary scoreboard. Strawberry abandoned his stoic routine and thrust his left fist into the air. The score now tied at four, Strawberry popped out of the dugout for a deafening curtain call. At last Shea Stadium was a quaking, shaking, electric zoo.

The Astros, though, immediately scored an unearned run off Aguilera to take a 5–4 lead, and when Backman (who replaced Teufel in the top half of the inning) prepared to lead off the bottom of the ninth, he had to get on by any means necessary. "It was my job as pest," he says. On the third pitch from Dave Smith, Backman dragged a bunt up the first base line. Davis charged in, scooped up the ball, and lunged toward Backman, who escaped by scampering several inches to the right of the line. Reaching for the bag, Backman tumbled into a cloud of dirt. First base umpire Dutch Rennert signaled *safe!* Lanier stormed from the dugout. His argument that Backman ran out of bounds and should immediately be ruled out was 100 percent correct—and 100 percent ignored. "I'm not gonna lie: The Astros had a pretty strong case," says Backman. "I just thought it was the best way to get there. Maybe the only way."

Two batters later the game ended. Having spent nearly the whole afternoon squirming on the bench, Dykstra had given up hope of making an impact. Of all the Mets, nobody abhorred watching baseball more than the pint-sized center fielder who knew in his heart that he was the biggest, baddest, toughest player in the world. Now here was his chance. Inserted 2 innings earlier, Dykstra approached the face-off against Smith with a single goal in mind: home run. From the bench Davey Johnson knew what was running through Dykstra's mind, and he hated him for it. All the Mets needed was a soft liner into the outfield for Backman to score the tying run. Heck, if he was ever to settle for singles, Dykstra could hit .320, maybe even .330. It was the classic case of a midget wanting to be a giant, and like Darling's wildness, it burned the manager's stomach. Dykstra hit 8 home runs in 1986. His goal was 500.

This time the runt knew what he was doing. Three months earlier Smith had faced Dykstra in a similar situation—ninth inning, runner on second—and threw him an inside fastball that was smoked off the fence for a game-tying double. "Here," Dykstra said, "I had a real gut feeling he'd throw a forkball." He was right. He swung with all the might he could muster, and as the ball cleared the right field fence, Dykstra danced around the base paths. Upon reaching home he was engulfed by a sea of arms and legs and bodies, the crowd chanting "Len-ny! Len-ny! Len-ny!" From his dugout Ashby watched in heartbroken disbelief. *Why did I call for the forkball, of all pitches?*

"The last time I hit a home run to win a game in the bottom of the ninth," Dykstra said, "was playing Strat-O-Matic against my brother, where you roll the dice. I rolled some good numbers."

So, it turns out, did Bud Harrelson, New York's third-base coach. Elevated by the euphoric high of a hard-fought, last-licks triumph, Harrelson went home that night and made love to his wife, Kim. Nine months later Troy Joseph Harrelson was born.

"Weird, isn't it?" says Harrelson, cracking a smile. "Lenny Dykstra put me in the mood."

———————

In the battle against fear, feigned indifference is the worst weapon. Talking about one's fear often makes things palpable. Confronting one's fear often lessens and/or eliminates the fear altogether. But when one pretends a fear does not exist and acts as if it is no more of an obstacle than a wall of Jell-O, that's when problems start.

On the night of October 12, 1986, the New York Mets were afraid, only nobody would admit it. In a matter of minutes Davey Johnson's team would again face Mike Scott. The Mets spent the preceding hours playing cards, dominoes, and handheld video golf, smoking cigarettes, and taking BP. Yet if the banter seemed upbeat, the inner thoughts were not. New York lost 54 games in the regular season. They had never been rendered completely helpless until the awful 1–0 Game 1 setback to Scott. "It was," says Backman, "a new experience for us."

Instead of focusing on ways to beat Scott, the Mets turned to a new obsession: catching him. In the lion's den that was Shea Stadium, the Astros would no longer be able to send *their* batboy to retrieve all of Scott's scuffed-up, out-of-play baseballs. Instead that duty would fall to the Mets' Mike Rufino, twenty-year-old batboy/Iona College student. Three years earlier Rufino had held the same position with the Yankees, making $5 per hour (not including tips) for a club that, with a few exceptions, offered the pizzazz and personality of a cardboard warehouse. When Charlie Samuels, the Shea Stadium equipment manager, offered Rufino a job across town, there was a tempting appeal to the new location. On a winter day following the '83 season, Rufino bumped into Bobby Valentine, the Mets' third-base coach, and asked his opinion. "Son," Valentine said, "do you want the elevator on the way up or the elevator on the way down?"

As the Mets jumped from sad to respectable to powerful in '84 and '85, Rufino was vindicated for trading in his dark pinstripes for the less glamorous blue and orange. He was leaving behind a stodgy world for whoopee cushions and roller skates. "It would be impossible to say how much more fun it was with the Mets," says Rufino. "The guys treated you with love and respect. Dwight Gooden bought us dinners. Bobby Ojeda made us T-shirts. We were important."

Especially now. Never before had Rufino accepted a greater baseball-related responsibility than in Game 4 when he was instructed by several Met players to retrieve every foul or discarded ball that originated from Scott's hand and return it to a milk crate in the home dugout. The plan was hatched before the game started. New York would gather up a slew of scuffed baseballs and hand them to Feeney, the league president. How could he not see the proof? "People ask if the guys were intimidated by Scott," says Rufino. "I don't think there's much doubt about it." After Ashby's two-run homer off New York starter Sid Fernandez cleared the left field fence in the second inning, the 55,038 fans in attendance had every reason to leave early. The Mets were dead.

Scott went 4⅔ innings before allowing a hit, but that didn't prevent dozens of used baseballs from winding up in the Mets' clutches. Throughout the game a debate raged along the Met bench: Who was responsible, Scott or Houston third baseman Phil Garner? Most Mets agreed with Hearn, who remains convinced that Scott had a small piece of sandpaper glued to his left index finger. "My younger brother, Tom, called me after Game 1 and begged me to look at the videotape of Scott," says Hearn. "When most pitchers rub up a ball, they spin it in their hand to take the sheen off the shine. Scott just rubbed it hard in one place. That's how you scuff."

Ojeda spent much of the evening with his eyes elsewhere. Like a character straight out of *Murder, She Wrote*, he swears by the less obvious theory. "The SOB who was doing it was Phil Garner at third," Ojeda says. "He's a rat. He had this thing in his glove, and when the ball was thrown around, he'd squeeze it and throw it to Scott. I'll go to my grave believing that."

"Is that a silly belief or what?" says Garner. "Completely untrue."

What mattered most was not *who* or *how* but *how often*—as in how often would a scuffed-up baseball find its way into the Mets clubhouse? At first they trickled in: two in the first inning, none in the second. But by the seventh inning Rufino had compiled a collection of seventeen baseballs bearing Oreo cookie–sized bruises, all in the exact same area. "That was the biggest thing," says Rufino, "the spot and the size. Every

suspicious ball had the two consistencies. It wasn't just a coincidence."
During Howard Johnson's pinch-hitting appearance in the eighth, a
baseball was softly fouled into the Mets dugout and the waiting hands
of Teufel. After looking over the ball, Teufel was seen on TV handing it
off to Santana, who pointed to a spot, frowned, and flipped it down to
Ojeda at the other end. Ojeda examined it, smirked in comical disbelief,
and tossed it into the Mike Scott Ball Bin.

When the game ended with a 3–1 Houston victory, New York's players walked into the clubhouse shaking their heads. The once patient, now
spooked Mets were swinging at first and second pitches as if they were
coin-stuffed pinatas. In the bottom of the fifth, with two down and
Knight on first, Santana popped Scott's first offering to Davis for an easy
out. In the bottom of the seventh, Carter and Strawberry each
grounded out on second pitches. In the bottom of the ninth, with Dykstra on third, Carter flew out to center to end the game. How did he work
over a tired Scott? By swinging at the first ball. "I let Scott get way too far
into my head," says Carter. "In that first game, after he struck me out
three times, I hit a little dribbler down the third base line, and I was happy.
I was happy to hit a dribbler! That's pathetic."

In a quiet postgame locker room, one man spoke up. Knight had just
gone 1 for 3 versus Scott, and he was sick and tired of his teammates
whining. "Guys," he said, "this is getting ridiculous. The umpires aren't
gonna do anything about it, so let's stop the stinkin' whining and make
an adjustment. Move up in the box. Start your swing earlier. Just stop
bitching about it, 'cause it ain't working!'"

On the morning of October 13 the members of the New York Mets
woke up to the sound of hell.

On the morning of October 13 the members of the Houston Astros
woke up to the sound of heaven.

The noise was raindrops, covering the New York–New Jersey metropolitan area in a slick coat of game-postponing moisture.

To Houston the delay meant two things. First, that a refreshed Ryan,
not Deshaies, would start Game 5 on October 14. Second, that Scott

would be even more rested and energized for a possible Game 7 in the Astrodome. This was not what the Mets needed.

It didn't help that as the rain was pouring down outside his New York office, inside Feeney was checking over the Mets' collections of allegedly scuffed baseballs and finding nothing. In what would forever be derided as the Dred Scott Decision, the NL president ignored blatant evidence and even suggested it was possible that the baseballs were tampered with *after* reaching the Mets. It was a pathetic moment for a beloved figure. As a young employee of the Giants in the 1940s and 1950s, Feeney urged team management to sign black and Latino players. In his role as NL president, Feeney argued vehemently against the DH and helped install the postseason playoff system. His every move seemed to convey integrity—until now.

Had Feeney ruled the baseballs illegal, Scott would likely have been banned from further playoff participation and Houston's two victories would have been forfeited. It would have required guts. "As far as we know, Mr. Scott is not guilty of this infraction," Feeney said in a written statement. "A man is innocent until proven guilty. However, we will be watching closely the next time he pitches and will take appropriate action if necessary."

Charlie Kerfeld was born to be a Met. On a team of choirboys, Houston's primary right-handed setup man was a tobacco-chewing, beer-swilling badass. At age twenty-three, Kerfeld retained just enough teenager to still lack the self-awareness that makes adults dull. When the Houston media discovered with delight that he wore a Jetsons T-shirt underneath his uniform, the six-foot-six Kerfeld, down 45 pounds from the previous winter's 295, hammed it up for all it was worth. On the mound he broke out a pair of black horn-rimmed sunglasses. Not because they were stylish or intimidating. Just because, well, he was a Kerfeld.

From a publicity standpoint the best thing about Kerfeld was his twenty-four-hour-a-day flapping tongue. "You never knew what Charlie was going to say," says Rob Matwick, the Astros' media relations head, "but he was always available to say it." Kerfeld would expound on anything, even if it was not in his team's best interests. For example, his thoughts on Gary Carter. Kerfeld did not know Carter, and he did not like Carter. "He's always looking for that camera," Kerfeld told a handful of reporters at the start of the series. "I don't think the number of endorsements equal his ability. It's sort of a joke."

In the eighth inning of Game 3, Carter hit a hard grounder to Kerfeld, who caught the ball behind his back and exuberantly pointed it at the Met catcher. From that point on Carter was dying for a chance at retribution. It was one thing to be humbled by Ryan or Knepper or even Scott, three men with lengthy major league careers. But who the heck was Charlie Kerfeld? A twenty-fourth-round pick out of Yavapai Junior College, a man dumped by the Phillies and Mariners, a fatso. "He was a big goofball," says Carter. "I'm just playing the game hard, and he makes those comments. Why?"

With the geriatric Ryan starting Game 5, Kerfeld knew he would be needed. He spent the afternoon on the edge of his bullpen seat, nervously watching Gooden and Ryan in a fascinating battle of new heat versus old heat. This time Gooden was dynamite, holding the Astros to one run over ten innings. In the second, Astros right fielder Kevin Bass led off with a single to center, and Cruz followed with a hit-and-run single of his own, sending Bass to third. When Ashby struck out, Reynolds, the .249-batting left-handed shortstop, came up. On Gooden's first pitch, a curveball, Reynolds hit a lazy bouncer to Backman, who pivoted toward second to start the double play. His toss to Santana was soft, however, and even though Cruz was out at second, Reynolds easily beat the throw to first. Bass crossed home plate, and Houston led, 1–0.

But wait . . .

First base umpire Fred Brocklander paused, then pumped his fist. Reynolds was out. The inning was over, the run nonexistent. A regular New Testament reader, Reynolds rarely had a bad word for umpires. But this was the playoffs. Upon hearing *out,* Reynolds ran toward Brocklander and let loose a string of explosive expletives. "If that play is called correctly, the whole game turns out differently," says Reynolds. "And if the whole game turns out differently, the whole series might turn out differently. He blew the call."

The Astros and Mets exchanged runs in the fifth in a classic pitchers' duel that—obscured by an epic series—history has forgotten. Gooden threw brilliantly. Ryan was even better. Exactly seventeen years after he preserved a Met shutout in the third game of the '69 World Series, Ryan allowed New York just 2 hits over 9 innings, striking out twelve. Days after the game, the Astros' PR staff admitted that Ryan had pitched with a hairline fracture of his left ankle. It was unheard of.

In the tenth inning of a 1–1 game, Kerfeld entered to raucous boos. More than fifty-five thousand Met loyalists saw what he had done to their catcher, and they didn't much care for it. Carter might have been a geek, but he was New York's geek.

For two innings Kerfeld held the Mets at bay while Gooden and Jesse Orosco did the same to the Astros. There was one out in the bottom of the twelfth when Backman drove a bullet toward third that Walling dropped and failed to pick up cleanly. With Hernandez at bat and the speedy Backman on first, Kerfeld threw a ball, a strike, and a pickoff attempt to Davis that bounced past first and into foul territory. Backman scampered to second, forcing an intentional walk for Hernandez to set up a double play. Up came Carter.

Until this point there had been no lousier player in the series. The Kid had gone 1 for 21, an .048 average. Even the most ardent Met loyalists began booing the catcher during Game 5. If it was just bad luck, people would understand. But Carter was being humiliated. "I stunk," he says. "And New York fans don't have much patience for guys who stink." As he approached the plate, a whirlwind of thoughts zipped through Carter's mind. He was thinking about the disrespect of an intentional walk. About the importance of winning this game and closing Houston out before another Scott start. Most of all he was thinking about Charlie Kerfeld showing him the ball in Game 3; about a future Hall of Famer being mocked by a flash-in-the-pan punk.

Kerfeld started Carter with three balls and a called strike. The next three pitches were fouled off. On the eighth offering, a fastball over the heart of the plate, Carter drove a ground ball straight up the middle and into center field. He raised both arms into the air and unleashed a primal scream.

As soon as Backman crossed the plate, handily beating the throw from Hatcher, a giant sigh of relief blew through Shea Stadium.

Win tomorrow's Game 6, and Mike Scott is insignificant.

Win tomorrow's Game 6, and move on to the World Series.

Because the rainout in New York ate away a would-be off-day, the Mets and Astros left Shea Stadium and immediately flew to Houston for the following afternoon's contest. Fatigue, glee, angst, pressure—whatever the cause, this was one of the rare team flights where most of New York's players plopped into seats, pulled down the eye masks, and fell fast asleep.

As the airplane started in its final descent into William P. Hobby Airport, Hernandez and McDowell popped out of two overhead storage compartments, hooting and hollering. Hernandez proceeded to act out a scene from the horror movie *Poltergeist*, only instead of JoBeth Williams, it starred Knepper, the Astros' Game 6 starter. With his teammates laughing hysterically, Hernandez portrayed Knepper nervously waiting for New York's plane to land. When the jet neared touchdown, Hernandez, in his best Knepper/*Poltergeist* voice, uttered the famous line: "*Theeeeeeeeey're baaaaaaaaaaaaack!*"

Confidence was not an issue.

That said, there was a ghostly presence hovering over every move the Mets made. He was big and powerful, and although Mookie Wilson was never sucked into a TV and Rafael Santana never had coffins pop up in his swimming pool, the specter of Mike Scott was very real. "If we don't win Game 6, we face Scott in Game 7," says Knight. "If we face Scott in Game 7, we lose. I hate to say that, but it's true. We don't go to the World Series."

As if New York needed any further reminder of their tormentor, before the game Judge Jon Lindsay, a member of Houston's Harris County Commission, was asked to throw out the ceremonial first pitch. Upon reaching the mound, Lindsay dug into his right pocket and held aloft a square of sandpaper. The crowd of 45,718 burst into a gleeful chant of "Beat New York! Beat New York!"

Warming up in the bullpen, Ojeda was troubled. After pitching a career-high 217⅓ innings in the regular season, he was left with an elbow that was suddenly throbbing. The two cortisone injections he had been given to ease the pain might as well have been Tylenols. Worse than the pain were the pitches. Throwing to bullpen catcher John Gibbons, Ojeda's stuff was as flat as a year-old bottle of Tab. His change-up, normally deceptive, looked like an ordinary slow fastball. His curve had no snap. "It just wasn't happening," he says, "but I didn't want to pull the shoot. I said, 'Gimme the ball, man. I'm gonna go out there. I'm gonna try.' That's the way I was built."

Doran led off the bottom of the first with a slashing single to right, but he was forced at second on Hatcher's grounder. Garner, batting third, took Ojeda to a one-ball, two-strikes count before doubling to the center field wall, scoring Hatcher for a 1–0 advantage. Davis followed with an RBI single to center, and after Bass walked, Cruz arrived at the plate. A sixteen-year veteran, Houston's left fielder had played in 2,189 games without reaching the World Series. Time was getting short. Cruz blooped a change-up down the right field line, in front of a charging Strawberry and behind Teufel and Hernandez. Davis scored to make Houston's lead 3–0, and Bass cruised into third.

Davey Johnson had Aguilera warming up. If Ashby was able to get Houston's fifth hit, Bobby O. would be sent to the showers.

Lanier fancied his team as a boxer going in for the kill. With the dominating Knepper as his starter, the Astros' manager knew he wouldn't need a slew of runs to win. So with New York's infield playing deep, Lanier called for the suicide squeeze.

When Ojeda began his delivery, Bass broke for home. Ashby squared and—*whooosh!*—a fastball zoomed past his bat and into Carter's glove. "I never expected that pitch," says Ashby. "It was the first one he threw me all series." Carter chucked the ball to Knight, who easily tagged out Bass at third. When Ashby lined out to Santana, the inning was over. "It could have been worse," says Ojeda. "And I was determined to bear down and fight."

Knepper, meanwhile, was masterful, keeping the Mets guessing with offspeed junk and an occasional fastball or two. Ojeda, too, found his composure, surrendering one hit over 4 innings. He was replaced by Aguilera in the sixth, and the trend continued. For 3 innings Aguilera limited Houston to one hit and no runs.

Still, the Mets entered the ninth inning in the ultimate pickle: down 3–0, with a hot pitcher on the mound and an unhittable pitcher sharpening his meat-carving knives for the following afternoon. Just in case anyone forgot what was at stake, the Astrodome patrons made it clear with a chant: Mike! Mike! Mike! Mike! "I didn't think we had a chance to come back," Strawberry would later say. "It ran across our minds that we were beaten." To lead off the inning, Davey Johnson followed a hunch and sent up the left-handed Dykstra to bat for Aguilera. It was a risky move, considering two switch hitters (Backman and Howard Johnson) and two right-handed hitters (Elster and Hearn) were available. On a two-strike count Dykstra drove Knepper's slider beyond Hatcher's reach to deep center field, rolling into third with a triple. Wilson followed with a single that glanced off the top of Doran's glove, and New York finally had a run. Knepper forced Mitchell to ground out to third for the first out, but Wilson, who was running on the play, advanced to second.

Watching from the on-deck circle, a simple thought crossed Hernandez's mind: *I'm gonna hit this guy.* Sure, he was 0 for 3, but how many times had Hernandez smelled the blood of a fatigued hurler and pounced? Hundreds? Thousands? Hell, it was what he preached to younger teammates. "Take advantage when the situation arises. Know when you've got the upper hand." With the count one ball, two strikes, Knepper threw a mistake high and over the plate, and New York's first baseman punched a line drive into right center for a double, scoring Wilson and cutting the lead to one. The Astrodome was silent.

Lanier came out to fetch Knepper and replace him with Smith. As the Houston closer warmed up, Carter and Strawberry stood to the side, sizing up a pitcher with impressive stats but less than intimidating stuff.

Smith saved 33 games in '86, utilizing an ordinary fastball and a wicked forkball. "I knew we were going to win that game," says Carter. "We could hit Smith." And frustrate him. Carter worked the count, and on three balls, two strikes, Smith threw a pitch that crossed the corner of the plate. Brocklander, the same umpire who had erroneously ruled Reynolds out at first in Game 5, called ball four. Smith blew up, paced around the mound, sulked, and stared down the ump. Strawberry followed by also walking, and with the bases loaded, Knight patiently took two balls and two borderline strikes. The next pitch appeared to follow the exact same path as the two called strikes, only this time Brocklander ruled it a ball. It was too much for Smith, who screamed, "What the fuck?" from the rubber toward home plate. Even the well-mannered Ashby groaned loudly. "How can two pitches be strikes and a third one, which is even better, be a ball?" Smith said after the game. Knight began jawing at Ashby, who, in turn, advised Knight to shut his face. Brocklander strolled toward the mound to calm everyone down, and shortstop Dickie Thon walked toward home and challenged Knight to a fight. "You yelling at me?" Knight barked.

"Yeah, fuck you!" replied Thon.

"Well," said Knight, "fuck you, too. Go back there and play shortstop!" Standing at the dugout's edge, Davey Johnson used the pause to pop two Excedrins. For the first time in twenty-five years of professional baseball he was suffering a headache during a game.

When things cooled down, Knight drove in Hernandez with a 375-foot sacrifice fly to right center field. The game was tied at three, and Carter and Strawberry had advanced to second and third. Smith intentionally walked Backman, loading the bases for Heep, a pinch hitter. Lost in much of the NLCS hype was the fact that four years earlier Heep had been acquired in exchange for Scott. In his time with New York, Heep became one of baseball's most underrated off-the-bench performers, leading the league with 4 pinch-hit home runs in 1983. Heep, though, was still known mostly as the man who two seasons later was Ryan's four thousandth strikeout victim. Here was the opportunity to change that.

Very few men, Heep would later note, have the honor of hitting with two outs and the bases loaded in the ninth inning, with your team one run away from the World Series. If he succeeded, Heep would be spoken of in New York with the same reverence of such clutch heroes as Brian Doyle, Phil Simms, and Joe Namath. With the count full, Smith threw an inside fastball. Instead of immortality, Heep settled for a cheap half-swing. Strike three, inning over.

By now it was obvious that this was a playoff match for the ages. On the New York bench indifferent chatter was replaced by a quiet, fatigued intensity. The game had been running for just nine innings, but it felt like four months. "It took everything out of me, and I wasn't even in it," says Hearn, the lone Met position player not participating. The Mets handed the ball to McDowell, and the funny man took things seriously. That morning *USA Today* had run a small box that read, "FACT: Roger McDowell was 0–3 with a 4.15 ERA versus Houston this season." Jogging to the mound, it was all McDowell could think of. Over the next 5 innings he allowed no walks and just one hit. So much for statistics.

Houston countered with Smith and long relievers Larry Andersen and Aurelio Lopez to keep New York scoreless through the thirteenth. This was no longer just a baseball game but a battle for survival. Benches were being emptied. Last-resort pitchers such as Houston's Jeff Calhoun and New York's Doug Sisk and Randy Niemann were on red alert.

New York finally broke through in the fourteenth as Backman singled home Strawberry with the go-ahead run. To preserve the agonizing victory, Davey Johnson dialed the bullpen for Orosco. "It was a Rolaids moment," says Johnson. "Roger was our most trusted guy. I gave him the tough assignments, and I gave all the cookies to Jesse." This was no cookie. It would be the left-hander's third appearance in four games, and his fingernails were down to nubs. Throughout most of the game Orosco had been darting back and forth through the long Astrodome visiting dugout, cheering excitedly and rarely sitting down. It had never occurred to him that he might be needed. "By the time Davey says, 'Jesse, get ready,' I'm already breathing hard," Orosco says. "That's a bad sign."

Orosco sucked it up, striking out Doran on a heavy sinker to start things off. That brought up Hatcher, owner of 8 home runs in 591 major league at-bats. On his way to the plate Hatcher spotted a young girl yelling to Doran from above the Astros dugout. "It's okay, Doran! Hatch's gonna hit a home run right now! I promise!" Orosco's first pitch was scorched foul down the left field line. He followed with another strike and three balls. Davey Johnson glanced over at pitching coach Mel Stottlemyre, who was a nervous shade of green. "Mel, it doesn't get any better than this," he said. "Why don't you enjoy it?" On cue, Orosco made the mistake of throwing a dead-fastball hitter a fastball. Oops. Hatcher hammered a high, deep drive down the left field line. It was fair. It was foul. It was fair. It was foul. It was fair. The baseball hit the screen attached to the foul pole—a legal, score-knotting dinger. "You're running around the bases, and you can't even hear yourself think, it's so loud," says Hatcher. "It was like winning the lottery."

Orosco settled down to retire Walling and Davis, and neither team scored in the fifteenth. But eventually fatigue, sloppiness, and dwindling resources did in the Astros. Lopez spent much of the '80s with Detroit as one of baseball's toughest long relievers, but by '86 Señor Smoke was old (thirty-eight) and overweight (235 pounds). Strawberry led off the inning with a high pop fly to center, and when Hatcher mistakenly broke back on the ball, it fell in for a double. An RBI single by Knight gave New York a 5–4 lead. Calhoun entered, walked Backman, threw two wild pitches (the second scoring Knight), and permitted an RBI single to Dykstra, lifting New York's lead to a comfortable 7–4. With the reliable Orosco in the game, it was over. Almost.

Reynolds struck out leading off, and a collective moan emerged from the once-electric crowd. When pinch hitter Davey Lopes walked, there was no stir. When Doran followed with a single, there was a little stir. When Hatcher followed with a single, scoring Lopes, there was a bigger stir. When Walling hit into a fielder's choice, forcing Hatcher out at second, there was another groan.

With two outs and runners on the corners, Davis—the Astros' big bopper—looped a single to center, sending Doran home and moving

Walling to second. Orosco, slowly pacing around the mound, was exhausted. Before he took the field for the sixteenth, Davey Johnson told him, "Jess, I'm gonna win it or lose it with you." These were big words. Even though he had saved 91 games in six seasons with New York, Orosco had never displayed the moxie of an Ojeda or a McDowell. He would get nervous at rough moments and often required a soothing word from Hernandez or Carter. "Davey's belief in me," he says, "meant everything."

With Bass due up, Hernandez, still livid over the pitch Hatcher hit for a home run, called time. Staring at Bass, he jogged over to Orosco, whose hands were quivering and whose eyes were as wide as pancakes. "Jess," he said, "I don't give a fuck what Gary calls. If you throw this guy one fuckin' fastball, I will kill you." Orosco nodded. Bass saw five pitches. All five were sliders. On a three-balls, two-strikes count, Orosco heaved a low slider that snapped perfectly off the plate. Bass stepped, swung, and found nothing but air.

Four hours and forty-two minutes after Knepper began the game by striking out Wilson, the Mets swarmed the field and swallowed Orosco. Mike Scott was named NLCS MVP. New York was going to the World Series.

It was time to destroy an airplane.

Chapter 15

THE PASSION OF BILL BUCKNER

Bill Buckner was not just a great player. He was a champion warrior.

—RAY KNIGHT, Mets third baseman

WHEN WILLIAM JOSEPH BUCKNER debuted as a professional baseball player, he liked to hit things. The year was 1968 (well before "anger management" became something of an American credo), and Buckner was a speedy eighteen-year-old outfielder for Ogden, Utah, of the Pioneer League. Even though he led all players with a .344 batting average, 88 hits, and 8 triples, it wasn't good enough.

When he whiffed or popped out or even hit a dink single that felt somewhat cheap, Buckner often lifted the helmet off his head and slammed it to the ground. At first this made his manager, a portly enthusiast named Tommy Lasorda, happy. The kid had passion, and that was important. But as more and more helmets wound up in Ogden trash cans, the skipper lost his cool. "Buck, no more goddamned helmet slamming!" he yelled. "We can't afford this shit!"

The following afternoon Buckner grounded out to end an inning, then retreated to a secluded spot behind the dugout. Bam! Bam! Bam! The noise was so loud that Lasorda dashed off to see what it was. When he reached Buckner, the rookie's forehead was dripping with blood. He had bashed his head into the concrete wall.

Buckner's helmet, lying on the ground, was in one piece, just as Lasorda had wanted.

For young baseball fans in the mid-1980s who watched Buckner play first base for Boston, it was impossible to envision the feisty adolescent from nearly two decades earlier. With the Red Sox, Buckner did not so much run as hobble. His joints creaked and his bones ached. In 1986, at age thirty-six, Buckner remained a dangerous batter. But when people recalled what he once was . . .

"Bill Buckner was an absolutely terrific athlete," says Knight. "He could run, he could hit to all fields, he played a great defensive outfield. He was an up-and-coming star." So athletic was the Vallejo, California, native that, coming out of Napa High, he was unsure which sport to pursue. On the one hand, he was a two-time All-State wide receiver being chased down by every Pac-10 university. "I was a good receiver because of my mentality," he says. "I would do whatever it takes to get the football, and that makes up for any deficiencies." On the other hand, Buckner's first love was the diamond.

So when the Dodgers offered him a $44,000 contract, Buckner jumped. He became part of what remains the best single-team draft in major league history. Of the seventy-one players that Los Angeles selected in 1968, a startling fourteen—including Buckner, Steve Garvey, Davey Lopes, Ron Cey, Bobby Valentine, Joe Ferguson, Tom Paciorek, and Geoff Zahn—would play for the Dodgers. Yet unlike most of his happy-go-lucky teammates at Ogden, Buckner played with a lionlike furor. Once, during his teenage years, Buckner was part of an amateur team that traveled inside the high-security walls of Vacaville State Prison to take on a squad of inmates. Except for the visitors, everyone affiliated with the game—spectators, ball fetchers, umpires—was doing hard time.

In a key at-bat late in the game, Buckner took a called third strike from the home plate ump. Buckner snapped, walked right up to the umpire's face, and screamed. "I thought he was going to hit him with a bat," Jimmy Buckner, Bill's brother, told Fox Sports. Luckily for Bill, his tirade was ignored.

While playing for Triple A Spokane in 1970, Buckner and Valentine smashed heads in an ugly outfield collision. Both men dropped to the ground, and Buckner left the game with a broken jaw. The Dodgers instructed Spokane's staff to keep Buckner out for five weeks. He missed one game.

"Buck wound up hitting .335," Lasorda told *Sports Illustrated*, "and he learned to spit and swear with his jaw wired shut."

From the end of the 1970 season through 1974, Buckner started in the outfield and thrilled Dodger fans with an uncommon combination of bat control, speed, defense, and aggressiveness. He was the ideal number 2 hitter behind Lopes, who had since developed into one of baseball's most dangerous base stealers. So nifty was Buckner with the bat that Walter Alston, the Dodgers' manager, would have him take two strikes so Lopes could swipe second. He trusted him to hit behind in the count.

Impressed by the way Lopes could slide into a bag then—SNAP!— pop back up in a millisecond, Buckner copied his base-stealing technique, which involved earlier extension of the lead leg. While attempting to swipe second against San Francisco in a game on April 18, 1975, Buckner began his new-style slide a tad late. His body continued forward, but his left foot caught under the bag. The result was ugly: Buckner writhing in pain on the ground, his ankle severely sprained.

He returned after a month-long stint on the DL, but the running-diving-graceful Bill Buckner was, at age twenty-five, gone. After the '75 season he had two surgeries, one to remove a tendon in his ankle and the other to remove bone chips. Before and after every contest Buckner spent hours icing down his ankles, partly to reduce the swelling, partly to numb the pain. Long after most teammates departed, Buckner would be alone in the dark clubhouse, legs draped over a table and in a bucket of arctic water. In November 1976, while having yet another surgery performed on his left ankle, Buckner suffered a staph infection that made the pain even worse.

For the Dodgers it was an erstwhile future star turned useless. Steve Garvey had established himself as the league's top first baseman, and Buckner was no longer capable of regularly playing the outfield. On January 11, 1977, Los Angeles traded Buckner, along with shortstop Ivan DeJesus and pitcher Jeff Albert, to the Cubs for outfielder Rick Monday and pitcher Mike Garman. "You think you're part of something special, and then it's pulled out from under you," Buckner says. "Being traded for the first time was a very, very hurtful experience."

In one of the great mistakes of his career, Buckner converted pain into stubbornness. When his new first baseman reported to spring training walking with a cane and unable to participate in the exhibitions, Cubs GM Bob Kennedy asked the National League to annul the deal, calling Buckner "damaged goods." Although it was true, this enraged Buckner. In Vero Beach, Florida, home of the Dodgers spring training, Lasorda was raving over Monday, who was roping balls left and right. Lord knows Bill Buckner was not going to be made a fool of by his replacement. He played in 122 games with the Cubs in 1977, a feat that deserves to be immortalized in the Courage Hall of Fame. He hit .284, drove in 60 runs, and stole 7 bases—with a pronounced limp that only got worse as the summer turned to fall. In late August the Dodgers went to Wrigley Field for a series that meant little to the floundering Cubs and everything to Buckner. In the first game, a 6–2 Chicago triumph, Buckner drove in 5 runs with 2 homers and a pair of singles. The next day he had 3 more hits and a home run in another win. "Buckner was pretty tough on his daddy," Chicago manager Herman Franks said with a chuckle in reference to Lasorda. "The guy's one feisty SOB."

Feistiness and intelligence do not always coincide. Buckner nearly ruined his career. The gimpy left ankle caused him to put excessive weight on his right leg, which led to a series of debilitating injuries. In 1977 alone, Buckner pulled both hamstrings, both quads, and both groins. By season's end he was on his feet only when he had to be; that is, when he was on a baseball field.

Over the next half-decade Buckner searched for good health. He tried acupuncture, anti-inflammatories, leg-numbing spinal injections, enzyme beverages, heat wraps, and mystical ointments. In 1978 a fan sent Buckner a booklet on the lower-body benefits of ballet. Within a month he was enrolled in a class. "I wanted to strengthen the back of my legs," he says. "And I didn't have to wear a tutu." The ensuing year the Cubs acquired outfielder Ken Henderson from the Reds, and he brought along yet another healing idea. In the late '70s the big kick was DMSO (dimethyl sulfoxide), a colorless liquid derived from Lignin, the natural material that bonds together the cells of trees. It was primarily used as a horse medication. Henderson, who at age thirty-three had his own problems with body breakdown, raved enough about DMSO's impact as a painkiller that Buckner gave it a try. "It was br*uuuuuu*tal," Buckner says. "It made your whole body stink like garlic, and it did very little to help."

The best Buckner could do was grit his teeth, tie the shoelaces extra tight, and play through the pain. Miraculously, he hit above .300 in four of his seven full seasons with the Cubs, even winning the 1980 batting crown. Buckner was now a spray-hitting machine who compensated for poor health by studying the league's opposing pitchers. He was grouped with Rod Carew, Bill Madlock, and Pete Rose as baseball's toughest outs. "My philosophy on hitting changed," he says. "It was trying to produce runs, not just trying to get on." What didn't alter was the Buckner intensity. In the sixth inning of an 8–2 loss at San Diego in 1982, he believed that Padres starter Tim Lollar had intentionally tried to hit him with a pitch. Buckner asked Cubs reliever Dan Larson to retaliate, and when he did so, Chicago manager Lee Elia stormed out of the dugout with a reprimand. At inning's end Buckner grabbed his skipper by the collar and threw a wild punch. For a player who prided himself on following the game's unofficial eye-for-an-eye code of justice, not protecting your own was akin to treason.

In a game at Montreal one month later, Buckner smashed his bat into the ground and accidentally broke the mask of Gary Carter, then the Expos catcher. When the teams met again at Wrigley, it was retribution time. Following a Buckner single, Carter picked up the left-behind bat and cracked it across home plate. The next inning, as Carter rounded first after flying out, the two adversaries bumped shoulders. Punches were exchanged, and both benches emptied.

"Gary irritated you as an opponent, so he wasn't the worst guy to brawl with," Buckner says. "But, looking back, the fights were kind of stupid."

By the end of the 1983 season, Buckner was no longer Chicago's model of the ideal first baseman. His .280 average was the lowest in eight years, and his thirteen errors at first tied for the league lead. The position was becoming all about power, and with just 16 home runs, power wasn't Buckner's game. Before every game Buckner would ice both knees, then cake his entire body with Red Hot, a muscle-loosening gel with a thousand times the burn (and odor) of Ben-Gay.

Upon reporting for the '84 season, Buckner was crushed to find that manager Jim Frey had handed the first base job to Leon (Bull) Durham, a powerful twenty-six-year-old. When the Boston Red Sox inquired about Buckner's availability, a trade didn't take long. On May 25 he was sent to Beantown in exchange for pitcher Dennis Eckersley and Mike Brumley, a minor league outfielder.

Nobody was better suited to Boston, a town of blue-collar diehards where baseball is as vital to living as oxygen and the Catholic Church. The Sox were eternal underdogs, and so was Buckner. He still limped, and to the Red Sox Nation this was more endearing than debilitating. "He was a hard-nosed, fierce warrior," says Lou Gorman, the Red Sox GM. "Most guys wouldn't have played 2 games with the injuries he had, but Buck refused to sit down."

Buckner was reborn. At the conclusion of the '84 season, during which he hit .278 with 11 homers and 66 RBIs in 114 games with the Red Sox, Buckner began working with Boston hitting coach Walt

Hriniak, who told his pupil, "If you'll shift your weight, you can hit homers." In fourteen major league seasons he had never hit more than sixteen balls out of the park or driven in more than 75 runs. The next year, playing in 162 games for the first time, he finished with a .299 average, 16 homers, and 110 RBIs, and then followed that up with an even better '86 (18 home runs, 102 RBIs). "For a while I felt like a kid again," Buckner says. "We were winning, I was relatively healthy. But then . . ."

The roof caved in. Midway through '86, Buckner's body broke down like a '58 Edsel. He batted just .267, and before every game he could be spotted in the trainer's room with even more packaging than usual—ice taped to his ankles, to his Achilles tendon, to his lower back, to his left elbow, to his shoulders. The left ankle he had injured eleven years earlier now throbbed like a transplanted heart.

On September 27 he caught the final out in a 2–0 win over Toronto to clinch the AL East title. Buckner squeezed the ball as if he were trying to mash every ounce of pulp from an orange. It had been twelve years since he last reached the playoffs with Los Angeles, and Bill Buckner wanted to savor the moment.

Chapter 16

BOSTON AND NEW YORK

If you listen to the experts, there's no reason for us to
show up. The Mets have it won.

—RED SOX MANAGER JOHN MCNAMARA,
before Game 1 of the World Series

IN HIS SPACIOUS OFFICE on the first floor of City Hall, Edward I.
Koch displayed very few—as he would say—tchotchkes. New York
City's mayor wasn't the type of person who had to keep every picture,
key chain, and Playbill that came his way. His was a startlingly clean
room, one of dust-free desks and blank walls.

As a result the man whose bald head and salty speech had become
as emblematic of the city as the Statue of Liberty offered nary a hint
that his town was home to not one but two major league baseball
teams. "When it comes to sports," the unathletic Koch once said, "I
have no opinion." This was hardly an exaggeration. On the invitation
of Nelson Doubleday, the co-owner of the Mets, Koch attended the
team's April 14 home opener against St. Louis, during which he was
introduced to the crowd of 47,752 as "New York's biggest baseball

fan." Laughably, New York's biggest baseball fan left after the first inning.

Yet the mayor knew big when he saw it, and this World Series was big. Koch was as much self-promoter as politician. Within the past two years he had made cameo appearances in movies (*The Muppets Take Manhattan*) and music videos (Ricky Skaggs' *Country Boy*), and his autobiography, *Mayor*, had soared to the top of the *New York Times* best-seller list. When the Mets asked him to attend a team-hosted World Series party at Pier 59 on the Hudson River, the mayor balked—until he learned the guest list included everyone from Glenn Close and Carly Simon to Hal Linden and Chita Rivera.

To the mayor, Boston-New York was just too good. True, he wouldn't have been able to distinguish between Jim Rice and Jerry Rice or a bowl of Rice-A-Roni. But as a self-proclaimed man of the people, Koch was aware that New Yorkers viewed Bostonians as effete losers and that Bostonians saw New Yorkers as Philistines. This was too easy. On the morning after the series matchup was set, Koch placed a phone call to Boston mayor Ray Flynn, and the two men bet apples and corned beef sandwiches against baked beans and New England clam chowder. They also agreed that the loser would fly the other team's flag above City Hall. "Even if you sent a fine corned beef sandwich to Boston," Koch quipped to *Newsday*, "they wouldn't appreciate it. But they'll never know. We're going to win."

In spite of his status as an unequivocal baseball moron, Koch was correct—this was no ordinary World Series. More than eleven hundred members of the news media were accredited, easily an event record. From the beginning of the playoffs, most experts agreed that the other prospective matchups, Houston-California or Houston-Boston or New York–California, just didn't have the zest of a Mets–Red Sox clash. As *Sports Illustrated* wrote:

"A Mets–Red Sox confrontation would be near-perfect theatre. It would be the first time since Fenway Park's inaugural season, 75 years ago, that a team named Boston met a team named New York in the Fall Classic. . . . It would raise the possibility of the Red Sox' first world championship since Babe Ruth pitched for them. It would bring together America's Sparta and Athens, and pull the men of letters, music and history out of the woods."

This was a World Series not just of fortune but of destiny (an over-used word but in this case appropriate). As stirring as New York's anti-Scott assault was in the triumph over Houston, nothing could match the dramatics of the Red Sox playoff triumph. Against California, Boston was out-pitched, out-hit, and out-managed for most of the first four contests, meekly falling behind three games to one. On the afternoon of October 12, the Angels appeared all but certain to reach the franchise's first World Series. Playing in front of a frenzied home crowd of 64,223, California led 5–2 heading into the ninth inning of Game 5. Even when Boston DH Don Baylor homered to cut the score to 5–4 with one out, California was still in control. Witt forced Dwight Evans, the Red Sox right fielder, to pop out to third, and now Angels manager Gene Mauch was minutes away from reaching the first World Series of his thirty-five-year major league career. As he stood on the top step of the dugout, DH Reggie Jackson by his side, Mauch reflected on three and a half decades of unfulfilled promise, of seasons that began with hope and died with horror. When reliever Gary Lucas plunked Red Sox catcher Rich Ged-man, putting the tying run on base, the manager refused to show dis-tress. He brought in closer Donnie Moore, whose 52 saves over the past two seasons established him as a good-as-done door slammer.

There was only one problem: Bothered by a chronic pain in his right shoulder throughout the season, Moore had taken a cortisone shot the night before the game. Generally, anywhere from thirty to fifty hours is required to recover from the injection's discomfort. Moore was pitching on perhaps twenty.

Moore's first pitch to Red Sox center fielder Dave Henderson was a fastball, for a called strike. The second pitch, also a fastball, was swung through. Strike two. Following two balls, Henderson fouled off a pair of pitches. Figuring the hitter was looking for a dead fastball, catcher Bob

Boone signaled for a splitter. Henderson launched the ball over the left center field wall for a home run, delivering the Sox a shocking 6–5 lead. Thousands of fans instantly went from standing on their feet, screaming and high-fiving, to mournful silence. Although the Angels battled back to tie, their mojo was officially crushed. The Red Sox won 7–6 in 11 innings, then returned to Boston and triumphed in two routs.

The Red Sox were in the World Series. Unlike fans in New York City, which is to baseball championships what Rome is to crucifixes, the stench of repeated failure clung to Bostonians like a million pounds of spoiled scrod. The Red Sox last captured the championship in 1918 when their ace left-hander was the hard-throwing George Herman Ruth. But when Harry Frazee, Boston's financially troubled owner, sold the Babe to the Yankees for $120,000 in December 1919, everything soured. As John Kuenster, the longtime *Baseball Digest* editor, wrote of the Sox in his book, *Heartbreakers,* "There was a longing for a soul-satisfying triumph that had gone unfulfilled so many times in the past."

Three days after they thumped California 8–1 at Fenway Park to win the American League pennant, the Red Sox were scheduled to face the Mets in Game 1 at Shea Stadium. Manager John McNamara's club could have used a month to recover from the emotional and physical tolls taken by a grueling ALCS. Clemens, the team's twenty-four-year-old ace, was suffering from an energy-sapping flu that had him applying ice packs to his face. Third baseman Wade Boggs, the American League batting champ with a .357 mark, was hampered by aches in his ankle, hamstring, and knee. Tom Seaver, the legendary Met acquired by the Red Sox to add wisdom and stability, was on the inactive list with partially torn cartilage in his right knee (thus killing a great story line). But the worst was Buckner. While beating out a slow grounder to short in Game 7 of the ALCS, Buckner had strained his right Achilles' tendon, leaving him unable to walk. On the night of the injury Buckner, already looking toward the World Series, had Red Sox team physician Arthur Pappas inject the tendon with a cortisone shot. Then the first baseman did something revolutionary to add support. Instead of wearing his normal spikes, Buckner had Nike send him by overnight express a pair of black high-tops straight out of the Bronko Nagurski Old School Museum. "Those shoes," wrote *Boston Globe* columnist Michael Madden, "looked pre-Crustacean, prehistoric, pre–night ball and not too pretty. There can be no vacillating in the World Series; truth must be told. Bill Buckner's shoes look ghastly on a baseball player."

The Mets had their own issues. On the morning before the opening game, Davey Johnson woke up at 6 o'clock to drive to the Meadow Brook Country Club where he, Bill Robinson, and Greg Pavlick gathered for eighteen holes of relaxation. Throughout the regular season Johnson often retreated to the links to escape the pressures of managing in New York. When he was at the ballpark, his mind was on baseball. When he was home, his mind was on family. When he was on the greens, his mind was on golf. It was a not-so-secret key to surviving. Those who live base-ball 24-7-365 don't live very long.

Yet one day before the start of his first World Series as a manager, Johnson's mind centered on the game. Ever since McNamara announced that left-hander Bruce Hurst would oppose Ron Darling as the Red Sox Game 1 starter, Johnson had gone back and forth on who should play second base.

When Backman batted second in the New York lineup, there was an electric juice to the Mets that Teufel could never provide. Backman was a hustler, a gamer. Having nurtured Backman from Triple A to New York, Johnson loved the second baseman as he did his own son. *If only,* the Met skipper thought to himself, *Wally could hit lefties.* Then again, how much better was Teufel? When Cashen made the trade with Minnesota, he assured the skeptical Johnson that a hole had been filled. "Tim Teufel has the power to hit 20 to 25 home runs," Cashen told his manager. "And he'll drive the ball against left-handers." But at the close of the '86 regular season, Teufel, with a .247 average, 4 home runs, and 31 RBIs, was a disappointment.

In the end it came down to Johnson's most trusted assistant: computer-generated logic. Based on his dynamic series against Houston, during which he hit .304, Johnson decided to let Dykstra, a left-handed hitter, start against Hurst. With Wilson leading off and Dykstra batting second, there was a greater need lower in the lineup for pop rather than speed. Though ordinary, Teufel remained more likely to slug a ball over the fence. On the sixteenth hole Johnson made up his mind: Teufel would play second base.

When Tim Teufel learned from Johnson that he would be starting Game 1 of the World Series, his reaction was simple: "Okay, Skip." In the midst of the Mets' oft-spastic clubhouse, Teufel was a firm believer in keeping things on an even keel. If he ever whooped or hollered, it was only because McDowell placed something squirmy in his jockstrap. "Never get too high, never get too low," he says. "It catches up with you."

Although New York projected a brash front, twenty-two of its twenty-four players had never before appeared in a Fall Classic. In a way that explains the explosive flight back from Houston when the Mets momentarily forgot that there was still one more step to take. "We had a big strut," says Ojeda, "but there was a lot of insecurity behind it." With good reason. Game 1 was being played in front of 55,076 live spectators, and the Mets looked pathetic. Unlike Scott, whose splitter burst here, there, and everywhere at sickening velocities, Hurst utilized a nasty forkball and a mean, late-breaking curveball that helped him win five straight September starts. Hurst mesmerized and frustrated New York's lineup, holding the team to 4 hits in 8 innings. Part of his success was due to a crafty veteran with a game plan. But much of the Mets' futility was a product of overanxious excitement. Even veterans like Hernandez, Knight, and Wilson seemed jittery on the sport's biggest stage.

Teufel, though, did not. He scorched a single to left in the second inning, then hit another one in the seventh. Defensively, he cleanly handled the one ball hit his way as Darling battled Hurst pitch for pitch, holding Boston scoreless through the first 6 innings.

The top of the seventh began roughly for New York. Left fielder Jim Rice led off with a walk and advanced to second on a wild pitch to right fielder Dwight Evans. When Evans grounded back to the mound, Rice was held at second and things appeared safe. Gedman, the powerful yet inconsistent catcher, came up. Although Darling was unfamiliar with the Boston lineup, here was a recognizable face. In the late 1970s when he was blooming as a pitcher for St. John's High School in Worcester, Massachusetts, Darling's team regularly squared off against crosstown rival St. Peter's, which won the '77 state championship behind a burly pitcher–first baseman named Gedman. "If anyone knew how to hit me," says Darling, "it was Rich." Not tonight. On the first pitch Gedman bounced an innocent grounder directly toward Teufel, who casually positioned his body to make the play. "As soon as he hit it," says Darling, "I thought, '*Wheeeew*, I'm out of this mess.'" At the last possible second Teufel's upper body jerked in anticipation of a high hop. *Pfffft*. The ball rolled under his glove, through his legs, and into right field. Rice scored the game's only run as an agonized Teufel raised his head to the sky. *Why? Why?* The Red Sox won, 1–0. "I don't know if I saw Tim Teufel miss a ground ball the entire year," says Knight. "He had the softest hands on our team."

Teufel slinked into the Mets' clubhouse, where he was attacked by an army of reporters. What began as his worst moment ended as one of his finest. Instead of hiding in the showers, Teufel fielded questions for forty-five minutes, seven times being asked the same thing: "Tim, what happened on that play?" Once, when a writer wanted to know what was wrong with New York's offense, Teufel declined to answer. "You could probably ask those questions of somebody else," he said. "I'll just field the error questions right now."

As he talked, Teufel ran a hand through his hair and covered his reddened eyes. "You get an error like that," he said, "and it's going to stick with you." He refused to budge until every journalist was done—not just the beat writers he had come to know, but everyone. "It was heartrending," he says. "When you have to stand there and know we lost because of my mess-up . . . just the worst."

Had he listened to talk radio on his fifty-minute drive to Greenwich, Connecticut, that night, Teufel would have heard every entry from the Book of Insults. In fact, as he was driving, editors in the newsroom of the *Daily News* were anointing him the Mets' number 1 goat for the following morning's paper. Upon arriving home, Teufel walked into the room of his two-month-old son, Shawn. "It made me feel better," says Teufel. "In my house I was still loved." A few minutes later Teufel received a phone call from Knight. "Teuf, it's no big deal," he said. "We've probably got five or six more games against these guys. So don't let it bother you."

It was like asking a high school kid not to mind the KICK ME sign stuck to his back for six periods. Teufel felt humiliated. Unless the Mets bounced back, he was doomed to be remembered for a single gaffe.

In the early evening before Game 2, several Mets, including Teufel, attended Sunday chapel in the empty Shea Stadium locker room once used by the New York Jets. According to the *Post*, Father Dan Murphy, the team chaplain and the pastor at Our Lady of Help of Christians in Bay Ridge, Brooklyn, assured the players that they were in good hands. "God is with us," he said in his sermon. "I can tell you, none of us will be here next week because we'll all be celebrating. But in life you win and you lose. Some days you're Bruce Hurst and some days you're Timmy Teufel."

Ouch.

In World Series history one would be hard-pressed to find a pitching matchup with the buildup and anticipation of Game 2: Dwight Gooden versus Roger Clemens. Oh, there had been some sizzlers back in the day: Philadelphia's Chief Bender versus Rube Marquard of the Giants in 1913. Detroit's Denny McClain versus the Cardinals' Bob Gibson in 1968. Oakland's Catfish Hunter versus the Mets' Tom Seaver in 1973.

Yet it was 1986, and the World Series was not only being played by teams in two of the game's top five media markets but it was receiving spectacular ratings. (A startling 65 million fans watched Game 2.) The buzz for Gooden versus Clemens transcended sport and turned into *an event*. It was good versus bad. It was black versus white. It was R&B versus country music. It was New York versus Boston. Because Shea

Stadium's fifty-five thousand seats were sold out, many fans brought barbecues and portable TVs to the parking lot, just to be close to history.

While the fear-evoking Gooden was a statistical memory, he still had the reputation as the most dominant pitcher in the National League. Much of this was due to the power of Madison Avenue, which transformed Dr. K into a brand and made Gooden infinitely greater in legend than modern-day reality. Yet whether New Yorkers cared to accept it or not, by the conclusion of the regular season it was clear the 24-year-old Clemens had replaced Gooden as baseball's top young pitcher. "The Rocket" was phenomenal, compiling a 24–4 record, striking out a league-best 238 in 254 innings, and winning both the Cy Young and MVP trophies. His defining moment came on April 29 against Seattle when he set a major league record with 20 strikeouts over 9 innings. "I watched perfect games by Catfish Hunter and Mike Witt," McNamara told *Sports Illustrated*, "but this was the most awesome performance I've ever seen."

In the days leading up to the World Series, Cashen's head throbbed as he thought of the Red Sox ace. Five years earlier when Clemens was concluding his sophomore season at San Jacinto Junior College, the Mets had selected him as their twelfth pick in the June amateur draft. While deciding between turning pro and accepting a scholarship to the University of Texas, Clemens worked out for manager Joe Torre and pitching coach Bob Gibson, the Hall of Famer to whom Clemens is often compared. The Rocket was understandably nervous, and his performance was less than noteworthy. Gibson was impressed but not wowed by the youngster's minimal assortment of pitches (fastball-curve) and advised Cashen not to waste too much of the organization's money on someone he expected would struggle. The Mets offered Clemens $25,000, which was quickly rejected. "Clemens and Gooden!" Cashen would mumble in anger. "Imagine that . . . Clemens *and* Gooden."

Like many grand theatrical events, the product fell woefully short of the anticipation. Clemens pitched terribly, Gooden brutally. The Doctor was hammered for 3 runs in the third inning, then surrendered homers to Dave Henderson and Dwight Evans in the fourth and fifth, respectively. As in the games against Houston, Gooden seemed jittery—touching, then pausing, then wiping, then tugging. By the time he left, the Red Sox had pounded Gooden for 8 hits and 6 runs over 5 innings. Clemens was only slightly better. New York scored 2 runs in the bottom of the third to cut Boston's lead to 3–2, and over $4\frac{1}{3}$ innings The Rocket walked 4 and allowed 3 runs.

Fortunately for the Red Sox, the Mets were a mess. Five pitchers—Gooden, Aguilera, Orosco, Fernandez, and Sisk—teamed up to permit 18 hits, 9 runs and 4 walks, giving Boston a 9–3 romp on a day when Clemens didn't have his best stuff. It was a devastating blow to the Mets and particularly for Davey Johnson. If his club lost the Series, Johnson's legacy would be Game 2 when, trailing 4–2 in the bottom of the fourth, he had a chance to bounce back. With Heep on second, Santana on first, and 2 outs, Johnson allowed Gooden, clearly off his game, to hit for himself. It was typical Johnson, and it bit him in the rear. As Mazzilli and Wilson, the Mets' potential pinch hitters, watched from the bench, Gooden softly grounded out to Buckner to end the inning. For the first time all night Shea Stadium's denizens booed. The noise was aimed straight at the dugout.

If the loss wasn't enough of a downer, it was accompanied by the uncharacteristically selfish rants of Knight, who became enraged when he learned that Howard Johnson would start at third. It was the manager's effort to shake up a struggling lineup (Heep replaced Wilson in left as well), and it burned Knight, whose parents, Charlie and Jessie Knight, had taken the train all the way from Albany, Georgia, to watch their son. Upon entering the clubhouse and reading the lineup card, Knight went to his locker and sat in silence. When he spotted Davey Johnson alone during BP, Knight went off. "You're making a mistake!" he said. "You really are! And I hate you for it. I truly hate you for it! I love you, but I hate you!" Knight proceeded to fill in the media, an inappropriate rant at an inappropriate time. "Here we are playing in the World Series," says Carter, "and Ray's thinking of himself. It was unfortunate."

"I'd like to have seen Gary's reaction if Davey had decided to start Ed Hearn," counters Knight. "It had nothing to do with selfishness. I was a better player than Hojo at that time, and I wanted to win the World Series."

Down 2 games, heading to Boston, the team was demoralized and snippy. The wheels were falling off the Mets' Destiny Express. It would take the spirit of revenge to make things right—a spirit embodied by one angry man.

Chapter 17

REVENGE

I would have rather eaten shit than lose to the Red Sox.

—BOBBY OJEDA, Mets pitcher

ON AUGUST 1, 1985, two hours before an evening game against the White Sox at Fenway Park, twenty-five members of the Boston Red Sox held a closed-door team meeting to debate the pros and cons of a potential players strike. One by one the team's veterans defended Haywood Sullivan and Jean Yawkey, the Red Sox owners, who fancied themselves the heads of a big, happy family. "I've been here for more than ten years," Dwight Evans said, "and they have our best interests at heart." As other old-timers nodded in agreement, one of the club's least popular members shook his head, a look of disbelief crossing his face. When it came time for him to speak, Bobby Ojeda held nothing back.

"You know, fuck the owners!" he said. "The owners don't give a fuck about us! I don't care what you say. They're gonna try and pay us as little as they can. Yeah, if you're older, you don't wanna miss a paycheck being on strike. But I'm young, and I say fuck 'em!"

When the gathering ended, Ojeda was confronted by several furious teammates, one of whom cornered the pitcher and said, "That's the stupidest thing I've ever heard."

"Fuck you," countered Ojeda. "And fuck your dumb-ass opinion."

Within a couple of hours word of the pitcher's uprising leaked back to the front office. Three months later the Red Sox pulled a blockbuster trade, sending Ojeda to the Mets in exchange for pitchers Calvin Schiraldi and Wes Gardner as well as two minor-leaguers. Officially, Boston loved Schiraldi's potential. Unofficially, Ojeda was a cancer. "I hated it in Boston," he says. "I didn't like the ownership, I didn't like John McNamara, I didn't particularly like Bill Buckner and those guys. They weren't my friends. And they didn't like me, either. It was mutual."

Upon arriving in New York, Ojeda found himself reborn. The pitcher had first visited the city for a Red Sox–Yankees series as a rookie in 1980, and he immediately fell in love. The catalyst? A swindling. On the morning before a game, Ojeda and Hurst were touring Manhattan when they stumbled upon a sidewalk three-card monte table. Hurst, hailing from the buzzing metropolis of St. George, Utah, jumped right in, excitedly pulling out a $100 bill in anticipation of an easy victory. As the card Hurst picked (predictably) turned out a dud, Ojeda burst into laughter. "I was like, 'I dig this place,'" he says. "'I dig the style.'" Six years later nothing had changed. Ojeda fit in perfectly with the screw-the-world Mets and their ragamuffin cast, and, more important, his 18–5 record and 2.57 ERA made him the top starter on baseball's top staff. When the Red Sox beat California to advance to the World Series, Ojeda was itching for revenge.

On the morning after Game 2, the Mets were scheduled to meet at Shea Stadium, then catch an 11 A.M. Eastern Airlines charter flight to Boston, and, upon arrival, head directly for Fenway. That plan changed when Davey Johnson took a long look at his battered troops. Johnson's greatest strength as a manager was understanding his players' psyche, and here was a perfect example. "Listen, men. When we get to Boston, the buses are supposed to meet us and take us to the stadium," he announced from the front of the plane. "Forget all that. No workout, no nothing. Go have yourselves a good time. Do whatever you need to." The words were met with applause. In a World Series filled with questionable strategy, the decision would go down as a masterpiece. The Mets had already been to Fenway for a charity exhibition game in early September, so Johnson felt his men were familiar enough with the dimensions. At the same time the Red Sox were slogging through their workouts and being swarmed by the media, the Mets were sleeping and watching TV. "To me that was the turning point," says Carter. "My wife and I went to the hotel, we took a nap, we ordered room service, and then we took another nap. When I came back the next day, I felt refreshed." The only player required at the stadium for media duties was Ojeda, who arrived, sat at a table for the standard pre-start press conference, and lied his head off. "To me this is just another game," he said with a straight face. "That's how I'm approaching it. There's nothing personal."

Naturally there was everything personal. Upon returning to the Sheraton from dinner that night, Ojeda was standing by the hotel elevator bank when he bumped into Haywood Sullivan and John Harrington, Boston's chief negotiator. The two men were laughing and puffing on thick cigars. "Hey, Bobby, good luck tomorrow," Sullivan said with a sly smile. It made Ojeda want to vomit. "I could see them thinking, 'This thing's over. You're gonna get lit up tomorrow night,'" he says. "I didn't like Haywood, and I didn't like Harrington, either. They were happy, and life couldn't be better for them, and they were about to break the Red Sox jinx. They're giggling away, and I'm thinking, *We'll see, you fuckin' douche bags. We'll fuckin' see.*"

Payback was sweet. Ojeda gave the performance of a lifetime, holding the Red Sox to one run and five hits over seven innings in the Mets' 7–1 trouncing. Equally gratifying was the drubbing New York handed Dennis (Oil Can) Boyd, the loudmouthed right-hander who, in his pregame press conference, questioned his opponent's strategy and derided its vaunted lineup. "Being down 2–0 and not checking out our ballpark, that doesn't show us too much respect," he said. "Them skipping a workout has to be to our advantage."

Boyd continued: "When I first looked at the Mets, I saw they had good power in the middle. But I feel I can master those guys." Boyd's boasts infuriated the Mets players, who considered Boyd a mediocre arm with a few loose screws. Earlier in the season Boyd engaged in a first-class meltdown when, after learning that he was not selected to the All-Star team, he charged into the Red Sox clubhouse, cursed out McNamara, then ripped off his uniform and drove off. Boyd made eight of the next thirteen front pages of the tabloid *Boston Herald*, and he was suspended for three days. The word was officially out: Oil Can was a live wire.

Just in case any Mets missed the BOYD IS BONKERS news flash, they received a prompt reminder. Before the game Backman and Hernandez were standing along the Fenway third base line, chatting with Rangers outfielder Tom Paciorek, a former New York teammate attending the series as a commentator. Paciorek knew Boyd well, and his advice was sound: "When you guys start the game, just keep screaming shit at Oil Can from the dugout, because he's got rabbit ears," Paciorek said. "He hears everything, and it really gets him frustrated. He'll start hanging shit, and then he'll start looking at you. He'll point at you when he strikes someone out. If that happens, you've got him."

Hernandez didn't have to be told twice. As soon as Boyd strolled to the mound to start his warmup pitches, the assault began. The players kneeled on towels lined up in front of the dugout's top step, just to be as close as possible. "Hey, Shit Can! Is that all you've got!? C'mon, throw harder than that, you pussy! Hey, Shit Can! You're nothing!"

On the third pitch of the game Dykstra hit Boyd's knee-high slider into the right field stands, prompting a chorus of "Shit Can! Shit Can!" from the New York dugout. Backman followed with a single to right (Boyd pounded the rosin bag), Hernandez singled to left center (Boyd paced around the mound), and Carter belted an RBI double, making the score 2–0 (Boyd glared toward the New York dugout). After Strawberry struck out for the seventeenth time in 29 postseason at-bats, a play unfolded that defined Boston's laughable evening. With Hernandez on third and Carter on second, Knight hit a grounder to third base, where

Boggs fielded the ball and threw home. As Hernandez was caught in a rundown between Boggs and Gedman, Carter broke for third. Hernandez then returned to third as well, stepping safely onto the base at the same time Carter dashed back for second. Boggs threw to shortstop Spike Owen, and Hernandez broke off third again, momentarily distracting Owen. Carter slid into second, Hernandez stepped on third, and everyone was safe. Heep's single to center drove in two more runs on the path to Romp Central.

"That game was the most proud I'd ever been on a baseball field," says Ojeda. "Because I didn't like the Red Sox. I had new friends, real friends. I had teammates who would fight and bleed for me. To do something important for my guys was awesome."

If anyone remained unconvinced that this was big enough to be literally a *World* Series, Ronald Reagan cleared things up. On the night of Game 3 the fortieth United States president was hosting a White House dinner in honor of West German Chancellor Helmut Kohl. "I'd like to pause for a little American thing that has to be addressed," Reagan said to his black-tie audience. "At the top of the fourth, the New York Mets are four, the Boston Red Sox one." Kohl laughed. Even though baseball was to West Germany what curling is to America, perhaps the chancellor was aware of the obvious: The Red Sox were in trouble.

All Kohl had to do was turn his minimal English comprehension skills to the next morning's sports pages, where Al Nipper was listed as Boston's Game 4 starting pitcher. This was the same Al Nipper who had a 10–12 record as the Sox number 4 starter, the same Al Nipper who hadn't appeared in a game since the final week of the season. McNamara made the decision because he believed bringing back Hurst on three days of rest was asking too much. The Mets were licking their chops. "They had Clemens and they had Hurst, and after that they had nothing," says Carter. "Al Nipper? He was meat."

On the afternoon of his big start, Nipper sat in his Boston apartment and watched *Witness*, a movie starring Harrison Ford as a detective thrown into a world he had no business visiting. If the flick had

been baseball-themed, it might have been entitled *Al*. The Boston
right-hander had as much right pitching in Game 4 of the World Series
as Spuds McKenzie did distributing political advice. Heading into the
ALCS, Nipper assumed that he would start against the Angels. Then,
two days before the series, McNamara removed him from the rotation.
Nipper sulked until the reality sank in: *I won only two of my final eight starts.
I was 3–5 with a 5.17 ERA at Fenway. I went winless for more than a month. I
am as intimidating as Snoopy. I am not very good.*

Now here he was, a former Division II All-American at Northeast
Missouri State University, asked to keep Boston's dreams afloat. As if
the odds on Nipper weren't long enough, the opposing pitcher would
be Darling, last seen in a top-notch Game 1 outing. Unlike Nipper,
Darling remained calm and levelheaded under the World Series spotlight. He again stifled Boston for seven innings, this time permitting
just four hits and no runs. Nipper, meanwhile, was, well, *Nipper*. He
held New York scoreless for 3 innings, fluttering an array of soft
curveballs and suspect sliders, and relying primarily on the advantage
of unfamiliarity. By the fourth, however, the magic was gone. The first
of Carter's two homers sailed over the Green Monster, driving in a pair
of runs to open up a 2–0 lead, and by the middle of the seventh the
score was 5–0. Perhaps the game's most memorable play was Dykstra's
homer to right off reliever Steve Crawford, which popped out of
Evans's glove and over the wall. The look on the right fielder's face—
a pained grimace—summed up the history of Red Sox postseason
baseball.

"The whole thing was my fault," says Nipper. "I threw Carter a slider
in his first at-bat, and he crushed it. To me that one pitch changed the
entire series. Maybe if he doesn't hit that home run, I buckle down and
win the game. Maybe . . ."

Maybe not. The Mets won easily, 6–2, and a city that two days earlier
was planning a victory parade now found itself in a familiar position:
home to yet another Red Sox team blowing its big chance.

The Mets were reinvigorated, both by the comeback and a vile Fenway experience. No city has uglier fans than Boston, where anger and beer mix into a bitter stew. Throughout the series Fenway's denizens went out of their way to be as crude as possible. Darling's wife and Gooden's fiancée both had their purses snatched, and Melissa Niemann, wife of reliever Randy Niemann, was pinched in the rear as she made her way through the stands. The next day extra police officers were assigned to the section designated for New York's wives.

With two decisive wins at Fenway under his team's belt, Davey Johnson saw no reason why the Mets couldn't sweep the Red Sox in their own yard. The Game 5 matchup was Gooden versus Hurst, one every Met thought was in their favor. In hindsight there was only one small problem: Gooden versus Hurst.

Ever since Fenway Park's debut in 1912, the majority of left-handers had quivered in the shadow of the Green Monster. It was a right-handed hitter's paradise, and Johnson made certain his lineup was filled with them. Yet for no logical reason, Hurst again silenced the Mets, brilliantly mixing his forkball and curve. His success—a complete-game 10-hit, 2-run masterpiece—was a mystery.

The only explanation is that Hurst possessed the one thing Gooden lacked: playoff guts. "I was on the mound during the World Series, and I had an epiphany," Hurst says. "As a kid I would be in my backyard, throwing balls against the wall. It would always be a big game in the World Series. Now I had the ball in my hand, and I said to myself, 'Wow, this is great. This is just so incredibly great.' I wasn't nervous. I was in the World Series, and my team needed me."

Just as the Mets needed Gooden. In what was by now standard ritual before and after each of his postseason appearances, Gooden was asked by reporters whether they should make a connection between playoff pressure and his mediocre performances. "No, I'm ready for this," Gooden said of his Game 5 start. "I was hoping to get another chance to prove myself."

In a span of 4 innings Gooden did. He proved himself to be a World Series flop. It wasn't that he surrendered 9 hits and 3 earned runs in a humbling 4–2 defeat; it was the way he did it. Trailing 1–0 in the third inning, Gooden faced Evans with runners on first and second. In the old days Dr. K would have busted the Boston veteran with one 96-mph fastball after another. But now? Gooden threw four straight curveballs (*curveballs?*) before Evans pounded the first heater to center for an RBI single.

"I remember asking Evans what he got on 3–2 [in the fifth inning], and he said, 'Changeup,'" Red Sox DH Don Baylor told the *Post*. "Changeup! I played in New York for three years, and [Gooden's] different now. The confidence he used to have wasn't there."

"Gooden once had one of those pretty motions," added Marty Barrett, Boston's second baseman. "Good, easy gas, they call it. Now he looks awkward on the mound. He's falling off toward first base, dropping his arm on the fastball. He's still got good stuff, but it's not unhittable like it was two years ago."

Six years later Strawberry suggested in his autobiography that Gooden might have been competing while under the influence of drugs. It was a charge the pitcher denied time and time again, and one that—under pressure—Strawberry eventually withdrew. But as the Mets returned to New York on the verge of elimination, it made as much sense as anything. In two World Series starts, Gooden allowed 8 earned runs and 17 hits. Especially disconcerting was Gooden's physical appearance before the big Game 5 start. After only five minutes of warming up in the bullpen, Gooden's face and hands were glistening from a thick layer of sweat. It was eerily similar to the look of a thoroughbred after receiving an injection of Lasix, the diuretic used to treat bleeding. The horse sweats profusely, a sure indicator that something isn't kosher.

Whether or not Gooden was using drugs, something in his performance was not kosher.

As columnist Dick Young wrote in the next day's *Post*:

The repeated "explanation" for Gooden's turned-down heat is that it was deliberate, that the Mets' strategists had decided he would throw more breaking balls, so that more grounders would be hit off him. More grounders, fewer strikeouts. Fewer strikeouts, fewer pitches thrown each game.

. . . If the decision to have him abandon the fastball is strategic, it is the worst strategy since the French-built Maginot Line. I suggest the Mets return Gooden to smoking the ball. That is, if he still can.

His name was Dwight Eugene Gooden. The heralded Dr. K was no more.

Chapter 18

NEAR DEATH

There are those who will say, whether it is fair, whether it is logical, whether it is reasonable, that if the Mets don't win it all, they have somehow failed.

—NBC's BOB COSTAS,
before Game 6 of the 1986 World Series

ON OCTOBER 22, 1986, a small-time actor named Michael Sergio was sitting on the couch of his Manhattan apartment, a bowl of chips by his side and his thirteen-inch color television tuned to NBC's coverage of Game 4 of the World Series. Though not a huge baseball fan, Sergio had spent much of his youth playfully running beneath the old outfield bleachers at Shea Stadium where his mother worked as a concessionaire. He was enough of a New Yorker to yank his hair out every time those damn Red Sox scored another run. "Something about Boston annoyed me," he says. "Just got under my skin." Maybe it was the accent— "Going to the *pahk* in my *cah*." Maybe it was the goofy-looking Green Monster. Maybe it was the balloons. Maybe it was . . .

Ah, the balloons. In the bottom of the second inning of an otherwise dull game, the action momentarily halted as a string of fifteen red, white, and blue balloons, attached to a sign reading GO SOX, floated from the upper deck toward the Fenway Park playing surface. Some 33,920 Red Sox fans leapt to their feet. It was a moment that, to Sergio, summed up the Boston faithful in one perfectly compact word: weenies.

Balloons? Puh-lease. Although he was best known to friends as the guy who played "Rick" in the feature film *The House on Sorority Row*, Sergio had another passion. Over the past decade he had made more than two thousand parachute leaps from airplanes, spending several years competing on a European jumping tour and performing at fairs and stunt shows across the United States. In 1981 he was hired by George Steinbrenner to plunge into Yankee Stadium before Game 1 of the World Series. Inclement weather canceled the gig.

As he watched the balloons gently glide through the crisp Boston air, Sergio—as any parachute-jumping star of *The House on Sorority Row* would—cringed. He immediately concocted an idea for what he believed would be the most stupendous, most outlandish, most high-profile stunt in modern sport. And it would take place on the grandest of stages: Live from New York, Game 6 of the World Series.

Although the Mets had won 108 regular-season contests as well as a gripping NLCS over Houston, all would prove meaningless should they falter in Game 6 to the underdog Red Sox. "For us to come in second would be a complete failure," says Ojeda. Just as nobody remembers who the Packers defeated to win their first two Super Bowls or the various runner-ups in Bjorn Borg's Grand Slam career, the Mets would go down as, well, nothing. The hoopla would concern Boston's first title since 1918. The NL champion Mets? Tired news.

Whether out of nervousness, concern, hope, or anticipation, 55,078 fans packed Shea for a Saturday night spectacle. Starting for Boston was Clemens, now "110 percent" (his estimate) recovered from the flu and, after five days of inactivity between starts, well rested. Clemens threw high, hard, and tight, and as Barrett noted in an interview with Bob Costas from the Red Sox dugout immediately before the game, New York's choice of Ojeda—no matter how effective he had been in Game 3—hardly put fear into the hearts of Boston's players. "They were having that Chicago Bear–type season for baseball," Barrett said. "But now we're ahead 3 games to 2 with our best man out on the hill. We *should* win."

During the later innings of Game 5, the Fenway faithful picked Strawberry as an easy target, chanting "*Daaaa-ryyyyy! Daaaa-ryyyyy! Daaaa-ryyyyy!*" repeatedly. While New York's right fielder pretended to be unfazed by the mocking, even going so far as to turn and wave his cap, it irked him. As payback the fans at Shea pounced on Clemens. As he warmed up in the bullpen before the game, everything from batteries to nickels to a soda bottle were chucked in his direction. He also heard what would become a familiar refrain:

Raaaah-gerrrr!
Raaaah-gerrrr!
Raaaah-gerrrr!

There had been big games at Shea over the years but precious few marquee moments. Here, after so many dry days, was something special. When Ojeda left the dugout to begin his walk toward the mound, he was greeted by the sound of thunder—55,078 people clapping and pounding on their chairs. Then with Boggs on first after a leadoff single, Buckner walked up to the plate, stepped in, and adjusted his cap. Suddenly, as if $100 bills were materializing from thin air, the masses erupted a thousand times louder than before. In the broadcast booth NBC's Vin Scully didn't understand. "Boy," he said, "this crowd came here to make some noise tonight."

Then Scully saw it. The players saw it. The umpires saw it. Everyone saw it. Emerging from the sky was the man in a white jumpsuit, suspended from a yellow parachute with a huge banner reading GO METS dangling from a ripcord. *It was a bird! It was a plane! It was . . . Mike Sergio!* And he was no weenie. "I heard this noise—*aaaarrrrrrr!*" he says. "I'm thinking, *Why the screaming?* Then I realized the people were reacting to me." Home plate umpire Dale Ford waved his arms to call time, and as he gently landed between the pitcher's mound and first base, where a pair of police officers were waiting to take him away, Sergio pumped both fists in the air. Ojeda shrugged his shoulders in disbelief. Buckner applauded. Evans, preparing for his at-bat, grinned. Sergio was led through the Mets dugout, where Darling offered a high-five.

Yes, he would eventually spend twenty-one days in the Metropolitan Correctional Center. But Sergio had pulled off the impossible. Thanks to his parachuting experience he had enough ties to have some local FAA folk look the other way for a couple of hours. With his TV connections (at the time, he was playing Sal on the ABC soap *Loving*), he made certain NBC Sports' cameramen would be in the right place at the right time. "When's the last time you saw a camera on the roof of a stadium?" he says. "I'll leave it at that."

In violating every conceivable FAA regulation and Shea Stadium security code, Mike Sergio had kick-started a World Series game.

Noise is a funny thing. At a Kiss concert it can burn your ears. At a baseball game it can inspire or tick off. The Red Sox were ticked. Nothing personal, really, just a team tired of the in-your-face Mets putting on *Chorus Line*–styled productions. After Buckner flew out to center, Ojeda walked Rice on four pitches, and up stepped Evans, the fifteen-year veteran. In the hundreds of look-backs at Game 6, much has been made of this play or that player. Mistakenly they forget *this* at-bat. On a one-ball, one-strike count, Evans smashed an Ojeda changeup to the left center field wall, sending Boggs and Rice charging toward home for a 2–0 lead.

Oh, wait.

Somehow, in a world where dogs guide the blind and paraplegics finish marathons, a two-out double to a wall 360 feet away failed to score Rice, who, Charles Scoggins of *The Lowell Sun* once wrote, "stops at each base to scrape the gum off his shoes." It was a shameless display of lazy base running. Had he run on Evans's contact, Rice would have scored. "I have no idea how he didn't come home," says Ojeda. "Little things make huge differences, though, don't they?"

It was the first of countless sloppy, mindless plays in a game that—except for the gritty performances by Clemens and Ojeda—was downright ugly. Boston did increase its lead to 2–0 on an RBI single by Barrett in the second, and with Clemens cruising and the fatigued Ojeda scuffling, things looked bad for the Mets. Clemens, 9–0 in the regular season with five or more days of rest, was throwing pure smoke. Through 4 innings he held New York hitless. In the Mets dugout Davey Johnson sat on the end of the bench, his hands in his jacket pockets and his mind forlornly racing. *This guy looks a lot like Mike Scott,* he thought to himself. *Only better.*

The Magic Met Fairy was listening. Strawberry led off the top of the fifth with a walk, then stole second. Knight's single to center drove in New York's first run, bringing Mookie Wilson to bat. Over the years the great criticism of the Mets' speedy outfielder was that, for all his burst and pizzazz, he possessed the patience of a five-year-old on Christmas Eve. Too many strikeouts (72 in '86), not enough walks (32). In this rare case, however, impatience was a virtue. Wilson swung at Clemens's first two pitches—both fastballs—and then laid off a pair of balls. Knowing Wilson's reputation for turning quick on fastballs, Gedman called for an inside slider. It was Clemens's second best pitch, but one that put an unusual amount of pressure on his right index finger. As he released the baseball, Clemens felt the popping of a blister. It hurt but wasn't quite as painful as watching Wilson lace a single to right field. Knight took off for second, and when Evans momentarily bobbled the ball, he raced safely to third.

With the tip of his index finger oozing, Clemens could no longer throw anything but fastballs and forkballs. In the midst of a managerial meltdown, Davey Johnson made things as easy as possible for him. Although there were still 4 more innings, the skipper pulled Santana, his smooth shortstop, and pinch-hit Heep. The logic was simple (Heep was the Mets' best lefty bat off the bench, and here was the chance to chase Boston's ace) but flawed. Though Santana batted just .218, he was a dead-fastball hitter who had singled twice off The Rocket in Game 2. Heep grounded into a 4–6–3 double play, scoring Knight to tie the game but killing any chances of a big inning.

And now the Mets were stuck. As Scully said at the start of the sixth,

"How would you like to be Kevin Elster? He's twenty-two years old. He was drafted by the Mets two years ago. Came up from Jackson Double A, and he's the shortstop in a must-win game of the World Series."

It was all true. Elster was just twenty-two. He was drafted by the Mets two years earlier out of Golden West Junior College and had spent all but nineteen games of the '86 season at Double A, where he batted only .269. And now he was here in the center of the storm.

Although usually a keen judge of men, Davey Johnson was off on this one. Inserting Elster was ludicrous. In one of his earliest major league games, Elster was pulled aside by Backman after an opposing player reached first. "Look at me between pitches," Backman told the rookie. "If my mouth is open, I cover second. If it's closed, you got it." Moments later the base runner attempted to steal, prompting a throw from Carter. The signal was a closed mouth. Elster didn't move. The ball sailed into center. "Rookie, what the hell are you doing!?" Backman screamed. Elster was dumbfounded. "You didn't give me the sig . . . *ooooooohhhhhh*. Sorry. I forgot, dude." It was the story of his brief tenure—a .167 average, zero RBIs and deep-fried nerves.

Now the pressure was at an entirely different level. When Elster jogged out to his position to start the sixth, he wasn't thinking about being the surprise hero. "I was like, 'Just don't hit the ball to me, just don't hit the ball to me, just don't hit the ball to me,'" he says. "It was being thrown into an ocean when you can't swim." Because his mitt had recently caved in, Elster was using Knight's spare glove. It was a disaster waiting to happen. A confident group of infielders now had to contend with a foreign element.

Davey Johnson brought in McDowell to start the seventh, and with one out and Barrett on second, he forced Rice to chop a soft grounder toward third. It was a play that in his ten years as a major leaguer Ray Knight had made at least ten thousand times. Now Knight suffered a case of the yips. He fielded the ball cleanly, but when he transferred it to his right hand, his fingers aligned with the seams, not across them. Two seconds later his throw sailed off the mitt of a leaping Hernandez, and Barrett reached third. He scored moments later on a fielder's choice. Boston again led, 3–2. "The thought immediately came into my mind, *We can't lose this thing. Not on that play,*" Knight says. "*If we lose because of that throw, I'm moving my family to Idaho.*"

Fortunately for Knight, Rice was again available to help New York's cause. Gedman, the next batter, hit a single toward Wilson in left that should have scored the Red Sox's fourth run. Based on Mookie's soft arm, third base coach Rene Lachemann waved Rice home from second. But as Peter Gammons perfectly described it in *Sports Illustrated*, "Rice cut the bag like a 16-wheeler turning into a McDonald's." Wilson's throw wasn't powerful, but it was perfect. Rice was dead by four steps.

Upon returning to the dugout, Knight walked up the tunnel toward the clubhouse and found a quiet spot. He uttered a prayer: "Dear God, baseball is a game of redeeming features. And if there's any chance, please give me the opportunity to redeem myself."

Someone was listening.

Through 7 innings Clemens was at his Cy Young–worthy best. Despite throwing a whopping 135 pitches, he managed to hold New York to 2 runs and 4 hits. It was an ace outing from an ace. Yet while facing Wilson with one out in the seventh, Clemens tore a fingernail on his right hand. He was now bleeding from both the index and middle fingers. At the end of the frame McNamara cornered Clemens and told him that should a rally start, he might be pinch-hit for. Clemens didn't argue, but his look was one of fury. *After all I've done, you're yanking me!?* It was a one-way conversation overheard by numerous players. "No way Roger wanted out of that game," says Hurst. "He was a fierce competitor."

For the next fifteen years McNamara maintained that Clemens had actually *asked* to be removed. "My pitcher told me he couldn't go any further," he said at the postgame press conference. It was a fib by the manager to save face. (*Sports Illustrated* reported that when Clemens was informed of McNamara's comments, he became enraged, storming off to confront his manager.) This hardly comes as a surprise to those who tracked the team on a daily basis. Gerry Callahan, the *Lowell Sun*'s beat writer at the time, calls McNamara "the single most miserable human being I've covered in my career. You could search your whole life and never find such a jerk." Adds Dan Shaughnessy of *The Boston Globe*: "McNamara was particularly nasty and petty and vile." To many of the Red Sox players the manager was an old, crotchety man. There was little love.

When Henderson led off the inning by reaching first on an Elster bobble and Owen sacrificed him to second, McNamara committed the worst sin of his managerial career. He pinch-hit rookie Mike Greenwell for Clemens, removing baseball's top starter from a World Series–clinching game and placing a slim lead in the hands of a worn bullpen. Greenwell, a year older than Elster but equally jittery, whiffed on three straight McDowell sinkers.

McNamara's next decision was equally inexplicable. Following his strikeout of Greenwell, McDowell intentionally walked Boggs, then walked Barrett on five pitches. With the bases loaded and Buckner due up, Davey Johnson had no choice but to insert the left-handed Orosco who held lefties to a .187 average in '86. Because Buckner was a .218 hitter against left-handers, McNamara informed him that Baylor, the veteran slugger, would pinch-hit. The move made perfect sense. One hundred and eight of Baylor's 315 career homers came against left-handers, and Dave Stapleton, a soft-handed utility player who had served as a late-game defensive replacement for Buckner in all 7 of Boston's playoff wins, was ready to step in.

Buckner battled back. "Skip, I can hit this guy," he told McNamara. "I know how to get Orosco." The fact was, Orosco dominated Buckner. Nineteen at-bats, 3 hits. Seven years earlier, in an eerily similar situation, Orosco made his major league debut. With the bases loaded, two outs, and the Mets leading the Cubs by 4 runs in the bottom of the ninth, the left-hander was called upon to face Buckner. A fly-out to the warning track ended the game.

McNamara was swayed. He stuck with Buckner, then cringed as a first-pitch fly-out to Dykstra killed the inning. Of the twenty-four Red Sox fighting to win a championship, only one understood the logic of the move. Buckner was his name.

From the beginning, Calvin Schiraldi was a hard thrower. But what would you expect? Like Nolan Ryan before him, he was Texas born and raised, which in the world of pitching means unstoppable strength is your birthright.

That was Calvin. A gunslinger on the hill. The boy was four years old when his father, Joe Schiraldi, began to notice that the baseball did not just depart from his son's hand, it exploded like a torpedo from a submarine. When he was twelve, Calvin's 65-mph heater soared past gangly preadolescents so often that he single-handedly pitched a team to the Texas Babe Ruth League title. Upon reaching the University of Texas, he was the number 1 starter on a staff whose number 2 was a kid named Clemens.

So why, one might ask, was Clemens selected thirteenth by Boston in the 1983 June amateur draft while Schiraldi dropped all the way to twenty-seventh, where the Mets used a compensatory pick between the first and second rounds?

Roger Clemens pitched with fire. Calvin Schiraldi did not.

There was something disconcerting about the lanky kid with the sleepy eyes, a softness that belied his six-foot-four, 200-pound stature. "Calvin was very mellow," says Billy Beane, a teammate and roommate at Double A Jackson. "We used to get on him about slugging around the house. We were all high-energy guys, and we'd make fun of him for leaving snail tracks around."

The Mets knew Schiraldi wasn't high energy at Texas, but his raw skills were too awe-inspiring to ignore. Yet when he struggled in brief big league appearances in '84 and '85, the Mets started to lose faith. His makeup was iffy. Prior to the Ojeda swap, Cashen took an informal poll of his staff. Not one person thought Schiraldi, though nearly five years younger, had a long-term future with the Mets. "We immediately jumped on the trade with Boston," says McIlvaine. "Bobby would be better for us than Calvin. We all believed it."

Converted into a reliever by the Sox, Schiraldi excelled, posting a team-low 1.41 ERA and striking out 55 batters in 51 innings. The Mets weren't concerned. From former teammates to scouts to decision makers, there was a firm belief that Schiraldi was not prime closer material. He was soft. He could be rattled. He felt the heat.

And now in the eighth inning of Game 6 of the World Series he was on the hill, asked by McNamara to take Boston home. When Mazzilli, pinch-hitting for Orosco, led off with a single to right and then Dykstra followed with a bunt that was thrown away by Schiraldi, Hearn, sitting alone in the New York dugout, could feel his heart thumping. Yes, he wanted a World Series ring, but at the expense of his best friend? When the two were teammates at Double A Jackson, Hearn served as an usher in Schiraldi's wedding, filling his honeymoon car with two hundred crickets, a thirty-five-inch rainbow trout, and a slab of Limburger cheese. So close were the pals that for much of '86, Hearn was dating Calvin's younger sister. Because each Met player was permitted to invite one significant other along for the forty-five-minute charter flight from Boston to New York after Game 5, Hearn's guest was, in as hushed tones as possible, Rhonda Schiraldi, kin of the enemy.

Backman, following Dykstra in the order, laid down a perfect sacrifice bunt, advancing Mazzilli, the tying run, to third. "I love Cal, but I told the guys the truth," says Hearn. "'If we're able to get to Schiraldi, he does not have the makeup to be a stopper. He's not psycho enough to come in late, and he gets on himself too much. We can beat him up and down.'"

Schiraldi walked Hernandez intentionally to pitch to Carter. With a three-ball count Carter swung mightily but just missed crushing the ball. Instead, his sacrifice fly to left drove in Mazzilli, who scampered home with his arms raised high in the air, the noise a deafening roar of glee. Strawberry flew out to end the inning, and the game was tied, 3–3.

Schiraldi had blown the lead, but his troubles were just beginning.

On his right wrist Darryl Strawberry wore a watch that would stop Stevie Wonder in his tracks. It was a top-of-the-line $10,000 Rolex, sprinkled with diamonds the size of peanuts. Wherever Strawberry went, the watch followed. It was as much a part of him as hamburgers and chewing tobacco.

One year while the Mets were in spring training, Vinny Greco tapped Strawberry on the shoulder and pointed to his timepiece. "That," Greco said, "is the most beautiful watch I've ever seen." Nearly eight months later Strawberry handed Greco a gift-wrapped box. Inside was the Rolex. "Straw, are you crazy?" Greco said. The slugger just smiled and proceeded to slip the assistant equipment manager an envelope filled with money, too. "That's how I always think of Straw," says Greco. "Just a big-hearted kid." Within the small fraternity that is the team's clubhouse staff, Strawberry goes down as one of New York's all-time great guys. The stories of compassion are countless, from lending out his car to buying dinners to gifts and large tips. While many teammates found their superstar to be as lovable as a cobra, low-level employees cherished him. "When it came down to what really mattered," says Greco, "you could almost always depend on Straw."

Almost.

When the Mets returned to the dugout after tying the game at 3–3, Davey Johnson told Strawberry that he was being pulled. To the thinking baseball fan it made sense. The manager would have Mazzilli play right and hit in the ninth hole, and insert Rick Aguilera, the new pitcher, in Strawberry's four spot. That way, with a bullpen now containing just two rested relievers—the nomadic Randy Niemann and the erratic Doug Sisk—Johnson would have time before having to pinch-hit for Aguilera.

Without muttering a word to his skipper, Strawberry stormed through the dugout, down the tunnel, past Greco, and into the clubhouse, where he sulked for the remainder of the evening. His teammates watched stupefied as the drama unfolded in front of their eyes: Here was the most selfish act in modern World Series history. "Darryl was flat-out wrong," says Knight. "Davey made a double switch at a point where the game was on the line. It's not about ego."

After the game Strawberry went off on his manager to the media. Did it matter that he was batting .200 with no home runs or RBIs? Uh, no. "I'm disturbed," he said. "I'm embarrassed. It made me look bad and showed me the manager doesn't have confidence in me. I've been helping the club all year, and I have to watch the last inning in the locker room."

Inside the New York clubhouse, Samuels, the equipment manager, tried consoling Strawberry. So did Greco—to no avail. It was life or death for the New York Mets, and their star was sitting on his stool, furiously smoking a cigarette.

Prior to the playoffs, a reporter from *The St. Louis Post-Dispatch* asked Hearn if he had any gut predictions. "I have a feeling," he said, "that before the end of the league championship series and World Series, the guy playing a big role for us will be Rick Aguilera." He was right. If Strawberry had been watching instead of sulking, he would have seen Aguilera coolly set down Rice, Evans, and Gedman in the top of the ninth. In many ways it was a vindication for Davey Johnson who, when the pitcher struggled with a 2–3 record and 5.40 ERA in the first half, resisted Cashen's demands to return him to Triple A Tidewater for more seasoning. With his manager's support, Aguilera went 8–4 in the second half of '86.

With the score tied at 3–3, the bottom of the ninth began promisingly for New York. Knight led off with a five-pitch walk, and thinking back to two innings earlier when his error nearly cost the Mets the Series, he gave an emphatic high-five to first base coach Bill Robinson. Wilson, the next batter, was greeted by the customary *Moooooo!* But this time it was louder, stronger. The fans could sense an ending, and they wanted the beloved Wilson to provide it. After fouling off strike one, Wilson laid down a sacrifice bunt in front of home plate. Gedman burst from his crouch, picked up the ball, and launched a rocket to second, where Owen stretched to make the catch. *Safe!* Umpire Jim Evans, perfectly positioned nearby, saw the shortstop's shoe inch off the bag. McNamara's protestations were expletive-packed, but the call was correct. New York was on the verge of a remarkable comeback—two on, no outs, and a stadium shaking on its foundation.

It was time for a manager to screw things up.

Due up for New York was Elster, the nervous-as-a-cat-in-a-wave-pool rookie. Davey Johnson had made his mark on the Mets by infusing the team with youth, but this wasn't a matchup he embraced. Santana, for all his weaknesses, could be trusted to lay down a sacrifice bunt. Elster couldn't—especially against the high heat of Schiraldi. As a result, Howard Johnson was called upon to pinch-hit.

Shortly after the Mets acquired Hojo from Detroit in December 1984, Davey Johnson called Tigers manager Sparky Anderson to learn about his new third baseman. "He's a great kid," Anderson said, "but I'm not so sure he can handle the pressure." In Detroit's '84 World Series triumph over San Diego, Hojo received just one at-bat. Davey Johnson took this as a challenge, promising himself that, given the stage, Hojo would see serious action.

As Schiraldi's first pitch, a fastball, approached, Johnson squared to bunt and flat-out missed. In 253 plate appearances in 1986, Hojo had attempted exactly two bunts, both unsuccessful. Davey Johnson recognized an ugly bunter when he saw one and immediately called off the sacrifice. Why this didn't occur to the skipper *before* he sent Hojo up is a mystery. Surely he knew that Hojo was no better suited to lay down a sacrifice than Frank Cashen. Now caught off guard, he flashed a signal to Harrelson at third, who relayed it to Hojo: swing away. Three pitches later Hojo foul-tipped strike three into Gedman's glove. When Mazzilli followed by hitting a deep fly ball to left, Shea Stadium collectively sighed in angst. Had Elster or Hojo or someone successfully sacrificed Knight to third, the game would have been over. Instead, Dykstra flew out to end the inning, and a golden opportunity had vanished.

From the NBC booth the masterful Scully, a future Hall of Fame announcer, committed his only gaffe of the game. Unaware that his microphone was still on at the end of the inning, he angrily barked, "If Howard Johnson was good enough to swing, how come he wasn't—" *Dead air.* Twenty-six million viewers filled in the rest: "—given more than one chance to sacrifice Knight to third?"

It was a great question.

Rick Aguilera pitched in 5 of the Mets' 13 playoff games, and before each appearance he would warm up in the bullpen and nervously ponder all the bad things that could happen. "It's the anticipation that kills you," he says. "Your mind races." As soon as he stepped onto the field, however, the fear slid away. Negative thoughts turned to intensity.

When he took the mound for the top of the tenth, Aguilera was at ease. He started Henderson off with a high fastball, which he swung through for strike one. Even though the center fielder had rescued Boston from ALCS elimination with his ninth inning dinger off Donnie Moore in Game 5, Henderson did not evoke fear in his opponents. He was a lifetime .255 hitter who had spent nearly all of his six-year career mired in the baseball sludge that was Seattle. Hence, Carter comfortably put down the one-finger signal for fastball and set up his glove on the inside corner. Aguilera threw the baseball. It was fast. It was hard. It was right over the heart of the plate. It was gone.

Henderson hopped high into the air, and while jogging backward down the first base line, he watched the ball soar through the sky and smack a *Newsday* sign above Wilson's head in left. Shea was a morgue. "It's so quiet in New York," said Scully, "you can almost hear Boston." With two outs Boggs doubled to left center and Barrett singled to give Boston a 5–3 lead. As soon as Aguilera forced Rice to fly out to right to end the inning, he walked into the dugout, put his head in his hands and realized the enormity of the situation. *We're the best team in the game*, he thought, *and I've blown it.*

Chapter 19

WORLD CHAMPS

The nightmares are that you're gonna let the winning run
score on a ground ball through your legs.

—BILL BUCKNER, in a TV interview before
Game 1 of the 1986 World Series

WITH BOSTON'S SERIES VICTORY now inevitable, John Rufino was
being ordered to take a cart holding New York's 20 cases of bubbly
and wheel it through Shea's concrete bowels and down to the visiting
side. "Assholes forget to bring champagne," the Mets assistant equipment manager mumbled, "and we've gotta give 'em ours." When he
reached the Red Sox clubhouse, John glanced up at the television
screen. He saw Backman, the leadoff hitter, fly out to Rice for the
first out.

"Johnny, c'mon! We gotta hurry!" The command came from Vinny
Greco, now busy hanging WORLD CHAMPION BOSTON RED SOX
T-shirts and hats in every locker, draping the walls with plastic, and
twisting the caps off the tops of the bottles. As his final act, Greco, for
five years the loyalist of Shea employees, found a blue Red Sox warm-

up jacket and pulled it over his Mets shirt. When New York made the final out, Greco was planning to sprint onto the field.

"I just wanted to be a part of the celebration," Greco says, sheepish embarrassment in his eyes. "Any celebration."

By the time Greco started his walk into the Red Sox dugout, Keith Hernandez had flown out to Henderson in center.

Two outs.

Just as Henderson was settling under Hernandez's fly ball, third base coach Bud Harrelson turned toward the Red Sox dugout and made eye contact with Seaver, his former Met teammate and longtime chum. Though inactive, Seaver still dressed and attended the games. With a cocky smile he waved to Harrelson from the top step. "I'll call you," he yelled.

Harrelson bristled.

In Shea Stadium's Video Scoreboard Control Room there are two monitors. To the left, the preview monitor allows one to see an image before it appears on the giant Diamond Vision. To the right, the program monitor displays the actual, live Diamond Vision view. It is extraordinarily simple. "You don't have to be a rocket scientist," says Mike Ryan.

This is good news because Ryan—though plenty smart—wasn't. In four years with the Mets, Ryan had shot up the company ladder, from marketing assistant to his high-ranking role as director of broadcasting. During games his primary duty was to make certain the messages appearing on the Diamond Vision were appropriate.

As soon as Backman flew out, Ryan ordered one of his employees to type up a "Well done" message for the soon-to-be-champion Red Sox and then display it on the *preview* monitor. While this was going on, Ryan's mind raced in a million different directions. Growing up in Pittsfield, Massachusetts, the home of Boston's Double A affiliate, Ryan marveled as future big leaguers like Carlton Fisk and Rick Miller passed through his town. That turned him into a die-hard Red Sox fan. So really, how could he not think about 1918 and the Curse of the Bambino and Bernie Carbo and Luis Tiant and . . .

CONGRATULATIONS RED SOX!

The three words flashed onto the Diamond Vision large enough for the world to see. There were two outs, and Gary Carter was strolling to the plate. The World Series was *not* 100 percent over. "Get that shit off now!" Ryan screamed. "Get it off!"

In total, CONGRATULATIONS RED SOX! lasted for no more than five seconds. Everybody saw it.

Keith Hernandez walked into the clubhouse, sat on a chair in Davey Johnson's office, lit up a Winston Light, and cracked open a Budweiser. He could not believe what was happening. In his head the New York Mets were one thousand times better than the Boston Red Sox. No, ten thousand times better. And yet they were about to lose.

Across from Hernandez sat Jay Horwitz, the media relations director, and Darrell Johnson, a Met scout and, oddly, manager of the '75 Red Sox, the last Boston team to reach the Series. Around the corner Mitchell, wearing a T-shirt and his underwear, was on the phone with his travel agent, making a reservation to fly home to San Diego. McDowell, sitting nearby, called Chris Dill, his best friend from Bowling Green. "Well," Hernandez muttered to no one in particular, "we've only got one thing going for us. Schiraldi is pitching."

Doug Sisk spent the past fifteen minutes warming up in the Mets bullpen just in case a rally started. For a couple of fleeting moments he thought he might have a chance to play hero. Not anymore. Sisk stepped off the mound and pulled on a jacket. "Doug, you'd better keep warming up," said Greg Pavlick, the assistant pitching coach.

"What for?" asked Sisk. "Next year?"

When they were roommates at Double A Jackson in 1983, Kevin Mitchell and Calvin Schiraldi used to stay up late and talk. The topics ran wide—best player you've ever seen, toughest catcher to steal against, worst ballpark, hottest actress, and so forth. One night Mitchell asked his friend how he would pitch him. "Mitch, you'd be easy," Schiraldi said. "I'd start you off with a fastball in, then throw you a slider away. Cake." The philosophy was this: Mitchell could hit Nolan Ryan's fastball blindfolded, but even the most elementary of sliders reduced him to Mario Mendoza.

Not that this was on Mitchell's mind. Not now, with his team about to lose the World Series. Hell, he just wanted to catch a flight home. But this damn travel agent, keeping him on hold, listening to elevator music . . .

"Mitch! Mitch!" It was John Rufino, sent back from the dugout by Davey Johnson. "You might have to pinch-hit for Aggie! They want you out there now!"

Mitchell hung up the phone, grabbed his pants, and—minus protective cup—pulled them on. Halfway onto the field, his zipper was still partially undone. He sprinted to the on-deck circle, which Gary Carter had just vacated.

Gary Carter never cursed. Never. To him expletives like "F-bomb" and "Gosh darn it!" were strong enough. But he saw CONGRATULATIONS RED SOX! and could hear Dennis Boyd cackling from the edge of the Boston dugout, mockingly waving good-bye to the Met players. The veteran catcher was pissed.

With a two-balls, one-strike count, Carter looked up at Schiraldi, whose brow was glistening with sweat. "The kid was scared," he says. "You could see it." (Schiraldi, by way of disagreeing with this assessment, says, "Gary Carter can suck my ass.") On the next pitch he lined a Schiraldi fastball to left for a single. Upon reaching first, Carter slapped Bill Robinson's hand. "I'll be damned," he said, "if I'm gonna make the last fuckin' out in this fuckin' World Series!"

With Carter on first, an announcement was made in the press box: "Boston pitcher Bruce Hurst has been named World Series MVP!"

———

Schiraldi's first pitch to Kevin Mitchell was a fastball, which he fouled off for strike one. Now, thinking back to that long-ago conversation, Mitchell *knew* what was coming. It helped that the slider was a sloppy one—soft, knee high, and over the heart of the dish. Mitchell's swing was pure, and as the ball nestled in center for a single, he rounded first and turned to Robinson. "Uncle Bill," he said, "there's no fuckin' way I'm gonna make the last fuckin' out of the World Series. Not me."

In the Mets clubhouse the superstitious Hernandez issued an order: "Everybody freeze!" You don't mess with a rally, especially one like this. McDowell was commanded to stay on the phone with Chris Dill. Horwitz and Johnson remained in their seats. Nearby, Darling, Ojeda, and Orosco, all of whom had also given up hope, were standing in the equipment manager's office. Charlie Samuels kept his collection of NFL helmets on a couple of wooden shelves, and the players had donned them as make-do rally caps. When Carter singled, the three celebrated with head butts. Now the helmets *had* to stay on. They were working.

"I'm not psychotic," says Hernandez, "I'm neurotic."

As he watched Mitchell's ball soar over his head, Schiraldi couldn't help but ponder the most negative of thoughts: *What the hell am I still doing out here?* It was a fair question. Before Henderson's homer in the top of the tenth, McNamara had planned to pinch-hit Baylor for Schiraldi (who was scheduled to bat third) and then insert veteran right-hander Bob Stanley. But with a lead, the Sox manager wanted his best reliever on the mound. Did it matter that Schiraldi had already pitched 2 long innings? That he was, as he says, "sucking some serious wind"?

"My thinking was simple," says McNamara. "Calvin Schiraldi was my best reliever, and I trusted him to finish them off. What else can I say?"

Before Ray Knight took his turn against Schiraldi, he glanced up into the stands where he saw Nancy Lopez, his wife, crying into a tissue. When their eyes met, he mouthed something to her: "I'm fine. I got it." Lopez continued to sob, but a calmness overtook the Mets' rugged third baseman. It was as if everything disappeared, and it was just him, his wife, and a cool October night in New York. "I've never been *that* locked in," he says. "It was my time."

Schiraldi's first pitch was a called strike, and the second was fouled off down the third base line. For the first time the New York Mets were down to their final strike.

Throughout the season any Boston pitcher who allowed a hit with a two-strike count was fined $100 in the team's Kangaroo Court. This made Schiraldi, earning just $75,000, especially cautious. In twenty-five regular-season appearances, not once did he have to pay up. Now, with two strikes on Knight, Schiraldi did something completely out of character. Instead of offering Knight a setup pitch out of the strike zone, he reared back and threw as hard as possible.

Smack!

Knight's bloop single to center scored Carter and sent Mitchell to third as the tying run. When he reached first, Knight gritted his teeth and looked into Robinson's eyes. "You know, Bill," he said, "there's no fuckin' way I was gonna make the last out of the World Series."

Even as everything was falling apart for the team he covered, John Dennis continued to believe the Red Sox would pull it out. The sports anchor for Boston's WHDH TV had witnessed some strange happenings and miraculous comebacks in his ten years with the network, but this seemed as good as over. Hence, he walked down to the Red Sox clubhouse to set up his postgame report. "I'm arranging this all in my mind," he says. "Babe Ruth and 1918, Pesky holding the ball. I've got this whole piece in my head." When he peeked inside the room, Dennis saw Bob Costas standing on a podium, the Commissioner's Trophy by his side. Jean Yawkey, one of Boston's owners, was sitting in a chair, moderately concerned but still smiling.

"They were ready for the celebration," says Dennis. "Everything was set."

Six months earlier when Red Sox fans were unmercifully heckling him at Fenway Park, Bob Stanley made a bold proclamation to a local TV station. "They may boo me now," he said, "but they'll love me when I'm standing on the mound when we win the World Series."

True though this might have been, very few Boston fans loved the sight of Stanley actually jogging in from the bullpen, his club still only one out away from the World Series title. It had been a rough stretch for the two-time all-star who was replaced by Schiraldi as the club's closer and relegated to a secondary role. Yet, as promised, here he was when it counted, the season in his right hand.

Before digging into the batter's box, Mookie Wilson, hitting left-handed, took a deep, calming breath. Was he nervous? "Of course I was," he says. "You're talking about a big moment here. That's what makes us all good—that fear of failing."

With toilet paper streaming down from the stands behind home plate, and the crowd boisterously screaming "*Moooooo!*" Stanley's first pitch was fouled off for strike one. Two high balls followed, and Wilson fouled the next one in the dirt, making the count two balls, two strikes. For the second time the Red Sox were one pitch away from a championship.

In the Boston dugout Clemens was sitting by himself, his palms rubbing together in prayer. Had it been only thirty minutes since he and Nipper were joyfully high-fiving in the bullpen, their World Series dream becoming a reality? Clemens even took the time to autograph a baseball for an elderly visiting bullpen attendant. Why not? The game was over.

Ever the hacker, Wilson hit the next two pitches into foul territory. Gedman, crouched behind the plate, gave the sign for Stanley's fabled palmball and shifted his body and glove to the outside corner. The pitch started wide-wide-wide, then—*snap!*—broke fiercely to the inside, past a leaping Wilson, past Gedman's stab, and back behind the plate. "Geddy made a mistake," says Stanley. "It happens." Wilson immediately fell to the ground, propped himself on one knee, and waved frantically for Mitchell to charge home. Stanley covered the plate, but there was never a play. As Mitchell scored, a new level of pandemonium engulfed the stadium. Against all odds, the game was tied.

To be a member of baseball's print media is to be a selfish SOB. You root for one thing: simplicity. The earlier the outcome is sealed, the more time you have to write a masterpiece.

For most of the 129 scribes on hand late in Game 6, this was an easy task. The Red Sox were about to capture the World Series for the first time since 1918. Dan Shaughnessy, the *Boston Globe* writer, already had his Dave Henderson column completed—on how the city would place his statue next to one of Sam Adams in Faneuil Hall.

"Everyone's heads were down, writing away," says Bob Nightengale, who was covering the event for the *Kansas City Star*. "And when the Mets scored to tie the game, it was complete bedlam."

This is what was heard: *Damn Red Sox! Dammit! Aw, hell! Fuck! Fuck! Fuck! Fuck!*

When it came time for his team to take the field for the bottom of the tenth, McNamara never even considered replacing Bill Buckner with dependable Dave Stapleton. Sure, Buckner was being held together by glue, spit, and little wads of bubble gum. And sure, Stapleton had served as a late-game defensive replacement throughout the regular season and playoffs. Buckner, however, was a warrior, a guy who had given the Red Sox his heart and guts. If anyone deserved to be on the field for the victory celebration, it was good old number 6.

Yet here McNamara was—the game tied, momentum dead, the stadium crazed, and Knight, the winning run, 180 feet away on second base. Buckner could have—*should have*—been pulled. He was a battered old man playing a boy's game. Now was not the time for sentimentality.

This will go down as the greatest managerial screwup in baseball history.

Following two more foul balls, Wilson hit a slow roller down the first base line. Had Stapleton been in the game, he could have charged the ball and easily made the play. Instead, Buckner hung back, watching the baseball bounce-bounce-bounce toward his glove. Then at the worst possible moment the ball didn't bounce. It skipped.

To the right of Buckner's mitt and through his legs. The ball rolled into shallow right field, a momentarily unclaimed piece of baseball history ignored in an ocean of emotions. As Knight, his arms circling like mini-windmills, scampered home from second with the decisive run, Buckner removed the glove from his right hand and walked back to the dugout. Every Met, from Knight to Davey Johnson to Mazzilli to Harrelson to Hernandez, Orosco, and the other superstition-minded men bound to the clubhouse, converged at home plate in a blue-and-orange mountain of bliss.

There are varying motivations for becoming a professional athlete, from the money to the fame to the women to the drive of competition. But on this night at this singular moment the Mets remembered what it was like to do something for pure love. They had accomplished the baseball impossible, and the result was euphoria.

When the ball passed Buckner, panic struck in the Red Sox clubhouse. A celebration-ready room that took thirty minutes to prepare had to be dismantled—*now!* "The whole clubhouse froze for a second," says Vinny Greco, "and then someone said, 'Holy shit! What are we gonna do?'" Here's what they did: Greco ripped down the plastic and rolled it into a large ball. Tony Carullo, the visiting clubhouse manager, plucked the hats and shirts out of each locker and tossed them in a nearby box. The platform, with the Commissioner's Trophy sitting on top, was pushed out the back door. John Rufino covered the cases of champagne bottles with a tarp and rolled them back down the hall.

One by one the Red Sox filed in. Nobody said a word. It smelled like bubbly. Baylor was the first to shower and change into street clothes. There was a locked box in the trainer's room for player valuables. "Has anybody got a key?" Baylor asked. "Anyone?" No one answered. Baylor grabbed the top of the box and barbarically ripped it off its hinges. Money and jewelry poured out.

"They were dead," says Greco. "Dead."

Shortly after the end of Game 6, Arthur Richman, New York's crusty travel secretary, popped his head into the umpires' locker room, where he was greeted by Ed Montague, who had just spent the evening positioned in right field. Montague handed Richman a baseball. "What's this?" Richman asked.

"It's the last ball of the game," said Montague. "You're with the Mets. Go get Mookie Wilson to sign it, and you'll have something to treasure."

Richman went into the clubhouse, and Wilson wrote, "To Arthur: This is the ball that won it. Mookie Wilson," and dated it 10/25/86.

The baseball sat on a shelf in Richman's Manhattan apartment for the next six years, until he was convinced to put it up for auction. On August 4, 1992, actor Charlie Sheen proved that his accepting the starring role in *Grizzly II: The Predator* was no fluke in judgment. He paid $93,500 for the ball, ten times the presale estimate. Richman donated the money to charity.

After the game Bobby Ojeda's car was (coincidentally) parked next to the bus that would take Boston's executives back to Manhattan's Grand Hyatt. Strolling toward his vehicle, Ojeda was granted what he considers one of the all-time great gifts. Standing there in the blustery cold were none other than Haywood Sullivan and John Harrington, the two Red Sox bigwigs last seen arrogantly puffing on cigars in the lobby of the Boston Sheraton. This time there were no stogies, no smiles, and no egos. Just a pair of deflated men. "To see them with their faces on the floor, like their dog just got hit by a car, was awesome," he says. "I was like, 'Fuck you and eat shit, assholes. And you know what? You're gonna lose tomorrow, too.'"

With the remarkable comeback providing thrust, the Mets refused to let anything rain on their parade. Literally. Game 7 was scheduled to be played the next evening, but when most New Yorkers awoke that Sunday morning, they were greeted by gray skies and heavy showers. At noon Al Harazin, the Mets assistant GM, and Red Sox GM Lou Gorman met at the Manhattan office of Commissioner Peter Ueberroth to determine whether baseball could be played.

As Ueberroth and Gorman sat in skeptical silence, Harazin began an uninterrupted ten-minute riff on Shea's Stadium's extraordinary powers of drainage and how "without any question" the field would be perfectly playable for the 8:25 P.M. first pitch.

It was pure B.S. Harazin knew the field was a mess, and he was an awful liar. If the Mets and Red Sox played that evening, Boston would again start Boyd, who was not only eight nickels short of a dollar but, as proven in Game 3, eminently beatable. Unfortunately for New York, if the game was postponed, McNamara would replace Boyd with Hurst. Harazin shuddered at the thought. "Really, our field is great. You won't even know it rained."

Four hours later Ueberroth headed to Shea to check things out for himself. It was the funniest of scenes: the New York assistant GM strolling around in loafers and without a coat, pretending he was on a beach in Tahiti, and the commissioner, an umbrella above his head, sloshing around the marshy infield in muck-walkers and rolled-up pants. "Al," he said, "why aren't you out here in your swim fins?"

Game 7 was postponed. It would be Darling versus Hurst.

On the morning of the most important start of his life, Darling spent two hours walking around Manhattan's Chinatown with his parents, Ron Sr. and Luciana. It was something of a stress release for the right-hander, with just one catch: There was no stress. Darling had stayed up until 3 A.M. the night before watching *The Hustler*, and not once during the movie did McNamara, Hurst, or Boston's lineup pop into his head. Just Paul Newman, six ball in the corner pocket.

If only everyone were so cool. As was World Series tradition, before the game the lineups for the two opposing teams were introduced on the field. When his name was called, Strawberry jogged directly past his manager as if the man didn't exist. Equally enraged at his teammates for their lack of support, he ignored tradition and refused to shake anyone's hand. Standing next to him in line, Carter couldn't help but think to himself,

What a pathetic show. Arms defiantly crossed, Strawberry stood tall, more proud than humbled.

When the game began, it quickly became clear that Darling did not have his best material. Boston scored 3 runs in the second, highlighted by back-to-back homers by Evans and Gedman. In a stroke of karma, the second of those soared deep into right field where Strawberry jumped, caught the ball, and—*pop!*—watched it wiggle out of his webbing and over the wall. It was an embarrassing moment for an arrogant man. Both baseballs went high, far, and deep, and not one Met was overly concerned. "We were like Popeye when he eats his spinach," says Ojeda. "He's getting his ass kicked, and he looks down and out. But he knows he's got his stash on the side. We knew that we had yet to eat our spinach."

If the power of momentum was reason number 1 for such optimism, then a close second was Sid Fernandez. At the start of the series Johnson made the decision to go with a three-man rotation of Darling-Gooden-Ojeda, excluding the Hawaiian who had won *only* 16 games and tied for fourth in the NL with 200 strikeouts. The move crushed Fernandez, who stormed out of Johnson's office, contemplating all the reasons he would be better off playing elsewhere in 1987. "You feel unappreciated and unloved," Fernandez says. "But after I thought about it, I realized I could mope or I could contribute."

When Gooden was hammered in the Game 5 loss, it was Fernandez who entered and held the Sox scoreless for 4 innings. Now he was being called upon to do so again. For 2⅓ innings Fernandez was masterful— no hits, no runs, no Boston clue. When he was twelve, Fernandez's Pony League team was invited to Dodger Stadium, where he had his photograph taken with one of his heroes: Bill Buckner. The picture hung in his house for years, and Fernandez always idolized Boston's first baseman. Now he was shutting down Buckner and his teammates.

In the sixth inning New York finally grasped Hurst. With one out, Mazzilli, pinch-hitting for Fernandez, singled to left, then moved to second on another single by Wilson. Hurst walked Teufel to load the bases for Hernandez, who was 1 for 7 against the Boston lefty. That morning while eating breakfast with his brother Gary, Hernandez made a prediction. "If I get up with men on base," he said, "I'm driving them in." As promised, he ripped a single to left-center, scoring 2 runs and bringing Shea Stadium to its feet. The Mets were down, 3–2.

Up came Gary Carter.

Though amicable, throughout their years together Carter and Hernandez were hardly holding hands and singing *Endless Love*. When Carter arrived in New York before the '85 season, he had to watch as pitchers turned to someone else for advice. Hernandez, meanwhile, found Carter's excitability grating. He especially bristled during the NLCS when Carter's anti-Scott rants made the team look like a bunch of sore losers.

And yet there was always a level of respect. Hernandez loved the way Carter called a game from behind the plate. And Carter was blown away by Hernandez's smooth glove at first. "Winning," says Hernandez, "brings opposites together."

Knowing New York's catcher thrived on heat, Hurst's first pitch was a drooping curveball that floated to the low-outside corner of the plate. Carter swung mightily, bopping a flare into right field. Evans charged in, dove, smothered the baseball with his glove, rolled over, and watched it pop out from under his body. Backman, pinch-running for Teufel, easily scored the tying run. Hernandez, however, had problems. With the ball obscured by Evans's torso, right field umpire Dale Ford delayed making a call. As a result, Hernandez paused between first and second and was tagged out by Owen. "Where was the damn call?" he yelled toward Ford.

Years later Carter, living up to his reputation as a me-first player, blamed his teammate for robbing him of greater glory. "If Keith Hernandez was watching what's going on, I end up hitting over .300," says Carter, who wound up with a .276 average. "But he gets thrown out, and that hurts my numbers."

When told of the criticism, Hernandez fumed. "That's typical Carter," he says. "And he would've got the MVP too, right? That's the main rip on Gary Carter. He should've been happy to get the monkey off his back because he was labeled a loser—me-me, I-I. And he just got the monkey off his back, and he's worried about being the MVP?

"I wasn't watching? He doesn't think I'm watching? Evans has a great arm, so if he comes up cleanly with the catch and then comes up throwing, I'm doubled off first and we don't get a run. The most important thing was the run, not Gary's numbers. He shouldn't have even been thinking about MVP of the World Series. And he was."

Two games, two stirring comebacks. Left with a tattered staff and a battered bullpen, McNamara brought out Schiraldi to start the bottom of the seventh. He might as well have handed New York the Commissioner's Trophy. With the crowd chanting *Caaaal-viiiin! Caaaal-viiiin! Caaaal-viiiin!* and the red-hot Knight at bat, there was only one way it could go. On a two-ball, one-strike pitch, Knight hammered the baseball over the left center field wall. The moment was greeted with such a sonic boom that Scully noted, "It's so noisy at Shea, you can't hear the airplanes."

The Mets scored 2 more runs to take a 6–3 lead, and even when the Red Sox made it 6–5 with an eighth-inning rally against McDowell, any lingering aspirations to breaking the Curse of the Bambino were swiftly erased. Strawberry led off the bottom of the inning against Nipper, fell behind no balls, two strikes, and proceeded to wallop the ball as high and as far as any hit in the series. This time Strawberry basked in the glow of the moment. He didn't so much jog as trot around the bases, making certain to inspect each fragment of dirt along the way. Nipper was infuriated, but he had the wrong idea. Strawberry's provocation was directed not at the Red Sox but at Johnson. When he entered the dugout, he walked right past the manager without saying a word.

One inning later it was all over. Orosco, the man acquired for Jerry Koosman seven years earlier, forced Ed Romero to pop up to Hernandez, then coerced Boggs into a groundout to Backman at second. Now Barrett stared out at Orosco, and the reckoning was at hand. A fan interrupted the action by throwing a smoke bomb into left field, and as the red clouds floated into the air, the symbolism was obvious.

With the count two balls, two strikes, Barrett swung through a high outside fastball that Manute Bol couldn't have reached. Orosco jumped, flipped his mitt into the air, fell to his knees, pounded the ground with both fists and—*whooooosh!*—was tackled by his entire team. Fifty mounted police officers immediately rode in from right field, and rolls of toilet paper rained from the upper decks. WORLD CHAMPS! flashed on the Diamond Vision.

On the Boston bench Boggs bit on his index finger, tears flowing down his puffy cheeks. Gedman stared in shock at the field. Before he joined the celebration, Harrelson again spotted his old pal Seaver, this time without a smile. "No," Harrelson yelled, "I'll call *you.*"

Amidst the champagne blasts and beer pouring and screams and shouts and laughter of the victorious clubhouse, Davey Johnson was asked whether the country could appreciate the greatness of his club.

"I'm not so sure," said the manager.

Why?

"Because," Johnson said, "the bad guys won."

Chapter 20

WHAT DYNASTY?

One of the saddest things in the world is wasted talent.

—AL HARAZIN, Mets assistant GM

THE OFFICIAL EXCUSE, relayed to the press via Mets media relations director Jay Horwitz, was illness. "Dwight Gooden wasn't feeling very well," Horwitz announced on the afternoon of October 28, 1986. "That's why he was absent."

The words rang hollower than a termite-carved tree. For three years Horwitz had been obliged to serve—in the words of *Boston Globe* columnist Leigh Montville—as Gooden's "Plexiglas shield," guarding the phenom from even the slightest hint of negativity. This, however, was too much. Overslept? *Overslept!* On the morning after Game 7 of the World Series, nearly every member of the New York Mets was able to shake off hangovers to make it to Battery Park in time for the largest sports victory parade in Manhattan's history, one attended by an estimated 2.2 million confetti-tossing, fist-pumping, blue-and-orange-clad spectators.

So where was Dwight Gooden?

Keith Hernandez and Bobby Ojeda spent the previous night bouncing around from bar to bar, beginning on Long Island at Finn MacCool's and then at The Columbus, a restaurant/bar on the Upper West Side of Manhattan. Everywhere they went the two men drank for free. At 7 A.M. when they finally stumbled into Hernandez's Upper East Side apartment, the Gold Glove first baseman and the left-handed starter were blitzed beyond comprehension. In three hours, they were due to report to Shea Stadium, where a police escort would lead the Mets' bus into Manhattan for a glorious Tuesday celebration, scheduled to begin at 12:30 P.M.

Ojeda, sleeping on the couch in Hernandez's den, was the first awake and hence the first to realize that he and his teammate were in deep shit. With a cotton-dry mouth and a brick-smashing hangover, Ojeda groggily rolled off the sofa and opened the blinds. "Holy crap!" he yelled, noticing the brilliant midday sun. "Mex! Mex! Wake up! It's 12 o'clock! It's 12 o'clock!"

Without showering, brushing, or changing clothes, the teammates darted outside, hailed a taxi, and rode downtown until the traffic began to thicken. When all movement ceased, they left the cab and sprinted through the streets. "And the crowds see us, and they all start yelling 'Yeeeeaaaahhhh!'" says Ojeda. "It's like me and Mex had our own little parade trying to get to the parade." Once they neared the starting point, Hernandez and Ojeda were confronted by a seven-foot iron fence that stood between them and their destination. "I'm thinking, 'Damn, all this way and we can't get through,'" says Ojeda. "Now what?" On an afternoon when the Mets were kings, a mob of their loyal subjects—fans standing nearby—lifted the two players over the fence. "And we made it," Ojeda says. "It was a minor miracle, but we were there for the greatest parade I've ever seen."

So where was Dwight Gooden??

It was the million-dollar question—and remains so. In his autobiography, *Heat,* Gooden insists that he spent the night of Game 7 club hopping, drinking to excess, but avoiding all illegal drugs. "It was a simple garden-variety hangover," he writes. "I finally put my head on the pillow at eight, foolishly thinking a few minutes of napping would refresh me."

At 10 A.M. Darryl Strawberry knocked on the door of his friend's Long Island home. "I'd had every intention of going," Gooden writes. "I told Jay Horwitz to save a spot for me in one of the lead cars, I was that excited about it. But now that I was feeling like death, there was no way I was leaving the house."

According to Gooden, he hid in his bedroom as Strawberry's knocking turned to pounding and then to yelling. *Doc, you coming? C'mon, we've got to get to the parade.* "I didn't want fans to see me in that condition," he wrote. "I didn't want anyone to know the humble, meek Doc was a drinker and could show up in public looking so bad. So I took the easy way out: I disappeared, I hid."

So where was Dwight Gooden?

To many in the front office of the 1986 New York Mets, this is not a question but an answer to another question:

When did the Mets' potential dynasty begin to crumble?

As soon as they learned that their young ace was a no-show, members of the Mets management team didn't feel the need to look too hard for answers. With rumors of Gooden's drug abuse running rampant, the assumption was an easy one. Accurate or not, they believed "fatigue" was a convenient synonym for "coke hangover." "There were rumors, but we didn't really know for sure that Gooden had a problem until the parade," says Harazin. "Not showing up was a pretty big indicator."

"Were we suspicious of Gooden when that happened?" adds Cashen. "I think we had to be."

Less than one month after the parade fiasco, Gooden's engagement to longtime girlfriend Carlene Pearson was called off when it was revealed that he had recently fathered a child with Debra Hamilton, a high school friend. Shortly thereafter Gooden and four friends were arrested in Tampa for a brawl with two police officers who pulled over his silver-blue Mercedes. (Gooden was placed on three years' probation and had to film a local "Say No to Drugs" commercial.) According to *Sports Illustrated,* around that time he also twice failed to show up for ceremonies retiring his uniform at Hillsborough High in Tampa.

From afar, Cashen found the repeated incidents troubling. Gooden's image might have remained untarnished to an adoring public, but within the paranoid confines of Shea Stadium's executive offices, something had to be done. So the beleaguered Cashen took the wimpy way out and found a convenient scapegoat.

On December 11, one day after Gooden's arrest, the Mets traded Kevin Mitchell to San Diego as part of a seven-player swap that brought outfielder Kevin McReynolds to New York. From a purely baseball standpoint, the move was a hard one to argue. Mitchell was promising, yet green, while McReynolds, who had 26 homers and 96 RBIs in '86, was an established power threat. McIlvaine had coveted the slugger since he scouted him as a collegiate star at the University of Arkansas and for more than a year had pushed his name on Cashen. Johnson, though, was furious and crushed. Mitchell was one of *his* guys. "I didn't want to trade Mitchell," says Johnson. "I knew what a pure hitter he was, and he could easily have settled into a starting job. But Cashen said he was going to get in too much trouble here. I had no say."

For the team's remaining African American players the move was a validation of the charges George Foster had made that August when he said, "When a ballclub can, they replace a George Foster or a Mookie Wilson with a more popular (white) player." Mitchell was a potential star thought of as "too black." With his gangster past and capped front teeth, Mitchell was never trusted by the front office. Behind closed doors they worried that the thug from San Diego was guiding Gooden and Strawberry down a wayward path, and they wanted him gone. It was, in an oncoming crush of miscalculations, New York's worst. The unofficial team barber, Mitchell was beloved by black and white team-mates alike. He was as much to blame for the substance abuse problems as was William Howard Taft. "I can't make a man go in there and suck on some white powder," says Mitchell. "How can I? I ain't never used any drugs in my life. I'm high off sex and I'm high off life. I rarely even dealt with Gooden and Strawberry off the field."

In McReynolds, Cashen and McIlvaine were cursed to get exactly what they had asked for. The team's new left fielder averaged 24 homers and 87 RBIs in the ensuing five seasons with the Mets, but his joyless approach turned teammates off. With New York trailing big in a 1989 game against the Cubs at Wrigley, McReynolds began changing into his street clothes before the end of the ninth inning. When the Mets rallied, he had to strip again and rush to the field to take another at-bat. He was fined $500. "McReynolds brought nothing to our club," says Ojeda. "He didn't want to be there, so it didn't matter to him. And Mitch, for all his faults, always wanted to be there. He was an intense ballplayer."

Equally hard-edged was Knight who, despite a magnificent season capped by the World Series MVP trophy, was deemed obsolete. The free-agent third baseman desperately wanted to stay in New York and was willing to accept substantially less money. To Cashen it was not an option. The Mets had Howard Johnson and Magadan waiting in the wings, as well as a hotshot nineteen-year-old minor leaguer named Gregg Jefferies. Why bring back a thirty-four-year-old journeyman? On the evening of November 2, the deadline for free agents to re-sign with their clubs, George Califedas, Knight's agent, met with Cashen and McIlvaine in a last-ditch effort to work something out. Before he left for the appointment, Califedas phoned his client. "If we get something done before midnight, I'll call you," he said. "If not, it's dead." That night Knight and his wife were returning from a golf tournament in Sarasota, Florida. At 11:55 P.M. Knight turned to his spouse, tears in his eyes.

Even though Howard Johnson had a fantastic '87 as the Mets' starting third baseman (32 stolen bases, 36 home runs, 99 RBIs), the team felt the absence of another major contributor to its former spunk. "Ray-Ray was a leader," says McDowell. "You can't get rid of leadership and expect things to stay the same."

Officially the Mets' descent began on March 26, 1987, the day Gooden took his first urine test after spending much of the winter denying incessant rumors of his drug abuse. Whether it was a cry for help or pure stupidity, Gooden actually insisted that he be subjected to screening, and he had the Mets place such a provision in his contract that winter. "It can be for a test every week, every two days, as often as they want," he told the *Tampa Tribune*. "Drugs? I never use them and I never will."

Four days later Cashen was informed that the first results indicated that Gooden had ingested cocaine within forty-eight hours. In one week the defending World Series champions were scheduled to open their season, and now their ace was suspended, off to twenty-eight days of rehab at the Smithers Alcoholism and Drug Treatment Center on Manhattan's Upper East Side. "I'll never forget Frank Cashen's announcement because I never, ever expected it," says Carter. "It was just a huge setback. It just wasn't the same feeling in the clubhouse. We still had chances to win, but the swagger was missing. Some of the magic was gone."

Very few tears were shed around the league. At the Phillies' spring training complex, a picture of the Mets was posted on the team's bulletin board. Across the grinning faces a question was written in fat black marker: CAN YOU BEAT THESE ASSHOLES?

The answer: yes. Between 1987 and 1990 the Mets won one division title. They placed second three times. "Immediacy of pleasure," says Rusty Staub, "has ruined a lot of good baseball teams."

Sitting ten rows behind home plate at the Mets' spring training facility in Port St. Lucie, Florida, Frank Cashen looks the part of the transplanted New York retiree, kicking back and enjoying some baseball. The year is 2002, and at age seventy-nine, sixteen years removed from the '86 title, he has nothing to do with the modern-day Mets of Mike Piazza and Mo Vaughn and their eight-figure salaries. Though his official title is vice president/consultant, Cashen's primary duties consist of very little. "I'm from another generation," he says softly. "Baseball is a young man's game."

Though his gait is slow, his skin wrinkled, and his hearing less than good, Cashen perks up from time to time. He enthusiastically rips the greed of the modern player and will expound for eons on his glorious run with the Baltimore Orioles. Yet nothing—not even talk of his seven kids and ten grandchildren—kick-starts the old ticker as does the reminder of Gooden, Strawberry, and their abuses.

"Dwight Gooden and Darryl Strawberry were the guys who really let us down," he says. "I built the goddamned team, and I built it around those guys. It's a tragedy when you think how many people try but aren't given the God-given talent. And for them to just waste it and fail . . ." Cashen pauses, sipping from the cup of water in his shaky right hand. The sun is shining, but inside Cashen's head it is pouring rain. In February 1990, three years after Gooden's first trip to Smithers, Strawberry, too, entered the facility to seek help with a substance abuse problem that had plagued him for several years. "That club should have won for the next three or four seasons without fail," Cashen says. "Those two men let not only themselves down but the teams and the fans of New York. That team was destined to be a dynasty. Maybe I take this too personally, but in my opinion those two men cost us years of success."

Between the end of 1986 and his retirement after the '91 season, Cashen—often following the advice of McIlvaine, his chief talent evaluator—completed one ill-advised transaction after another, stripping the Mets of almost all ties to the glory year. The man who built the Mets ruined the Mets. Now that New York was on top, the thinking changed. Minor leaguers were used primarily as trading chips. Older players were everywhere. The Mets' time was now, and they felt compelled to jump on it. As Gooden told *Sports Illustrated* in 1990, "Maybe we've made too many trades for guys who are used to getting their asses kicked. The guys who used to snap—Wally, Lenny, Ray, Keith, Mitch—they're gone."

By the beginning of the 1988 regular season, Santana was playing shortstop for the Yankees, and Heep, Orosco and Sisk, once known as the Scum Bunch, were scumming elsewhere. On December 12, 1988, just two months after his club was upset by the Dodgers in the NLCS, Cashen sent Backman to the Twins in exchange for Toby Nivens, Steve Gasser, and Jeff Bumgarner. It was a debacle, and not because the acquired players failed to reach the big leagues. No, when Cashen traded the fiery Backman, he did so to open up a spot for Gregg Jefferies, the most highly touted prospect in baseball during the 1980s.

Along with his remarkable hitting skills, Jefferies brought to Shea Stadium an attitude foreign to past clubs. Unlike Backman, he was meek, whiney, and aloof; "a clean-uniform guy," says McDowell, as well as a softie with the booze. He also had the misfortune of replacing a clubhouse favorite, and his .276 average and 42 homers in 465 career games as a

Met hardly justified his status. "Wally was real popular with the fans and his teammates, and all of a sudden he was out the door," says Dave Magadan. "So instead of embracing Gregg, it was 'He took a job from our friend and he's a baby.' There were a lot of players who took anonymous shots through the press at him, and that wasn't fair." On May 24, 1991, Jefferies asked that a letter—pleading his case as a misunderstood victim—be read on WFAN, New York's sports radio station.

Jefferies wrote: "When a pitcher is having trouble getting players out, when a hitter is having trouble hitting, or when a player makes an error, I try to support them in whatever way I can. I don't run to the media to belittle them or to draw more attention to their difficult times.

"I can only hope that one day those teammates who have found it convenient to criticize me will realize that we are all in this together. If only we can concentrate more on the games than complaining and bickering and pointing fingers, we would all be better off."

The letter went against one of baseball's oldest, most important rules (What's said in the clubhouse stays in the clubhouse), and it backfired miserably. Jefferies turned into even more of a team leper.

By the time he was shipped to Kansas City before the '92 season, he was one of the most disliked players in team history. "Gregg Jefferies killed us," says McDowell. "He was treated as an outcast because he was an arrogant kid who thought he was better than everyone else. Other than wearing a uniform, he was not part of that club."

Within an eight-month span after the Backman transaction, Cashen authorized three more deals that imploded. By August 1989 Dykstra and McDowell were exchanged for Philadelphia's Juan Samuel, Wilson went to Toronto for reliever Jeff Musselman, and Aguilera, along with four prospects (including future all-star pitcher Kevin Tapani), brought left-handed starter Frank Viola from Minnesota. None of the new players lasted more than two and a half years in New York. Age, meanwhile, caught up with Carter and Hernandez, both of whom departed as free agents at the end of the '89 season. By 1991, Darling, Fernandez, Gooden, Howard Johnson, and Teufel were the only remaining regulars from the '86 Amazin's.

"If you give us credit for any of the success, then you have to give us blame for the downfall," says Harazin. "But it's impossible to keep the exact personnel all the time. Change in baseball is inevitable. You have no choice."

When Cashen stepped down after the '91 season that saw the Mets go 77–84 and finish in fifth place in the NL East, he left what he found upon arrival eleven years earlier: rubble. The Mets were one of eight teams ever to finish first or second for seven consecutive seasons but the only one of that group not to capture more than one pennant. Despite a stockpile of young pitching, the most prospect-packed farm system in baseball, and a lineup of muscular long-ball specialists, the Mets failed to return to the World Series for fourteen years. By the time they did, 1986 was a distant image, reduced to a couple of faded pictures hanging in the Shea Stadium walkways. The most memorable team in New York history had been forgotten.

Like a parade in Dwight Gooden's mind.

Epilogue

With baseball players you don't worry about the fame, you worry about life after the fame. How are they going to live their lives when nobody knows them? How will they handle not having free meals and not having everybody buying them drinks and not having everybody wanting to talk to them? How do you handle it when that's what you've thrived on?

—DAVEY JOHNSON, Mets manager

SOMETIME IN THE EARLY MONTHS of 2002, I flew out to San Francisco to meet with Kevin Mitchell, who was about to begin his first season as manager of the Sonoma County Crushers of the independent Western Baseball League. For two and a half hours Mitchell was everything one could hope for in an interview subject: Gregarious. Funny. Loud. Poignant. Chock full of stories.

Near the end of our sit-down, I asked Mitchell to expound on an anecdote that appeared in Dwight Gooden's 1999 autobiography, *Heat*. Before I even mentioned what exactly the anecdote was,

Mitchell's mood went from sunny summer day to winter storm. "Lemme tell you one thing," he said somewhat menacingly. "I didn't do that shit."

That shit was cutting the head off a cat with a twelve-inch kitchen knife. According to *Heat*, in 1986 Gooden and a friend were visiting Mitchell's Long Island home, and in the middle of a dispute with his girlfriend, the Mets outfielder picked up a small kitten and slashed it across the throat. The body fell to the ground. "I was horrified by the sight," Gooden writes. "Blood pouring out from where the head once was, limbs still twitching."

Shortly after the book was released, Mitchell received a call from a friend who informed him that Jim Rome was telling feline mutilation stories on his radio program. Mitchell phoned Rome at his office. "I asked him why he was making false allegations about me," Mitchell said. "Rome said, 'Hey, Mitch, I'm getting it straight from the horse's mouth, Dwight Gooden.'"

Mitchell was furious. "How could I cut off a cat's head with a kitchen knife? Hell, I love animals," he told me. "I'm not the one who went out there and sucked up some lines, like Dwight Gooden did. I'm a decent guy." For three years Mitchell waited patiently to face Gooden in person. He says he initially considered a lawsuit, then good old-fashioned violence. At the least, a tongue-lashing would suffice.

The moment finally arrived on the afternoon of November 8, 2002, when the two men were scheduled to attend a memorabilia-signing event in New Rochelle, New York. Gooden arrived first, then Mitchell. It didn't take long.

MITCHELL: "Why did you write that I cut off a cat's head?"
GOODEN: "It wasn't me."
MITCHELL: "It wasn't?"
GOODEN: "Nope."
MITCHELL: "Okay. We're cool."

Moments later I asked Mitchell about the encounter. "Doc said he wasn't responsible," he said. "I guess I believe him." *But*, I pointed out, *it's right there . . . in HIS autobiography.*

Mitchell didn't flinch. All anger was gone. "I said my piece," he said. "It's over."

Remarkably, it was.

Did Mitchell, in fact, slice a cat's head off? Or was it Gooden, embarrassed by years of substance abuse and underachievement, trying to deflect attention onto an innocent teammate? Truthfully, we'll probably never know. And after spending way too much time researching the team and its legacy, I genuinely wonder if the players themselves will ever know. In 1986 the New York Mets spent every day under the giant-sized tent of the Big Apple Circus. Things moved at 10,000 mph—a hard-to-track swirl of baseball and booze and women and drugs and cars and fans and wins. Stories are told with such dead-serious intensity—"Aw, you had to be there to see this . . ."—that you'd think a Bible was underhand. Yet it often takes four, five, or six witnesses to confirm whether the yarn is fact, fiction, or somewhere in between. Did Mitchell slice a cat's head off? Does it really matter?

Even today, chaos rules. The 1986 Mets hold a reunion/memorabilia show every two years or so, and like that magical season, you never know what you're gonna get. Mitchell versus Gooden. Carter mocking. X-rated stories. At an autograph gig in New Jersey several years back, an irate fan approached Ed Hearn, who was sitting behind a table. "Where's Tim Teufel?" the man yelled. "I'm gonna kick his ass! He's trying to pick up my wife!"

Hearn, an admirer of the quiet, religious Teufel, was shocked. "Tim's trying to pick up your wife?" he said. "What makes you say that?"

The man handed Hearn a baseball bearing Teufel's signature. "Look," he said. "He signed it for her and put his room number on the ball!"

Hearn laughed hysterically. The ball read: Rom. 116, as in Bible verse Romans 1:16.

Only the '86 Mets . . .

WHAT BECAME OF THE 1986 NEW YORK METS

After being traded to Minnesota midway through the '89 season as part of a package for Frank Viola, **Rick Aguilera** emerged as one of baseball's elite closers, saving 30 plus games six times and appearing in three All-Star Games. When he retired in 2001, Aguilera ranked eighth on the all-time save list with 318. He now lives in San Diego and serves as a part-time pitching coach at Santa Fe Christian, the school attended by his two children, Rachel, 12, and Austin, 7.

Pitcher **Rick Anderson** was a throw-in in the Ed Hearn-for-David Cone trade with Kansas City in 1987, and he retired two years later. As a first-year pitching coach for the Minnesota Twins in 2002, Anderson helped guide his team to the American League Championship Series. He is considered one of the game's bright young minds.

Wally Backman went on to enjoy a fruitful career with the Twins, Pirates, Phillies, and Mariners before retiring after 1993 with a .275 average and 893 hits. Hired by the Chicago White Sox in 2001 as a minor-league manager, he led Class AA Birmingham to the 2002 Southern League title by playing an aggressive brand of baseball termed "Wally-ball." He is now the manager of the Lancaster JetHawks, the Class A affiliate of the Arizona Diamondbacks.

When he began the '86 season by winning his first two decisions, pitcher **Bruce Berenyi** was depicted in a Bill Gallo *Daily News* cartoon as one of New York's five "great starters." Owing to injuries and inconsistencies, he was dumped three months later. He retired with a 44–55 record and oodles of untapped potential.

Today Berenyi works in the bag room of a golf club in Florida. He plays golf four times a week and is trying to catch on with the Celebrity Players' Tour.

Gary Carter retired with 324 homers, 1,225 RBIs, and a reputation as something of a phony. Perhaps that is why it took one of the greatest offensive catchers in baseball history three tries to get into the Hall of Fame, which he finally entered in 2003. These days Carter serves as a full-time minor league catching instructor with the Mets and oversees The Gary Carter Foundation, a not-for-profit charitable organization that contributes to myriad causes.

Infielder **Tim Corcoran**'s career never quite took off after leading the AL with 10 pinch hits as a rookie with Detroit in 1977. He went hitless in seven at-bats with the '86 Mets before a June release.

Pitcher **Ron Darling** enjoyed several more years of success with the Mets, winning 50 games from 1987 to 1990. He was traded to Montreal midway through '91 and spent his final four and a half seasons with Oakland. Darling has dabbled as a sports reporter for Fox Sports and as an actor. In 2001 he appeared in *Shallow Hal*, a film starring Gwyneth Paltrow.

Following his trade to Philadelphia in 1989, outfielder **Lenny Dykstra** became a star. Nails enjoyed an MVP-caliber season in '90, leading the league with 192 hits while batting .325. He again paced the NL with 194 hits in '93 as the Phillies reached the World Series.

While driving home from teammate John Kruk's bachelor party in May 1991, Dykstra smashed his car into a tree. Police said the accident was alcohol related, and it left the outfielder with broken ribs, a broken cheekbone, and a broken collarbone. Years later Dykstra called the crash a "blessing" in that it forced him to reexamine his life. Dykstra was hired by the Cincinnati Reds to manage its Class A Mudville team in 2001, but he quit after two weeks. He now presides over Lenny Dykstra's Car Wash & Auto Repair in Los Angeles.

Shortstop **Kevin Elster** set a major league record by going 88 straight games without an error in 1989 but never hit enough to establish himself with the Mets. Elster had a startling career revival with Texas in 1996, slugging 24 homers and driving in 99 runs. On April 11, 2000, while playing for the Dodgers, he hit 3 home runs against San Francisco in the first-ever game at Pac Bell Park. When he temporarily became bored with the game, Elster ventured into Hollywood. In his only major role he played Twins shortstop Pat Corning in the 1994 film *Little Big League*. Today Elster lives in Las Vegas where he happily spends much time by the pool.

In a five-team, fifteen-year career, pitcher **Sid Fernandez** struggled to command a weight problem that at times had him as heavy as 260 pounds. In 2001, four years after his retirement because of a mysterious pain in his biceps, Fernandez attended spring training with the Yankees and signed a $500,000 contract. When it was suggested that he start the season in the minors, Fernandez officially called it a career. He lives in Honolulu.

When he became eligible for the Baseball Hall of Fame in 1992, the notoriously moody **George Foster** turned Mr. Happy, calling several newspaper writers who had covered his career to "just check in and see how my old pal is doing." It didn't work. Foster received 24 votes, well short of the necessary 323.

Foster spent four years as an assistant baseball coach at Brunswick High in Connecticut and now lives in Vero Beach, Florida, where he operates a youth baseball academy.

It is a little-known fact that the Mets' leading hitter in 1986 was catcher **John Gibbons**, who batted a Cobb-esque .474—*in 19 at-bats*. He was traded to the Dodgers in 1988 for infielder Craig Shipley and spent the remaining three years of his career bouncing around the minor leagues. Gibbons is now the first base coach with the Toronto Blue Jays.

Although he enjoyed several more good seasons with the Mets, **Dwight Gooden** was never the same. On November 4, 1994, Commissioner

Bud Selig suspended him for the entire '95 season for violating the league's aftercare drug policy. According to Gooden, the day after the ruling was handed out, he sat in his bedroom with a nine-millimeter gun to his head, contemplating suicide.

Yankees owner George Steinbrenner gave Gooden a second chance, signing him for the '96 season. On May 14, as his father lay dying in a Tampa hospital, Gooden threw an emotional no-hitter against the Mariners at Yankee Stadium. He was carried off the field a hero.

Gooden retired on March 23, 2001, with a 194–112 record and a 3.51 ERA. Gooden lives in Tampa with his wife, Monica, and his five children, and works as a minor league pitching coach with the Yankees.

Since his retirement in 1991, **Ed Hearn** has undergone three kidney transplants. In 1993, depressed by his floundering health, he took a loaded .357 Magnum into the basement of his Kansas City home and contemplated suicide. Hearn put the gun down, told his wife, Tricia, of his intentions, and sought counseling.

Later that year Hearn was asked to be a guest speaker at the Overland Park Rotary Club. Thrilled by the reaction to his talk, he became a full-time inspirational speaker and authored a book, *Conquering Life's Curves*. On May 6, 2002, Hearn received a kidney from his childhood friend, Chuck Satterwhite. The procedure was a success. Hearn is healthy for the first time in years and lives happily in Kansas City with his wife and son.

Danny Heep won his second world championship with the Dodgers in 1988 and retired after the '91 season with 503 hits and a .257 average. He now lives in San Antonio with his wife and two kids, and is the head baseball coach at the University of the Incarnate Word.

A five-time all-star and eleven-time Gold Glove winner, **Keith Hernandez** retired after a dreadful '90 season in Cleveland, during which he batted .200 in 43 games. He has since thrived in a variety of roles, including actor (to see Hernandez in the *Sesame Street* skit, "Put Down the Duckie," is to know thespian greatness), hair product pitch man, and, since 1999, a part-time color commentator for Met broadcasts. In 2002, Hernandez blasted the Mets' sloppy play in a column on the MSG Web site, and then meekly apologized to the team when it caused an uproar. Catcher Mike Piazza led the countercharge, telling Mike Morrissey of the *Post*, "Personally, I'm not going to come back five years [after retirement] and rip guys. That shows my envy and jealousy. If I'm doing that, just shoot me."

Once New York's top outfield prospect, **Stanley Jefferson** was unable to handle big league pitching. In parts of six seasons he never appeared in more than 116 games or batted above .276. He retired in 1991 with a .216 lifetime average.

In 1998 Jefferson fulfilled his lifelong dream and became an officer with the New York City Police Department.

Beginning in 1987, **Howard Johnson** hit at least 23 homers for five straight seasons. He called it quits in 1995 after batting just .195 with the Chicago Cubs, took a job coaching with Tampa Bay's affiliate in Butte, Montana, and then made a failed spring training comeback with the Mets. Johnson worked in the Mets scouting department from 1997 to 2001, he managed the Brooklyn Cyclones of the Class A New York–Penn League in 2002, and now is the hitting coach at Class AA Binghamton. He is married and has two daughters.

The Mets' decision to sever ties with third baseman **Ray Knight** after the 1986 season proved to be, statistically speaking, a wise one. Following two sub-mediocre years in Baltimore and Detroit, respectively, Knight retired. He rejoined Davey Johnson in '93, this time as a coach with the Cincinnati Reds. When Johnson was canned, Knight managed the team for one and a half seasons, compiling a 124–137 mark. Following a 3–2 win over the Dodgers on May 6, 1997, Knight fined himself $250 for not knowing how many outs there were when he called for a bunt. He was fired two months later. Before the 2002 season, Knight was rehired by manager Bob Boone as the Reds' third-base coach, a position he held for two years.

With his rubber arm and unorthodox sidewinder delivery, reliever **Terry Leach** became a very valuable man at Shea Stadium. In 1987, one season after appearing in just 6 games for the Mets, Leach went 11–1 with a 3.22 ERA. Today, Leach lives in Palm Beach, Florida, and is the owner of a successful interior design business. He is the author of an inspirational autobiography, *Things Happen for a Reason*.

The Mets traded **Ed Lynch**, and he went 2–9 with the Cubs in 1987, then retired at age thirty-one. Shortly thereafter he enrolled in the University of Miami's law school and received his degree in 1990. From 1994 to 2000, Lynch served as the general manager of the Cubs. He resigned midway through the 2000 season and now works as an assistant with the club.

In Biloxi, Mississippi, catcher **Barry Lyons** is Mr. Baseball. After spending three years as a color commentator for the Triple A Nashville Sounds, Lyons returned to his hometown in June 2002. He was immediately inducted into the Biloxi American Little League Hall of Fame. In Biloxi, Lyons opened the Barry Lyons Baseball Academy, which he hopes to use as a developmental tool for young athletes.

Although **Dave Magadan** never developed the power Cashen had anticipated, he enjoyed a solid seven-team, fifteen-year career, retiring after the 2000 season with a .288 average, 1,197 hits, and only 42 homers. He now serves as the hitting coach for the San Diego Padres.

In 1992, just three years after retiring from a fourteen-year major league career, **Lee Mazzilli** starred as Tony in the long-running off-Broadway comedy *Tony N' Tina's Wedding*. Over the years he has hosted a New York sports show on Channel 5, served as commissioner of the independent Northeast Baseball League, and opened Lee Mazzilli's Sports

Café. In 1997 the Yankees hired Mazzilli to manage their Class A Tampa affiliate. By 2000 he was back in the majors, coaching first base for the Bronx Bombers. He is now the manager of the Baltimore Orioles.

Certified nut **Roger McDowell** pitched for twelve years in the majors, but he is best known for a stunt pulled at Dodger Stadium in 1987 when he put his full Mets uniform on upside down and walked out onto the field, his pants over his head and his shoes on his hands. McDowell saved 159 games with the Mets, Phillies, Dodgers, Rangers, and Orioles before retiring with a shoulder injury in 1996. He now serves as the pitching coach for the Dodgers' Triple A Las Vegas club.

John Mitchell never developed into much of a major league pitcher, compiling a 9–14 mark in parts of five seasons with the Mets and Orioles. Today he sells municipal castings in his hometown of Nashville, Tennessee.

When he traded him to San Diego after the '86 season, Mets GM Frank Cashen never could have imagined that only three years later **Kevin Mitchell** would be the most feared slugger in the National League. In 1989, Mitchell, then with San Francisco, won the NL MVP Award, bopping 47 homers, driving in 125 runs, and batting .291. Unfortunately for the Giants, Mariners, Reds, Red Sox, Indians, and A's (his employers over the years), Mitchell never regained the explosiveness and struggled with durability.

In 2002 Mitchell took over the reins of the independent Sonoma County Crushers of the Western Baseball League, guiding the club to a 49–41 record in his only season. He is single and lives outside San Francisco.

Randy Myers saved 30-plus games six times, including a career-high 53 with the Cubs in 1993. He pitched for six franchises before retiring after the 1998 season with a torn rotator cuff. He lives in relative seclusion in Vancouver, Washington, where he hunts, fishes, and practices martial arts.

One year after riding the wave as a spare part for the world champion '86 Mets, reliever **Randy Niemann** rode the wave as a spare part for the world champion '87 Twins, appearing in 6 games and compiling an 8.44 ERA. Niemann retired the next season and has enjoyed two stints as the Mets' bullpen coach (1997–1999 and 2000–2002). He lives in Port St. Lucie, Florida, with his wife and three children and works as the pitching coach at Class AAA Norfolk.

The magic of '86 never returned for pitcher **Bobby Ojeda**, who, like Hearn, has suffered multiple miseries since the world championship. On September 21, 1988, Ojeda jeopardized his career when he severed the tip of the middle finger on his left hand with an electric hedge clipper. Incredibly, he came back to pitch the following season.

On March 23, 1993, Ojeda and two teammates with the Cleveland Indians, pitchers Tim Crews and Steve Olin, took a boat trip out onto Lake Nellie, near the Tribe's Winter Haven, Florida, spring training site. It was dark, and the boat struck a long wooden pier. Crews and Olin were killed. Ojeda returned to pitch in 9 games with Cleveland in '93, and then 2 more with the Yankees in '94 before being released.

After retirement, Ojeda traveled extensively, hiking through Norway and biking up the Alps. He is now the pitching coach at Class AA Binghamton. He is married and has five daughters.

In 1988, *Sports Illustrated*'s Peter Gammons wrote that **Jesse Orosco** was "widely perceived to be over the hill." Fifteen seasons later, Orosco was thriving as the Minnesota Twins' forty-six-year-old left-handed specialist. Orosco retired after the 2003 season as baseball's all-time leader in games pitched. He was one of four players (along with Tim Raines, Rickey Henderson, and Mike Morgan) to debut in the 1970s and last through the turn of the century. His secret? "A positive outlook," he says, "and good eating."

On December 11, 1987, the Mets traded shortstop **Rafael Santana** to the Yankees for outfielder Darren Reed and two other players, marking

the first deal between the crosstown rivals in eight years. Upon completion, Yankee GM Lou Piniella hailed a new era of communication
between the clubs. Santana lasted just one season with the Bronx
Bombers and retired after 7 games with Cleveland in 1990. He coached
in the minors from 1992 to 2002 and now serves as the White Sox's first
base coach.

Doug Sisk pitched moderately well for the Orioles in 1988, but manager Frank Robinson had even less patience than Davey Johnson,
openly questioning the right-handed reliever's fortitude and guts. He
lasted only one season in Baltimore, then sat out all of '89 with frayed
ligaments in his knees. After a brief comeback with the Braves, Sisk
retired in '91 with a 22–20 career record and an unmatched legacy of fan
antagonism.

He lives in Tacoma, Washington, and works as the athletic director
at a local Boys and Girls Club.

There have been many disappointments in baseball history, but few so
profound as **Darryl Strawberry**. He enjoyed four more all-star seasons
with the Mets, but on February 3, 1990, less than two weeks after being
arrested for assaulting his wife with a deadly weapon, Strawberry
entered the Smithers Alcohol and Drug Treatment Center.

He signed with the Dodgers as a free agent on November 8, 1990.
Strawberry hit 28 homers and drove in 99 runs in his first season with
LA, but that was the last time he resembled a superstar. He appeared
in only 43 games in 1992, and 32 in 1993. On September 4, 1993, he
was arrested for allegedly hitting twenty-six-year-old Charisse Simon,
his future wife. (No charges were filed.) Six months later he was
investigated by the IRS for allegedly failing to pay taxes on income in
excess of $300,000 from memorabilia shows (he and agent Eric
Goldschmidt were indicted on tax evasion charges; Goldschmidt was
acquitted).

Strawberry entered the Betty Ford Center in April 1994 for twenty-
eight-day care, and one month later he was cut by the Dodgers.

On April 24, 1995, Strawberry was sentenced to six months of home confinement on charges of tax evasion. He was forced to pay the U.S. government $350,000 in back taxes.

Citing his big heart and eagerness to provide second chances, Yankees owner George Steinbrenner signed Strawberry on June 19, 1995. On July 28, 1996, Strawberry hit his three hundredth career home run in the ninth inning of a 3–2 victory over Kansas City. He played a useful role on several Yankee championship teams.

Strawberry was diagnosed with colon cancer in 1998, and the following year was charged with possession of cocaine and soliciting a prostitute. (He entered no-contest pleas to both charges.)

On March 1, 2000, Strawberry checked himself into a drug rehabilitation clinic for the third time, then bolted after three months. Over the next two years he committed a dizzying array of similar infractions, ranging from drugs to alcohol to auto accidents.

He recently served eleven months in the Florida Department of Corrections for cocaine possession. In November 2003, Strawberry was hired by the Yankees to work as a player development instructor. He quit after four months to devote more time to his church.

Tim Teufel's five-and-a-half-year New York tenure proved to be a productive one. Along with playing a solid second base, Teufel was responsible for a certifiable Shea dance craze, the Teufel Shuffle. While watching Phillies third baseman Mike Schmidt take BP before an '86 game, Teufel noticed that the all-star wiggled his butt prior to each pitch. The next season Teufel batted a career-high .308, shuffling his way to success.

Teufel retired in 1993 and spent several years working for a financial investment company in San Diego. He now manages at Class A St. Lucie of the Florida State League.

Mookie Wilson's real name is William Hayward Wilson, but many fans call him "Mookie '86." Wilson played three more seasons at Shea before being traded to Toronto. He retired after the 1991 season with a lifetime .274 average and 1,397 hits. Wilson was appointed the Mets' first base/outfield coach on October 17, 1996, and held the position through the 2002 season. He now manages the Mets' Class A team in Kingsport, Tennessee.

Through the years Wilson has appeared at numerous autograph shows with Buckner, and a signed picture of the infamous Game 6 play is one of the hottest sellers in the memorabilia business.

Speaking of which . . .

In 1992 Mets GM Al Harazin was sitting in his office, drinking a cup of coffee and reviewing some scouting reports. The intercom buzzed. "Al," said Jean Coen, his secretary, "I've got **Bill Buckner** on the line." It had been six years since Buckner's error, and Harazin had heard this one, oh, ten thousand times.

"Jean, it's just someone playing a joke. Hang up on him."

Twenty seconds later Harazin was buzzed again. "Al, I really think it's Bill Buckner."

"Jean, gimme a break," said Harazin. "It's someone messing with us. Take my word for it."

One minute later Coen buzzed a final time. "Al, I'm telling you. This is Bill Buckner. Pick up!"

When Harazin answered the phone, it was in fact *the* Bill Buckner, out of baseball and looking for a major league coaching job. "Do you realize the story that could have been?" says Harazin, who had no open positions. "I mean, the New York Mets hire Bill Buckner after what happened in '86. Could you imagine?"

Afterword

"WILL WE EVER SEE ANOTHER TEAM like the '86 New York Mets?"

Back in the summer of 2004, when I was first promoting *The Bad Guys Won*, that was the question every media type seemed to ask me. On radio. On TV. On the Web.

"Sports has changed so drastically," one interviewer noted. "Could a group as wild and crazy and open as those Mets survive in the modern age?"

Because I was young and dumb and sort of clichéd, I offered up the mindless boilerplate response of, "Well, it happened once, so it can probably happen again. . . ."

Which, in hindsight, was utter nonsense.

In the seven years since *The Bad Guys Won* hit bookshelves, professional sports have taken an increasingly odious path toward blandness. Back in 2002, in my final year as a baseball writer for *Sports Illustrated*, the magazine assigned me to tag along with the supposedly wild and crazy Oakland Athletics as they journeyed from California to New York. Having anticipated drunken parties and pie-in-the-face zaniness, I was struck (and severely bummed) by the glaring lameness of it all. As soon as the players boarded the airplane, nearly all of them covered their ears with headphones. For six-straight hours, the only sound to be heard was that of the engine. No shouting. No yelling. No primal screams.

The engine.

Well, it's only gotten worse. With corporate America's increasingly powerful tentacles wrapping themselves around the sporting world, professional athletes have grown, in a word, lame. Once upon a time, a post-game baseball clubhouse was akin to a frat basement. Cold beers would be passed from player to player. Cigarette butts piled up in scattered ashtrays. Wads of chewed-up tobacco goop laced the floors. Without so much as changing out of their uniforms, ballplayers would kick back and talk about the game. What had gone right. What had gone wrong. *Shit. Fuck. Goddamned ass-wipe pussy motherfucker.* They would stick around for hours, well after the members of the media left and the stadium lights were shut off and the adrenaline subsided. Though it went unsaid, the athletes wanted the buzz to last forever. This was their dream—to be paid to play a kid's game—and nobody was in a particular rush to return home to the wife and kiddies.

"It's strange to say, but there was an innocence," says Ron Darling, the former Mets starting pitcher. "We grew up together as baseball players and we simply enjoyed each other's company. We wanted it to last forever."

Nowadays, however, professional athletes seem to take their cues from LeBron James and Tom Brady and Albert Pujols—every word measured, every move mechanically orchestrated to inspire contentedness from the highest-bidding sponsor. Jon Wertheim, my friend and longtime *Sports Illustrated* colleague, likes to tell the story of the time the magazine sent him to spring training to profile Alex Rodriguez when he was still the Texas Rangers' star short stop. Leaning against a wall near A-Rod's locker, Wertheim listened in as another reporter wrapped up an interview. He was surprised to hear the notoriously pre-fabricated Rodriguez reel off a couple of funny stories from the top of his head. "Maybe," Wertheim thought to himself, "this guy's gotten a bad rap."

When it was his turn to talk, Wertheim pulled up a stool and, no

matter the questions, heard Rodriguez tell the exact same stories—
verbatim.

"That," I later told Wertheim, "is baseball in the 2000s."

Recently, the spirit of the '86 Mets seemed to return to the Big Apple
with the rise of the 2010 New York Jets. In Coach Rex Ryan, the city
had a man unafraid to brag and boast and sling large quantities of shit.
Like Davey Johnson, he told his men that nothing short of a championship would do. The Mets and Jets shared myriad similarities: Hotshot
youngster (Dwight Gooden, quarterback Mark Sanchez), accomplished
veterans brought in to lead (Keith Hernandez and Gary Carter, Jason
Taylor and LaDainian Tomlinson), flashy hot dogs with questionable
judgment (Darryl Strawberry, Braylon Edwards). There was, however,
one enormous difference.

The '86 Mets won it all.

Twenty-five years have passed, and here are five amazing facts about the
members of the '86 Amazin' Mets:

- Despite the severe substance-abuse issues, all thirty-six men who
  played for the team are *not* dead (aka: alive).
- Darryl Strawberry seems to be enjoying a prolonged period of
  sobriety.
- Keith Hernandez, the player unofficially voted Most Likely to
  Become a Manager by, well, everyone, has managed nary a single
  game.
- Danny Heep, leader of the Scum Bunch, is the head baseball
  coach at the University of the Incarnate Word, an extremely religious private Catholic university in Texas.
- Lenny Dykstra went on to a career as a Wall Street investor.

Wait. Stop. Lenny Dykstra—an investor? The man who reveled in
driving 120 mph and farting in the faces of priests? The man who lost
countless amounts in poker games and who boasted the attention span
of a third grader?

Lenny Dykstra? An investor?

"When I heard that," says Ed Hearn, the backup catcher, "my reaction was, 'What?' Huh? What?'"

Indeed, throughout the early to mid-2000s, Dykstra stood out as one of the most unlikely and perplexing post-baseball success stories of all time. His chain of California-based car washes, Lenny Dykstra's Car Wash & Auto Repair, reportedly generated huge profits. He partnered with Castrol in Team Dykstra Quick Lube Centers, owned a real estate development company, started a magazine for athletes, and began developing a handful of "I Sold It on eBay" stores throughout Southern California. He regularly appeared on Fox News and his stock-picking skills were praised by CNBC's Jim Cramer ("He's a stock guru!"), who had Dykstra write an investment column for TheStreet.com. In 2008, Dykstra's net worth was estimated to be a whopping $58 million, and HBO's *Real Sports* profiled him in a glowing feature. "Honestly, I couldn't believe it," says Hearn. "If you knew Lenny back in 1986, there's no way you'd say to yourself, 'One day this man is going to be a financial wizard.'"

In September 2008, Dykstra started a high-end jet charter company, the latest brick in his growing empire. His story was being told with increasing frequency—the baseball fuckup who made it big. He paid $18.5 million for the Thousand Oaks, California, estate belonging to Wayne Gretzky, and delighted in offering a guided tour to all who asked. He drove a black Rolls-Royce Phantom with an extended wheelbase and flew from Point A to Point B in his own Gulfstream II jet. Once dismissed as too small, too limited, too . . . *everything*, Dykstra seemed to delight in the neon largeness of his existence. "People invested with me made 250-large last year," he boasted to ESPN's Mike Fish in 2009. "That's $250,000."

(Deadpanned Fish: "Which, if true, should earn him a front-row seat in the Obama cabinet.")

"To see Lenny doing so well," said Doug Sisk, a Mets relief pitcher, "was wonderful."

One problem: It was all a lie.

Well, maybe not a lie, per se. But an illusion, not unlike a David Blaine rope trick or the path of a Charlie Hough knuckler.

Faster than one can say *George Bamberger*, Dykstra's so-called genius was being exposed as fraudulence. Between 2007–2009, he was the subject of at least twenty-four legal actions. According to ESPN, he was sued by three different groups of pilots and a litigation consulting firm that had offered testimony on his behalf for a lawsuit. He was even sued by his own family members.

By the end of 2009, Dykstra was living out of his car. According to multiple reports, the home he purchased from Gretzky was vacant, overrun by water damage and rotted wood. A second home was also uninhabitable because of mold. He had his '86 World Series ring auctioned off for $56,762, which helped reduce his $31 million in debt.

By the end of 2010, an adult film star named Monica Foster was accusing Dykstra of hiring her as an escort, then bouncing the check.

In other words, Nails was back.

Fortunately for the team's legacy, for every Dykstra there is an Ed Hearn, a successful motivational speaker with a wife and son. For every Gooden and Strawberry (whose up-and-down lives have been well chronicled) there's Hernandez and Darling, who work side by side broadcasting Mets games on the SNY network.

For every down, there is an up.

Like, unexpectedly, Wally Backman.

Not all that long ago, the former second baseman could be grouped with the other Mets whose lives had spiraled out of control. Never a wallflower, Backman imbibed to excess and partied wildly. In 2000 he was arrested for DUI, and a year later he was apprehended again, this time for a domestic violence incident involving his wife, Sandi. He was once even forced to file for bankruptcy, an embarrassing turn based on a handful of poor business decisions.

Through it all, however, Backman boasted one strength: He could manage his ass off. In his first season as a minor league skipper, with

Catskill of the Northern League, Backman went 3–23—an aberration in an otherwise stellar career. Over the next six years, Backman suffered but one sub-.500 campaign. In 2004, he led the Class A Lancaster JetHawks to an 86–54 mark and was named the *Sporting News*'s minor league manager of the year.

"He's the best manager I ever played for," said Steve Garrabrants, a former Lancaster outfielder. "First, the man would take a bullet for one of his players. I mean that—a bullet. But he was more than that. I would watch the things he did, the signs he put on. It seemed like he always did the right thing at the right time. He put pressure on defense. He creates havoc on the other team. Other managers had to be thinking, 'What's Wally gonna do now?'"

With his aggressive, run-run-run approach to the game, Backman's style came to be known as "Wally Ball." In short, opposing teams would either stop him, or die of 1,000 needles.

"It's all about aggressiveness," Backman said. "Power is great and I'm happy to have it. But I love manufacturing runs and always applying pressure."

In October 2004, the Arizona Diamondbacks, coming off of a dreary 51–111 season, brought in Backman to interview for the vacant managerial position. Joe Garagiola Jr., the organization's general manager, was blown away by the candidate's enthusiasm and energy; passion and knowledge. Backman was exactly what the Diamondbacks needed. A jolt of electricity. A boost of adrenaline.

On November 1, the Diamondbacks held a press conference to introduce Backman as the fourth manager in franchise history. After holding up a pinstriped number 6 jersey, Backman spoke of his plans. "This is not a rebuilding program," he said. "I'm here to win. That's what I've always been about and that's what the Diamondbacks are about. And we will get back to the Diamondback ways of the past as soon as we possibly can. We will make some changes and this team will compete. That's one thing that every team that I've ever managed does."

Two days after Backman was hired, the *New York Times* ran a lengthy piece detailing his legal problems. On November 5, admitting they hadn't properly researched Backman's background, the Diamondbacks fired him.

"It's obviously a mistake on our part to have made a decision without having done the proper background work that could have been done, should have been done," said Ken Kendrick, the team's managing partner. "I take full responsibility for that, and I'm very sorry. We determined that it wasn't in the Diamondbacks' interest or our fans' interest that Wally be our manager."

Backman's four-day tenure is one of the shortest in major league history. The ensuing weeks and months were nightmarish ones. Backman returned home to Prineville, Oregon, and did . . . well, nothing. He sat. He slept. He drank. He ate. Nothing.

"When they told me they were taking away the job, it was like a death in the family . . . the death of a dream," Backman said. "The pain is still raw. All I wanted to do was manage a major league baseball team."

Over the ensuing two years, Backman searched for meaning. He hunted and fished and even opened up Prineville's first authentic deli, the New York on Seventh Street Café. It didn't last.

Finally, in 2007, he begrudgingly agreed to manage the South Georgia Peanuts of the fledgling South Coast League, an independent operation with few fans, few dollars, and few hopes. The league was beneath Backman, and he knew it. He hated the long bus rides and the empty stands and the clueless umpires. He hated feeling as if he were being perpetually punished for long-ago mistakes.

Then, in a June game against South Carolina's the Anderson Joes, Backman lost it. After one of his players was ejected for arguing balls and strikes, he stormed the field and chewed out umpire Tom Height. Backman then returned to the dugout, grabbed twenty-two bats and threw them toward home plate. Just in case the point wasn't made, he emptied a bucket of baseballs down the third base line. Watching from above in a rickety press box, Mike Janela, the Joes' radio announcer, questioned Backman's professionalism and lambasted him as "an embarrassment."

Upon being informed of the criticism, Backman suspended all judgment and climbed the press box steps. "Mike," he screamed at Janela, "if you ever call me an embarrassment again, I will kick your fucking ass!"

"But Wally . . ."

"No," Backman shouted. "I don't care if it was one hundred fucking bats. If you do that one more time I will shove your mic up your ass."

Janela was a twenty-two-year-old recent college graduate who lived at home with his parents. There were, at most, five hundred people listening to the game.

Word of the exchange zoomed across the Internet. Before long Backman was, once again, a public embarrassment. A punch line. He was given another opportunity by the Joliet Jackhammers of the Northern League, but with his team in sixth place with a 24–42 mark, he was canned.

Surely, Backman's career as a manager was over. Surely, he'd be reduced to Holiday Inn autograph shows and tutoring sessions at a local batting cage.

Then, the New York Mets called.

In October 2009, the franchise that Backman cherished asked him to manage its Class A team, the Brooklyn Cyclones. He jumped at the opportunity, and guided the team to a league-best 51–24 record. When New York manager Jerry Manuel was fired following the 2010 season, Sandy Alderson, the new GM, interviewed Backman for the position.

Though the job was eventually offered to Terry Collins, Backman was once again praised for his knowledge and enthusiasm. He will spend the 2011 season leading the Mets' Double A Binghamton club. "My goal is definitely to reach the majors as a manager and to succeed there," he says. "But I'm content, and grateful to the Mets. They've looked out for me and they've given me a chance to make good. How can I ever complain?"

If Backman, or any of the '86 Mets, were to complain, it would be about love. Or, to be more precise, the lack thereof.

In the aftermath of that remarkable world championship season, the franchise went to great (and somewhat inexplicable) lengths to distance itself from the debauchery of a team gone wild. From the trading of Kevin Mitchell to San Diego to the nightmarish Dykstra and Roger

McDowell for Juan Samuel swap to the eventual ridding itself of Davey Johnson, the Mets seemed to want nothing more than to move on. With every drug-related misstep by Gooden or Strawberry (and there were many), the organization shuddered. Sure, '86 was a good time. A great time. But did the Mets want to be remembered for such slimy behavior?

In a word: No.

Beneath their breaths, members of the team complained to one another about the lack of outreach from the organization. The ten-year anniversary came and went with little note, as did the fifteenth. When the old Mets got together, it was usually at the behest of Mead Chasky, a memorabilia peddler who paid the players to sit in various rooms and sign baseballs. In 2005, the organization was approached by Trevor Engelson, a founding partner of Underground Films & Management, a production and management company based in Los Angeles. Engelson had purchased the movie rights to *The Bad Guys Won*, and came to the Mets armed with potential directors, producers, and actors.

The Bad Guys Won: The Movie? The organization wanted nothing to do with the idea.

Then, in 2006, something seemed to change. In August of that year, the organization invited every member of the '86 team back for a twentieth anniversary celebration (seven Mets were unable to attend, including Gooden, who was in jail). The players were flown to New York, placed in a Times Square hotel, fed, and entertained. On the night of August 19, before the current Mets were scheduled to face the Rockies, Shea Stadium hosted a truly remarkable gala. As each player was introduced, he walked through the stands, slapping hands en route toward the field. "The hair on the back of my neck stood up," says Doug Sisk, the relief pitcher. "For a night we traveled back in time."

"It was terrific," says Darling. "To be brought back like that and made to feel like kings was terrific. I think we were all touched because people remembered.

"All those years gone by, and people still remember."

Acknowledgments

WRITING A BOOK IS A NIGHTMARE. I learned this quickly: On day two of the project, with some one hundred thousand words waiting to be written, my computer screen was blank, and I couldn't pry myself away from *A-Team* reruns on TNT. I had no clue what I was doing. So I did what I always do in times of trouble: I called home.

"Boy," my father said, "look at it this way. If you don't finish, what's the worst that can happen?"

I made a list:

- Next book deal includes $21.53 bonus to ghostwrite *MC Hammer: Can't Touch Me*
- Forever known as the guy who took two-month *SI* sabbatical to play X-Box
- Wasted 12,471 pieces of paper on Kevin Elster transcript
- Promises to make Ed Hearn "bigger than Elvis" go unfulfilled

Fortunately, after much hard work and countless nights of statistical analysis and clip digging and video rewinding, *The Bad Guys Won* exists. But it sure wasn't easy.

My greatest gratitude goes to Jay Horwitz, the Mets' hard-nosed publicist, who to this day continues to take my phone calls. In a profession that too often relies on media manipulation, Jay is a straight shooter and a vat of information. Strawberry, Piazza, Seaver, and Koosman are all legendary Shea denizens, but Jay is truly Mr. Met.

David Hirshey and Nick Trautwein of HarperCollins are as smooth and savvy word editors as one could ask for. When I needed a kick in the pants, David provided it. When I needed a reassuring word, David offered that, too. Mazel tov!

My thanks to Marty Beiser for his deft surgery on my original draft, which was slightly longer than *Ulysses*.

My agent, Susan Reed of IMG, was something. I had a mental image of what an agent does for a client, but Susan completely redefined that.

This book is a tribute to the 187 people who took time to share their memories of a wonderful season. It's not always easy going back nearly two decades, especially when some of the images can be painful. But from stars like Keith Hernandez and Gary Carter to role players such as John Gibbons and Terry Leach, the members of the '86 Mets couldn't have been any more cooperative. Equally essential were the behind-the-scenes guys who after years of anonymity seemed thrilled to step on the stage: Paul and Vinny Greco, John and Michael Rufino, Steve Garland, Scott Capro, Bob Mandt, Jackie Pamlanye, and Charlie Samuels. A thousand thanks for your insights.

I have been blessed over the years to work with some amazing journalists, many of whom contributed profoundly to *The Bad Guys Won*. I am especially grateful for the insight of my good friend and colleague, *Sports Illustrated* senior writer Jon Wertheim, who willingly shared the experiences of writing his own book, the excellent *Venus Envy*. Equally essential was another *SI* chum, Brian Cazeneuve, a hell of a writer and, from what I hear, an even better batboy. In addition I need to tip my cap to *SI*'s Steve Cannella, my cohort on the baseball beat for four years. When I started calling Steve more often than my wife, I knew baseball had completely overtaken my brain. I am grateful to several other grand *SI* folk, including Bill Colson, Rich O'Brien, Hank Hersh, Gabe Miller,

Linda Wachtel, Karen Carpenter, Andrea Woo, George Amores, and the phenomenal Linda-Ann Marsch, queen of accuracy.

Writing and researching this book was made infinitely easier by the assistance and thoughtful suggestions of peers like Michael Lewis of the *Glen Falls Post-Star*, Joe Lombardi of *The Journal News*, Patrick Connolly of *The (Nashville) Tennessean*, Jennifer Wulff of *People*, Greg Orlando of *X-Box Nation*, Bill Fleischman of the *Philadelphia Daily News*, Bev Oden of Fox Sports, Laura Fasbach of *The Bergen Record*, Jody Berger of *The Rocky Mountain News*, Adrienne Mand and Robyn Furman of *The Delaware Review*, and Gary Miller of *Canine Digest*. I will also never forget the aid of Paul Duer, my old college roommate and a dazzling word editor, as well as Daniel Monaghan, co-captain of Edna's Edibles, and Stanley Herz, author of *Conquering the Corporate Career*.

I have been blessed with a supportive family. There are no better role models than my parents, Joan and Stan Pearlman, who kicked off my journalistic journey sixteen years ago by listening patiently as I read every *Chieftain* article aloud. I am equally indebted to my brother, David (Doovie) Pearlman; my uncle, Marty Pearlman; and my cousin, Daniel Pearlman, for their backing, as well as the boosting of Richard, Susan, and Jessica Guggenheimer; Laura and Rodney Cole; Leah, Reggie, and Jordan Williams; and Norma Shapiro, my Florida publicist.

When I was a kid, two adults took me in and shared their enthusiasm for the game. It was on Vinny Gargano's couch that I first appreciated the roar of a Gooden fastball and the power of a George Foster homer. And it was in front of John Ballerini's TV that I first heard the words "Davey Johnson sucks!" Thanks, Mr. Gargano. And to the Ballerini family: Your husband/father isn't forgotten.

Finally, a word about my wife: It is a cliché to say "I never could have done this without so-and-so's support," but in this case it's entirely true. Earlie, you were my editor, coach, critic, cheerleader, chef, guardian, back scratcher, and, most important, friend. Never before had I experienced the direct impact of such unconditional love. Everyone needs a PH #1.

ALSO BY JEFF PEARLMAN

THE ROCKET THAT FELL TO EARTH
Roger Clemens and the Rage for Baseball Immortality

"Pearlman's book develops a stark, unsparing picture of Clemens's life that surpasses anything that's come before."

—*Boston Globe*

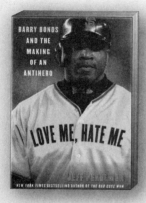

LOVE ME, HATE ME
Barry Bonds and the Making of an Antihero

"Pearlman paint[s] the picture of Barry Bonds— son, father, husband, baseball player, jerk. . . . An impressive piece of reporting [and] a nuanced picture of a complicated man."

—*Baseball America*

BOYS WILL BE BOYS
The Glory Days and Party Nights of the Dallas Cowboys Dynasty

"With vivid details that place you in the Dallas huddle—and in the team hotel rooms— Pearlman expertly peels the hedonistic layers off the unforgettable characters of the dynastic Cowboys."

—*Sports Illustrated*

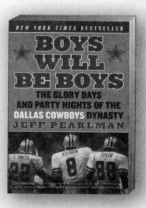

itbooks
AN IMPRINT OF HARPERCOLLINS PUBLISHERS